The Best
AMERICAN
ESSAYS
1990

1-9016

The Best AMERICAN ESSAYS 1990

Edited and with an Introduction
by Justin Kaplan

Robert Atwan,
Series Editor

Ticknor & Fields · new york · 1990

ISSN 0888-3742
ISBN 0-89919-927-5
ISBN 0-89919-937-2 (PBK.)

Printed in the United States of America

HAD 10 9 8 7 6 5 4 3 2 1

"Armenian Journal" by Michael Arlen. First published in *The Nation*. Copyright © 1989 by Michael Arlen. Reprinted by permission of the author.

"The Paradoxes of Creativity" by Jacques Barzun. First published in *The American Scholar*. Copyright © 1989 by Jacques Barzun. Reprinted by permission of the author.

"Intoxicated by My Illness" by Anatole Broyard. First published in *The New York Times Magazine*. Copyright © 1989 by The New York Times Company. Reprinted by permission of the publisher.

"Shouting 'Fire!'" by Alan M. Dershowitz. First published in *The Atlantic Monthly*. Copyright © 1989 by Alan M. Dershowitz. Reprinted by permission of the author.

"The Stunt Pilot" by Annie Dillard. First published in *Esquire*. Copyright © 1989 by Annie Dillard. Reprinted by permission of the author.

"At the Academy Awards" by Stanley Elkin. First published in *Harper's Magazine* with the title "In Darkest Hollywood." Copyright © 1989 by Stanley Elkin. Reprinted by permission of the author.

"A Few Kind Words for Envy" by Joseph Epstein. First published in *The American Scholar*. Copyright © 1989 by Joseph Epstein. Reprinted by permission of the author.

"The Creation Myths of Cooperstown" by Stephen Jay Gould. First published in *Natural History*. Copyright © 1989 by Stephen Jay Gould. Reprinted by permission of the author.

"No Wonder They Call Me a Bitch" by Ann Hodgman. First published in *Spy*. Copyright © 1989 by Ann Hodgman. Reprinted by permission of the author.

Contents

Foreword

EACH YEAR *The Best American Essays* confronts its guest editor with two critical challenges. One, of course, is to decide the twenty or so outstanding essays that will make up the annual edition. The other challenge — equally difficult but far less visible to readers — is to decide which of the numerous candidates for the volume are truly essays. Many prose pieces that look like essays are really reviews, reports, features, commentary, interviews, or profiles — in a word, what newspapers and magazines routinely call articles.

If it's impossible to come up with an airtight definition of an essay, it's equally impossible to define an article. This all-purpose literary label has a long, complex history, one that would make an interesting article in itself. The word goes back to the Latin term for a joint *(artus)* connecting two parts of a body, and its literal use was gradually extended to include the component parts of writing and discourse. By the early eighteenth century, "article" was being used regularly for literary compositions that treated a specific topic. According to the *OED,* the essayist Joseph Addison was the first to use the word in its modern journalistic sense.

Articles require not just a topic, but a topical topic. Unlike essays, articles are usually (a) about something specific, and (b) about something of current interest. Essays, on the other hand, can take large liberties with subject, theme, sources of information, organization, and point of view. Essayists tend to be personal, reflective, leisurely, digressive; article writers — should we revive the old term and call them "articlers"? — usually stay close to the facts, rarely stray from "the point," and seldom interrupt the flow of information with personal opinion. The essayist, too, will feel comfortable writing about various general topics — friendship, envy, nature, manners. The articler — whether the piece is inspired or required — is usually looking for an angle or "hook" to tie it up with some current event or fashionable trend.

Assign the topic of revenge to two writers, an essayist and an articler. Chances are the essayist will take a first-person, reflective look at the nature of revenge, blending together literary allusions and personal experience; the articler will most likely shape several interviews with psychologists into an informative piece assuring readers that revenge is a perfectly normal feeling and offering them six ways to cope with it. These are extremes, to be sure, but they suggest the divergent routes of the essay and article in today's literary marketplace. Or try this test: pick up a magazine and flip open to a page of text. Skim the page; do you detect a large proportion of interview quotations, a high percentage of names in the news, do you see catchy subheads, teasers, bulleted lists, statistics, abbreviations, and acronyms? If so, then it's about 99 percent certain you have an article in your hands.

But, as Justin Kaplan reminds us, writing is a slippery commodity and can easily elude the most carefully constructed editorial categories. At either end of the spectrum, it's fairly simple to distinguish an essay from an article. As we move toward the center, however, the distinctions grow less clear. Here we begin to find a compositional mix: personal essays that depend on research and reporting; topical articles that display a personal voice and viewpoint. These literary hybrids are becoming increasingly prevalent in the general magazines.

A large part of the distinction between an essay and an article rests on the writing's apparent durability. Many timely magazine articles, no matter how immediately engaging or skillfully crafted, have a painfully brief rack life. As public interest in a trend or topic fades, so does interest in the article. The names are no longer in the news, the issues irrelevant, the acronyms meaningless, the statistics hopelessly dated. How many fine articles by good writers hold up for five years? How many stay fresh even after one year? How to treat the immediate moment — to deal concretely and intelligently with the issues and topics of one's time — and still be read with pleasure long after that moment? That is an essential question for anyone who hopes to write enduring nonfiction.

It's a question Justin Kaplan carefully considered as he shaped this year's edition around public, rather than personal, essays. Though several personal and familiar essays appear in the book, the focus here is on writers working within the arena of topics and issues: a national disaster, the environment, AIDS, the First Amendment, the Academy Awards, the origins of baseball, Elvis sightings, Andy Warhol's legacy, the tensions between Blacks and Jews, the American novel. In all of these selections, the writers move between the topical requirements of an article and the literary demands of an essay, adroitly balancing fact and observation with the nuances of voice and style, irony and wit.

The Best American Essays features a selection of the year's outstanding essays, essays of literary achievement that show an awareness of craft and a forcefulness of thought. Roughly 300 essays are gathered from a wide variety of regional and national publications. These essays are then screened and turned over to a distinguished guest editor, who may add a few personal favorites to the list and who makes the final selections.

To qualify for selection, the essays must be works of respectable literary quality intended as fully developed, independent essays (not excerpts or reviews) on subjects of general interest (not specialized scholarship), originally written in English (or translated by the author) for first appearance in an American periodical during the calendar year. Publications that want to make sure their contributions will be considered each year should include the series on their subscription list (Robert Atwan, *The Best American Essays*, P.O. Box 1074, Maplewood, New Jersey 07040).

For this volume, I'd like to thank Charles Christensen for the many excellent suggestions he has provided the series since its inception. I'm grateful to Jane Jubilee once again for her timely help in putting the manuscript together. As guest editor, Justin Kaplan proceeded in the spirit of the great essayists. His openness to divergent opinions, sense of humor, resistance to cant and pomposity, and his commitment to public discourse are qualities that — however we define the genre — will always remain at the heart of the essay.

R.A.

Introduction

THIS DELICIOUS editorial assignment — to read, more or less at leisure, essays published during the past year in American magazines and select twenty or so from among them — nevertheless awakened some old apprehensions in me. They have to do with the aura and essence of the word "essay" and with recollections of Sunday afternoons darkened by the knowledge that I had one due at school the next day. Even now, on certain Sunday afternoons, especially during the winter, I feel in a shadowy way some of the same dread along with a pounding pulse and elevated skin temperature. The root of this early misery was not the work of writing but the indeterminacy of what was expected: an essay, but an essay about *what?* Why didn't they give us a subject? That would have been a humane thing to do. Instead, the word "essay," like Keats's word "forlorn," became a tolling bell.

What made those school assignments even more daunting was some of the models our teachers held up to us: Francis Bacon, Addison and Steele, Charles Lamb, William Hazlitt, Robert Louis Stevenson, Logan Pearsall Smith. Once in a while these highly respected authors did in fact get their essays going with something definite — a prizefight for Hazlitt, a pig roast for Lamb. But even then their work had a certain hermetic, self-referential quality, and their covert subject, no matter what their titles said, was the act of writing itself. These essays were ultimately triumphs of pure writing, of style, even, as C. S. Lewis said about Bacon, of "stylistic illusion." We all thought we understood Bacon's celebrated opening sentence, "What is truth? said jesting Pilate, and would not stay for an answer." But I wondered then whether Bacon himself could have told me what he was driving at in the next sentence: "Certainly there be that delight in giddiness, and count it a bondage to fix a belief; affecting free-will in thinking, as well as in acting." Was this the same Francis Bacon so dedicated to clear empiricism that he was to catch his death of cold in an experiment with preserving dead chickens in the snow?

At a time long before the New Journalism invited the writer to take center stage, the whole business of writing essays without a set topic seemed one of the "paradoxes of creativity" Jacques Barzun discusses here: "Producing something where nothing was before — making a thing out of nothing," even though science and common sense tell us that "nothing can be made from nothing." I don't know how in my greenness and nothing-ness I should have been expected to generate a thousand words that wouldn't give me a seizure to reread, and yet it had to be done, and it *was* done. On my first day as a college freshman I learned that I had already demonstrated enough competence to be excused from all required composition courses. At that moment the tolling bell stopped tolling, and pleasure ever since has prevailed over all my other feelings about the essay.

The old, nagging question remains unanswered, however. What *is* an essay, and what, if anything, is it *about?* "Formal" and "informal," "personal," "familiar," "review-essay," "article-essay," "critical essay," essays literary, biographical, polemic, and historical — the standard lit-crit lexicon and similar attempts at genre definition and subclassification in the end simply tell you how like an eel this essay creature is. It wriggles between narcissism and detachment, opinion and fact, the private party and the public meeting, omphalos and brain, analysis and polemics, confession and reportage, persuasion and provocation. All you can safely say is that it's not poetry and it's not fiction.

Given the confusion of genre minglings and overlaps, what finally distinguishes an essay from an article may just be the author's gumption, the extent to which personal voice, vision, and style are the prime movers and shapers, even though the authorial "I" may be only a remote energy, nowhere visible but everywhere present. ("We commonly do not remember," Thoreau wrote in the opening paragraphs of *Walden,* "that it is, after all, always the first person that is speaking.") Taking a cue from Annie Dillard's piece here, I suggest that the personal, familiar, informal essay — Joseph Epstein's "A Few Kind Words for Envy," for example — is a kind of stunt flying, a public display of energy and spirit, a sequence of loops, rolls, arabesques, and linked improvisations that never loses its line. (Stephen Jay Gould's collocation of baseball, creation myth, and evolutionary theory is also stunt flying.) The journalist or article writer, on the other hand, travels an assigned, scheduled course from one place to another, is answerable to editorial ground controllers, and has to deliver the people and goods on the manifest. Most of the essays in this collection fall between stunt flying and scheduled air traffic. They tend to be "about" something that exists independently of their authors' feelings and experiences, and this exercise of personal editorial taste, I have to acknowledge, may be my form of restitution for Sunday afternoons.

"Although the Essay seems to be undergoing the mildest of revivals just now," Wilfred Sheed recently said, "and occasional books have the nerve to call themselves collections of essays, the form has been in virtual eclipse for most of my writing life, squeezed to a shadow by the adjoining landmasses of the Article and the Review, not to mention its own dwarf love child, the column. One would feel unbearably precious calling oneself an essayist these days, but anyway they won't let you." Despite the evasive title, and his suggestion that the essay is in danger of extinction, Sheed's *Essays in Disguise* (1990) is one of those admirably nervy collections; others are Gore Vidal's *At Home*, reissued this year in paperback, and the late John Clive's book of historical essays in the grand discursive manner of Gibbon and Macaulay, *Not by Fact Alone*. Although no one could claim that with these exceptions, as well as the work of Lewis Thomas and a few others, esssay collections as a publishing commodity enjoy the boom of short story collections, the essay itself, as I think the pieces below demonstrate, is far from being in "virtual eclipse."

A remarkably large number of this year's essays are about illness and medical emergencies. I've included four: Anatole Broyard's "Intoxicated by My Illness," Natalie Kusz's "Vital Signs," Randy Shilts's "Talking AIDS to Death," and Paul West's "Portrait of the Artist as a Lion on Stilts." (A fifth, William Styron's piece about depression, "Darkness Visible," is listed among this year's "Notable Essays.") That we see so many distinctive pieces — sardonic, unflinching, even celebratory in a somber and grateful way — on this one topic may well be the flip side of our national obsession with fitness, diet, and conditioning; perhaps, AIDS aside, modern medicine gives us more survivors to contemplate the dynamics of survival; the AIDS tragedy in itself has forced us into a broader confrontation with what used to be denied or disguised. (Even *New York Times* obituaries, traditionally exercises in elision and circumlocution, now tell you what people died of — cancer, for example, is cancer and not a "long illness" — and who their significant companions were.) These essays are also an implicit attack on the kind of murk-making "insincerity" George Orwell identified in his essay "Politics and the English Language" (1946). Along with cliché, "euphemism, question-begging, and sheer, cloudy vagueness," he wrote, fall "upon the facts like soft snow, blurring the outlines and covering up all the details" and giving "an appearance of solidity to pure wind."

Other essays in this collection deal in different ways with the sort of cant Orwell had in his sights. "People say, 'I'm having trouble with my relationship,'" Leonard Michaels writes, "as though the trouble were not with Penelope or Max but with an object, like a BMW, a sort of container or psychological condition into which they enter and relate." He is just as hard on "mothering," "parenting," and the all-purpose banality "I can relate to that." "Environment," Joy Williams writes ("Save the Whales, Screw the Shrimp")—"Such a bloodless word. A flat-footed word with a shrunken heart. A word increasingly disengaged from its association with the natural world." She argues that "the ecological crisis cannot be resolved by politics. It cannot be solved by science or technology. It is a crisis caused by culture and character, and a deep change in personal consciousness is needed." The problem is how to rescue the environmental issue from degenerating into another fashionable cause taken up by politicians, image manipulators, and corporate advertisers gearing up to worship what Gore Vidal calls "the new world god, Green" with "environmentally friendly" products and proclamations that "every day is Earth Day with nuclear energy."

Alan Dershowitz's "Shouting 'Fire!' " examines Justice Oliver Wendell Holmes's frequently quoted, fundamentally mischievous example of unprotected speech under the First Amendment — perhaps "the only jurisprudential analogy that has assumed the status of a folk argument." Barzun targets "creativity," along with "innovation" one of contemporary culture's favorite buzz words. As a biographer who has done more than his share of penitential reading in the psychological literature about "creativity" and "the creative personality," and discovered that little in it holds up under intelligent scrutiny, I applaud Barzun for saying, "It is characteristic of a technological age to imagine that creation is a series of steps that can be discovered and analyzed like digestion or photosynthesis."

Ann Hodgman's hilarious report on her ordeal in Alpo-land, Stanley Elkin's "At the Academy Awards," and Michael Pollan's "Why Mow? The Case Against Lawns" are first-rate examples of topical humor and satire. But 1989 turns out not to have been a good year for political humor in the essay (as distinguished from the column), despite the fact that the fields received a good manuring from the bafflements of Dan Quayle, S & L scandals, insider memoirs, astrology, and the transition from one president who couldn't remember anything he did to another who in fifteen months hasn't done anything anyone else remembers (aside from invading Panama and denouncing broccoli). American satirists and humorists, from Mark Twain to Lenny Bruce and after, practice a profession that, in several senses, is a punishing one. They occupy a queer position in this country — that of clowns and entertainers when they don't inflict pain, cranks and sociopaths when they do.

Cynthia Ozick's "T. S. Eliot at 101," published in *The New Yorker*, was not only a literary essay, in every sense of the term, but also a personal one, its subtext (as I understand it) being the story of Ms. Ozick (as Sinbad the Sailor) dislodging the Old Man of the Sea (Eliot) from her shoulders. For reasons of length and permissions alone, her piece had to be left out of this collection. Another omission I regret is that of Julian Barnes's "Shipwreck" (*The New Yorker*), despite appearances to the contrary an excerpt from a novel, *A History of the World in 10½ Chapters*. Tom Wolfe's "Stalking the Billion-Footed Beast," the last selection here, was surely one of the noisier literary events of 1989. An advertisement for himself (and for *The Bonfire of the Vanities*) transparently disguised as a "manifesto for the new social novel," Wolfe's piece is frankly outrageous although, as always with this writer, stylistically supercharged and distinctive. It is a joy to read, however violently one takes issue with it. Many writers did. In the Letters column of *Harper's* three months after Wolfe's appearance in the magazine, Mary Gordon scored his "ignorance" and "narcissism," claimed that his "theory of realism would make a college freshman blush," and concluded that he was "the thinking man's redneck." For John Hawkes, Wolfe's stand on post–World War II fiction was "essentially reactionary and anti-intellectual," a familiar form of "literary America firstism." Alison Lurie pointed out that of the forty-eight writers mentioned in his article only two were women, a proportion suggesting that for Wolfe "literature is an almost exclusively masculine field." Wolfe's "billion-footed beast" struck Jim Harrison as "an origami pussycat . . . the Babbittry of Art in a new, white suit." In a more calmly argued response (in *The New York Times Book Review*) Robert Tower called the entire manifesto an "exercise in philistinism." And so on. If Wolfe had set out only to perform a provocative test, as doctors call it, on the thinking of American fiction writers today, he could scarcely have done a better job.

At the beginning of 1989, a year of extraordinary, even (until then) unimaginable changes and events, Robert Heilbroner declared in *The New Yorker* that "the contest between capitalism and socialism is over: capitalism has won." During the summer Francis Fukuyama stirred up a dust storm in *The National Interest* with "The End of History?" — the question mark at the end of his title being a sort of wild card. Had ideology finally died, or was the coming new order merely the triumph of K Mart over G.U.M.? Was "the end of history," as one respondent asked, "the political equivalent of global warming"? Fukuyama's critics thought that his account of the slaying of ideology at the hands of "economic and political liberalism" had got its paws tangled in a leash of semantic ambiguity ("history," "liberalism") and Hegelian dialectic. The new year opened with the publication (in the winter issue of *Daedalus*) of a companion piece to Fukuyama's in sogginess and pontification, "To the Stalin Mausoleum." This one derived a considerable portion of its front-page news value from the fact that the author was identified only as a mysterious "Z" (which, in turn, recalled an important 1947 essay by "X" — George Kennan — credited with enunciating "containment" as American cold war policy). Fukuyama and "Z" may have been only "intellectual flavors of the month," as Mark Feeney of the *Boston Globe* observed, but in their brief transit through the public mind they stimulated a certain amount of thinking, and this is no small achievement.

As it turned out, however, the signal events of 1989 — Tiananmen Square, the Wall, the stirrings of German reunification, the far-reaching effects of *perestroika*, the shrinking of Soviet hegemony, the promise of a "peace dividend" — simply moved too fast, too overwhelmingly, for the essay. But events of this size and velocity may not be the territory of the essay to begin with but that of reportage, articles, think pieces, and "thumb suckers." These are all of a day and serve a purpose. But essays on grand issues private as well as public require time, distance, distillation, and percolation through a subsoil of style and sensibility. What they may lack in todayness they make up in staying power.

JUSTIN KAPLAN

The Best
AMERICAN
ESSAYS
1990

MICHAEL ARLEN

Armenian Journal

FROM THE NATION

THESE DAYS, the way most people get to Armenia — though let's briefly call it by its proper name, the Soviet Socialist Republic of Armenia — is by flying in via dreary Moscow. Lumpish Moscow; fog in the air, snow underfoot. Typical of the city's gracious charm is the practice at the main tourist hotels of refusing entry to all Muscovites, except hookers. Though not all hookers; only those deemed worthy of earning hard currency — hard-currency hookers. Tonight, they occupy most of the tables in the fabulously tacky Lowenbrau Deluxe Bar and Eating Area, scaring the daylights out of a Dutch tour group. Nearby there are pinball machines and many opportunities to buy junk souvenirs. It's always a pleasure to get out of Moscow, though not always easy. At 4 P.M., a flight is scheduled to depart for Yerevan, the capital of Armenia. Out one is trundled to the airport the inevitable several hours before departure only to find that Aeroflot departures are in a fluid mode that day. Our flight is announced for midnight, leaves at 5 A.M. A huge plane crammed with Armenians. Also, an Armenian pilot, Armenian stewardesses. We fly noisily through night and dawn, three hours, one time zone, and blow a tire on landing — a loud pop, though nobody on board seems much interested. The plane speeds and skids and does a little spinning around on some grass and finally stops, and everyone gets off.

Yerevan. A million and a quarter people, probably more nowadays since many of the earthquake survivors are living here, in hospitals or with relatives. There are some attractive tree-lined streets, although most of the trees look pretty bare and scrawny. Boring official buildings made out of tufa, the local pink stone. Too many cars. Too much exhaust. Dust in the air. The usual cluster of large, shabby Soviet-style apartment buildings, with grimy windows and wash hanging from the balconies. The city seems normal, workaday, men and women going about their business. Also, numerous policemen in their good-looking blue greatcoats, by their faces not Armenian; these are the new police brought in from elsewhere — Greater Russia. Also Soviet soldiers, neither few nor many. They seem to walk about in threes, some wearing what appear to be flak jackets. Here and there you see a tank, not giant tanks but still tanks — city tanks with eight rubber tires and a gun mounted in a turret.

The lobby of the Hotel Armenia is like a movie set, not precisely *Casablanca* but one of those settings, part seedy, part exotic, with an air of faded grandeur, and with many strange people hanging about, mostly men in dark suits drinking little cups of that sweet, syrupy coffee — definitely not called "Turkish coffee" here — their heads lowered in presumably interesting and purposive conversation. Upstairs, there are several cavernous restaurants, none of them with any food to speak of, though with much in the way of brownish bread and green onions and slices of cold, hard cheese and unlabeled bottles of soft drinks described as "limonade," but which taste of mint and something difficult to identify. Also upstairs are the hotel rooms, randomly doled out — tiny chambers or large suites of three or four rooms, with beds never quite made up and a thick layer of dust pretty much everywhere — and always in the corridors, maids slowly chugging along, carrying armfuls of cleaning equipment.

We head out to the earthquake zone early in the morning — a warm morning, almost springlike but rapidly cooling off as we drive north toward Leninakan. We're in a fine yellow van belonging to Karekin Nercissian, otherwise known as the bishop of Yerevan. He's head of the Armenian church's relief operations here, fortyish, with a grizzled beard, a sporty black leather greatcoat. There's also Miriam, an Armenian aid worker from New York; Vartan, an architect from Chicago; and Ardashat, an old friend from Yerevan, a musician, a teacher of languages — a lifelong student, as he puts it.

Leninakan is about two hours' drive from Yerevan, at least it is today, with the road narrow and a soft misty rain beginning to fall. On either side of us lies the Armenian countryside — mostly stones and rocks and patches of bare field, with here and there a modest orchard of apple and apricot trees, their dark wispy branches still leafless. Far in the distance there are mountains, snow-covered, half hidden in haze. What are we going to find in Leninakan today? Dramatic examples of horrendous devastation? Or perhaps no devastation at all, since we are nearly three months after the fact. Perhaps dramatic examples of Soviet rebuilding.

Vartan and Karekin are discussing details of the earthquake. "December 7, at 11:41 in the morning," says Karekin. "The first shock. Thirty-two seconds."

"I thought it was longer," says Vartan.

"At 11:54 there was the second shock," says Karekin. "More than a minute."

On that December morning, Leninakan was the second largest city in Armenia, with about 290,000 people living there. It was once called Alexandropol, after the dreadful Czar Alexander, who had seized the region from the Ottoman Turks, thereby "protecting" the Christian Armenians from the infidel. Before that, it was known by its Armenian name, Gumry — this in those bygone days that drive Armenians mad to think about, when an Armenia existed that stretched from this barren, stony, rock-strewn north, down across the vast and fertile high-mountain plateau of what is now eastern Turkey.

"How many finally dead?" asks Miriam.

"The authorities still say fifty thousand," says Karekin, "but by all the signs we have, it was close to twice that number."

What I remember of Leninakan some years ago was a not exactly pretty city — too many of those ubiquitous Soviet-style apartment blocks for prettiness. But a dense and vigorous place. Old and new buildings. Busy thoroughfares. A sense of mass and people. Today, what one first notices is that the mass has been removed. Where once there was density there is now a

strange, damp, melancholy . . . openness. The city has been,
as they say, opened up: two thirds of the buildings are gone.
First they crashed to the ground in a murderous jumble of concrete and brick and kitchen sinks and human bodies. Then this
so-called rubble was removed, is in fact still being removed as we
stand there.

You see small groups of soldiers working in a desultory fashion beside the road, but are they building up or tearing down?
It's hard to say. An occasional truck lumbers by. There are some
heavy cranes in the distance.

We run into Etienne S., a doctor with a French relief team
that brought ten dialysis machines to the local hospital. "I don't
know what was the worst part," he is saying. "That they didn't
have any machinery to lift the concrete off the people who were
trapped and crushed? Or that they didn't have the surgical
equipment to perform the amputations? Of course, they performed them anyway, trying to save lives in those first days, using, how do you say, carpentry saws, saws for cutting logs."

Here and there you see clusters of olive-drab canvas tents volunteered by the army. People live in some of them. In others
there is a school — the sixty or so children remaining from an
elementary school of nearly two hundred.

We stop at the church — what used to be the church. Two
huge stone cupolas lie upside down, relatively unbroken,
embedded in the mud where they landed.

A freight train is on a siding. People are living in the freight
train.

A woman walks up to Miriam. From her appearance, she doesn't
seem bad off — wears a decent overcoat, hat, boots. Suddenly
she starts to scream at Miriam. "How can I live like this? How
can I take care of my children?" Miriam doesn't know what to
do or say. Karekin talks with the woman, asks if she has received
her monthly allotment of rubles from the government. "It wasn't
the money," he says afterward. "She has enough money. But I
think all her children are dead."

We walk along the muddy empty streets. Here much of the
rubble hasn't been cleared away. Great piles of concrete slabs
and broken stone and wire cables that didn't hold. Also a smell,
not strong, almost below consciousness, but not far enough below.

"It's happening," says Ardashat, sniffing the air. "It's warming up. The other day, my brother told me, the rats had found parts of a body and were dragging it into the street."

Vartan has come here to check out the prefab housing that has been brought in to house survivors. "There've been all sorts of strides in prefab design in the past few years," he says optimistically. But what we find isn't inspiring. There's a stretch of muddy ground about the size of a football field covered with green rectangular metal boxes. Five hundred green metal boxes. Some have a tiny window in the back, some don't. In a certain disconnected sense, the green of the boxes — bright and deep and shiny — is quite striking, almost pretty. But the prospect is depressing beyond belief. A man called Souren meets us, a sturdy, barrel-chested fellow in his fifties with a reddish face and a cut above one eye. He wants to show us his new home, takes us to the door of one of the green boxes and steps inside. There's almost nothing in it: a mattress on the floor, a bath mat for carpeting, two straight-backed chairs. "We don't have the electricity yet," says Souren, who seems alternately hearty and in a daze. "What about water?" asks Vartan. "We don't have the water yet," says Souren. Miriam tries to ask Ardashat discreetly how many members of Souren's family might be living there. Ardashat and Souren exchange a few brisk phrases and Ardashat says, "Only three. His wife is still in the hospital and two daughters were killed. But he has a little girl and a boy left." Souren wishes to offer us coffee but remembers that there is no way yet to make it. He stands at the door of his green metal box waving goodbye. "They'll be living there for at least two years," says Ardashat. "Probably three."

Dr. Etienne talks about crush syndrome. "I said they had a problem not having enough machinery to lift the concrete. But when they got the machinery they had a problem not knowing how to do things. You see, if you have a person, especially a child, lying under a slab of concrete and you lift off the concrete without first wrapping the crushed limb very tightly, what happens is that all the toxins gathered around the injury then rush back out and into the body, and often the kidneys can't handle this and they fail. You can do something about this if you have dialysis machines, but they didn't, at least none that worked, and so people were being rescued — from the rubble, that is — and then dying of kidney failure. It's called crush syndrome. But now we have machines here and in Yerevan, and we're getting some quite good recoveries."

Back in Yerevan, inside the Hotel Armenia, a tall, bespectacled Soviet army colonel whispers with two blue-coated policemen. The usual suspects sip their coffee. Miriam and Bishop Karekin are trying to explain the hotel's eccentric room-assignment policy to Bud, a new arrival from the United States — a gruff, middle-aged Armenian from Detroit who has come to Yerevan to try to interest "local industry," as he puts it, in a plan for manufacturing bathroom fixtures, specifically faucets. Just then, a plump young man walks by us — a local guy, sideburns, dark glasses, a fleece-lined denim jacket. "Hey, that's my jacket!" yells Karekin, and chases after him into the street. Moments later he comes back puffing, empty-handed. "I asked him where he got it. I mean, I *know* it's from our relief supplies. Who else has fleece-lined denim jackets here? He told me, 'I paid fifty rubles for it!' 'Fifty rubles!' I said. 'Who to?' 'To a friend,' he said."

There are plenty of stories about relief aid not getting through. Of shipments being skimmed off in Los Angeles, in Moscow, or even (or especially) in Yerevan. Two nights ago, Dr. N., a Boston surgeon expecting a shipment of blood analyzers, went out to the airport at midnight, as soon as he'd been told the plane had landed, only to find half his boxes already opened in the plane's cargo hold and two airport workers busily opening the rest. "What in hell are you guys doing?" said Dr. N. "We're just making sure things got here safely," one of the airport workers replied.

On the whole, the French and the Italians have the best record of getting aid into the country and into the right hands. "It's because they have a shorter distance to travel," says Miriam. "It's because they're smarter," says Vartan. "They send their people right on the plane with the stuff." So far, the French have brought in ten thousand tons of aid; the Americans, three hundred tons. But the three hundreds tons, mostly clothing, seems to have fallen into good hands with Bishop Karekin, who clearly runs a tight operation. On the wall outside his church in the center of Yerevan is an immense list of forty-five thousand names of needy survivors compiled by hand by Karekin and his priests. Inside the parish house are rooms full of clothing supplies — the fleece-lined jackets, and sweaters, jeans, and thermal underwear. Families troop in from the earthquake zone bringing with them their passports for identification, and Karekin doles out the stuff. "It works pretty well," he says. "Of course, the priests are furious, having to work for the first time in their lives. Also, some of our victims are very picky about what they want. The villagers really hate that thermal underwear."

"Let's play earthquake, children!" says Professor Dr. M. H. Alexeyev, an impressive, motherly woman with a broad face and tousled red hair. We are in a building called the Pedagogical Institute, inside an old-fashioned little classroom with wooden desks, and Dr. Alexeyev is standing in the center of a circle of eight young children, each one of them a shock victim of the earthquake. The children have begun to jump up and down, stamping their feet. "Make it louder, I can't hear you," says Dr. Alexeyev. The feet jump up and down. "Make the sound of fear," says Dr. Alexeyev. Now from the jumping children comes an eerie moaning sound. "That's right," says Dr. Alexeyev. "It's beginning, isn't it? But make it louder. I want to hear how terrible it is." The moaning of the children grows louder, higher, like some strange wind. "Now, touch hands together," says Dr. Alexeyev. "Eyes closed." Hands touch. The moaning dies down. The feet stop jumping. The children stand quietly in a circle, arms raised. "Like birds we are at rest," says Dr. Alexeyev. "We are alive."

Ardashat tells me we should have dinner at one of the new co-operative restaurants, one of the few visible indications of the much-advertised (literally, on posters glued to walls and office buildings) *perestroika*. It's a nice little place, the downstairs of an old town house. Ardashat has brought along his friend Kevork, a thirtyish professor of philology at the university. Ardashat asks me if I am outraged by the presence of martial law in Yerevan. Unwisely, I say that the soldiers I've seen seem to be trying hard to stay out of the way. "But they're *here!*" says Ardashat sternly. "It's a slap in the face." Kevork wants to know if the American people were angry at Gorbachev's repressing the Karabakh movement, the movement that drew those huge, peaceable crowds into the streets of Yerevan last year to demand the reunification with Armenia of an area usually and ponderously described as the autonomous region of Nagorno-Karabakh, an area populated mainly by 150,000 Armenians but located perversely by Stalin within the borders of Moslem Azerbaijan. I'm not sure how to reply to Kevork. The truth is often a good idea, but in this instance the truth I know is that most Americans, including most of my friends, don't know where or what Armenia is, let alone any autonomous region of Nagorno-Karabakh. While I am making up my mind, Kevork answers his own question, touching my arm in a brotherly fashion. "I know the American people cared very much," he says. Do I look doubtful? Ardashat says, "What Kevork means is the American intelligentsia. Of course the American intelligentsia cared very much."

Another morning, another trip scheduled to the earthquake zone, this time to the town (or former town) of Spitak. But there are problems of transportation. The sudden absence of a tire, or perhaps a wheel. While these are being attended to in an unconvincing way, I run into Bud rushing through the lobby with his salesman's suitcases. "How's the faucet business?" I ask. "It's a nightmare," Bud says cheerfully. "Businesswise, they're in the stone age here. But I've finally made contact with some of their technical people. One of their top honchos. In fact, I've got a meeting in a few minutes. Want to come along?" Bud checks his watch. "Don't mind carrying that, do you?" I pick up a suitcase that seems filled with bricks. "Faucet parts," explains Bud. Off we go, Bud carrying the other satchel. Spitak can wait, I figure, especially since it's ruins.

A ministerial car takes us to a gloomy building on the outskirts of Yerevan known as the Technological Center. At least, according to Bud. "Maybe it's only a technical center," he says, once inside. It is full of marble and the usual dust balls on the floor, and has three elevators, none of which work. Bud is undismayed. "I sense we're going to make a deal here," he says as we climb the stairs.

On the second floor we are met by three men in black suits, each one clearly a honcho. They shake Bud's hand and then my hand in firm ministerial style and announce that they will take us first to their "display center."

"I don't think I need to see any display center," says Bud. "Let's just talk faucets."

"Of course, we will talk faucets," says what is apparently the senior minister with a cloudy smile. "Faucets are the easy part. First, we will show you our manufactures."

Off we march down a long corridor — more marble, more dust balls. Through one door, tightly locked. The door is unlocked with much bravura by an underling. Another door, another lock. Then we are inside a darkened room. A light is switched on. "I'll be damned," says Bud. We have apparently stumbled into some kind of Soviet version of a gigantic Caribbean bazaar. Shelves from floor to ceiling filled with the most amazing bric-a-brac. Little plastic sandals in Day-Glo colors. Kiddy toys on the order of shovels and pails. Hula hoops. Very many brass light fixtures of garish design. Glassware. Nightmare table lamps. Many, many little metal trays.

My heart sinks. Even though I am not here to do serious business, these are my kinsmen after all — both the ministers and the invisible workers in this bizarre establishment who have produced such a treasury of unparalleled junk. I trudge behind Bud, who is trying to maintain a positive tone. "Goddamn, I've never seen so many metal trays in my life," he says. The senior minister beams at us and beckons us through another door. Now we are in a conference chamber, very large and long. Portraits of Lenin and Gorbachev. A vast table of shiny wood. Chairs of apparent Spanish design. We sit down in serious conference fashion, they on one side, Bud and I on the other. Bud asks for the suitcase, opens it, and places on the table a cardboard box with "World's Best Faucet" printed on it.

"First we have some pastry," says the senior minister.

Indeed, two large women appear with trays of pastries, then bowls of tangerines, then bottles of vodka, then apples, then bottles of cognac. Glasses are filled. Toasts are proposed and drunk: *perestroika* and so on. After the third ministerial toast, Bud starts to unpack the box. The senior minister immediately seizes two of the larger parts and hands them to his colleagues, who examine them in what strikes me as a nontechnological, or even nontechnical, fashion by rubbing their hands over the surfaces. "You give us these," says the senior minister, "and we will manufacture the rest."

Bud looks doubtful but he pushes the box toward the ministers. Inside it are dozens of little plastic bags, each one containing a faucet part — a washer or plastic ring or valve. The three ministers dip into the box like children, pull out the plastic bags, inspect their contents with a quick glance, smile, and say, "You give us this one, too." One hour later, much of the cognac and vodka have disappeared, also some of the pastries, though none of the apples and tangerines, and it is clear that the ministers have no plans to manufacture any of the faucet parts, or indeed to manufacture any faucets, but wouldn't mind being handed a couple of thousand of the finished product, as a gift. On the way back to the hotel I ask Bud if he's discouraged. "I still believe in *perestroika* even if they don't," he says. "Next time, I've got to get closer to the top."

There's an unexpected demonstration near the university. The occasion is International Women's Day, and more than a thousand women have assembled in the street. At first, speeches are made by several female candidates for the upcoming Soviet elections, though when a speaker goes on at too great a length the women clap their hands and tell her to shut up. In the background, soldiers and police look on impassively. Demonstrations are supposedly forbidden by martial law, but apparently only male demonstrations. Now the women begin to move off in the semblance of a march, heading toward Abovian Street, which leads to Lenin Square. They are protesting the jailing of the twelve leaders of the Karabakh movement, which happened right after the earthquake. The military aren't sure what to do about this development. Should they keep in the background or try to stop the march? Both tactics are tried but the women shuffle forward anyway, spreading out across Abovian Street, stopping traffic, causing passers-by to raise their right arms in solidarity. Now a group of several hundred men appear in a side street. They want to protect the women. From what? a fair-haired Soviet army lieutenant asks one of them. But even as they speak four tanks appear in the distance — no, eight — rumbling down the middle of Abovian Street. Also four trucks filled with soldiers and a large, weird-looking van that must be a military communications truck.

Now the men have something to protect the women from. The soldiers get out of the trucks but keep their distance — young boys from faraway places, they seem, many of them with Asiatic eyes and cheekbones. The tanks stop. Soon the men and the women are milling around in the middle of the street, and even on the sidewalks, talking and gesticulating and now and then pushing at some of the soldiers, but basically going nowhere. "All we want to do is go to the ministry and make our protest," says one of the women. "We don't care what the men do." An army major shakes his head. Prohibited. Nearby on the sidewalk are a half-dozen men in typical KGB outfits, black raincoats and hats, as easy to spot in a crowd as our FBI agents. The KGB men are clearly Armenian, as is everyone else in the street except the soldiers. "How can you live with yourself?" a woman yells at one of the KGB men. He shrugs. "That's not an answer," the woman calls back. "What do you expect me to do?" the KGB man says.

We are trying to have dinner in the hotel dining room. The problem isn't the food, which isn't a problem unless one was really expecting something to eat. Rather, it's the deafening blast of antiquated music, an ear-shattering mishmash of early-1970s disco, Armenian style, as some might say, which comes from a sweaty, sequined group onstage and appears to be greatly enjoyed by our fellow diners, who appear to be Armenian yuppies. They throng the dance floor, clapping their hands above their heads — men dancing with women, men dancing with men, women dancing with women. "Black market trash," says Ardashat. Miriam says she wants to go to Karabakh. Vartan the architect says he wants to go to Karabakh. Everyone wants to see Karabakh — this symbol of our people, this politically explosive autonomous region. "Of course you must go," says Ardashat. "But it's impossible. No visitors have been allowed into Karabakh. Not even Tom Brokaw."

An exhibition of drawings at the Pedagogical Institute. These are drawings made by some of Dr. Alexeyev's charges. A nine-

year-old girl whose feet have been amputated draws pictures of
a young girl with two clear, rounded stumps instead of feet who
is skipping rope. The girl in the drawing is high in the air, as if
soaring above the ground with her footless legs. A boy without
any legs draws a picture of a boy without legs jumping a horse
over a stream. Many of the children have taken their pens or
crayons and simply filled the page with chaotic scrawls. They
title these pictures "Earthquake."

I travel out to Spitak in the earthquake zone with Ardashat and
Vartan, who is trying to put together a report of construction
recommendations. Spitak is about a half-hour drive east of Leninakan, closer to the mountains. It was a much smaller town,
perhaps thirty thousand inhabitants, but it was closer to the ep-
icenter of the earthquake. Now there is nothing there. No, that's
not altogether true. As you come over a hill, heading down a
small valley toward Spitak, what you see in the distance, where
Spitak used to be, are scattered piles of rubble: a city plan where
the buildings are represented by flattened squares of debris. There
are no structures still standing in Spitak, unless you count a few
houses where the crumbled fragment of a single wall remains.
Vartan is scrambling around examining the broken concrete.
Nobody seems to be trying to clear up the mess; after all, who
would build another Spitak here? "Goddamn, they did so many
things wrong," he says. "First, they used volcanic ash in their
cement — cutting costs, of course. Only volcanic ash has a chemical reaction that makes it unbind from concrete. They didn't
pour the concrete continuously. Didn't stir it. They never rein-
forced their columns laterally. Worst of all, their ceilings — they
built these apartment buildings, ten stories, fourteen stories, following the accepted Moscow construction practices, not really
attaching the floor above to the columns that were meant to support it. They just made a little ledge — a shelf — on one side of
the columns and set the floor on the ledge. All the way up. Little
ledges. So when the quake hit, all the floors came crashing down
together. The French call it the *mille-feuille* effect."
      "The what?" says Ardashat.
      "It's a French pastry," says Vartan, sitting on a broken piece
of concrete with a wild look in his eye.

                                              *

We're over at the university late one evening talking politics. "At least it's something that we can do this," says Kevork. "I hate that attitude," says Levon, a mathematician. "Why should we be happy to be doing something we should have been able to do anyway?"

"You're a firebrand," says Kevork, as if explaining him.

"No, I'm not," says Levon. "I don't want anybody killed. I live under the Armenian curse. I believe in the idea of acting justly. Of course, it's so foolish and naïve, this notion that a person who acts justly carries an umbrella over his head, protecting him from the elements. But it's the only thing worth believing in, isn't it?"

Later, Kevork talks about the Karabakh committee, the twelve men, mostly teachers and professional people and so on, who guided the demonstrations before the crackdown. "You know, it started as an ecological movement, very small, to protest the pollution — all those chemical plants the central government has dumped in our country, the nuclear power plant designed by the same genius who designed Chernobyl. Then Karabakh asked for our support and that became a bigger issue. And then the Azerbaijani Turks massacred our people in Sumgait and that became a much bigger issue still."

"And then came the earthquake," says Levon, "and Gorbachev flew in from Bloomingdale's, all tears and sensitivity, and used this moment of national calamity to put all the committee members in jail."

"Gorbachev's not so bad," says Kevork.

"Who knows?" says Levon. "He's the only hope we have. But he put our best people in jail, these dangerous professors and writers. Nobody knows where they are. In Moscow, probably. Not even their families have been allowed to see them."

Soon it's close to midnight and the gathering starts to break up. "I hate the curfew," says Kevork. "Everyone hates the curfew," says Levon.

Visitors from outer space show up one morning in the lobby of the Hotel Armenia. Swimmers. Some months or years ago, at any rate before the earthquake, an international swimming competition was scheduled to take place in Yerevan, and so here they are, swimmers from many lands, unbelievably youthful and fit, standing around in their jumpsuits amid the haggard French doctors and weary Italian and American relief people, radiating prettiness and self-absorption like a magic force. I hear two Team U.S.A. girls in discussion at the newsstand, which is always closed and has nothing to sell anyway. *"Armenia?"* says one of them. "I mean, are we in Russia or what?"

"Coach says they were in the news," says the other. "Floods."

"Oh, God," says the first.

At this point, Bud heaves into view, not going out but coming in, still lugging his suitcases — the spirit of what made America great in the glory days before too much prettiness and the Japanese. "I'm off to Karabakh," he says.

It's true. Bud has gained entrée to the mysterious region, forbidden even to Tom Brokaw. At noon, a plane is to fly him to Stepanakert, the capital of Karabakh, to meet with no less a honcho than Arkady Volsky, Gorbachev's new man in charge. "You want to come?" he says. Of course I do. Miriam and Vartan also want to come. Conveniently, an aide from the trade ministry has been hovering in the background, surrounded by swimmers, clutching an armful of Bud's brochures on bathroom faucets. Miriam is given the brochures to hold, and the aide is dispatched to a telephone to negotiate new arrangements with those in charge. Apparently, it works. Even the aide is surprised. "I guess 'joint venture' is the password around here," says Bud.

We head off to the airport in a ministerial van. "Should I have packed something?" Miriam asks. "It's only a short hop across the border," says Vartan. Clearly, none of us knows much about where we are going. Once at the airport we are sequestered in what is said to be the VIP lounge — a forlorn chamber containing a few pieces of ancient hotel furniture, a two-month-old German newspaper, and the usual dust balls. A portly minister joins us. Then there is much waiting and ministerial telephoning. It seems that when Gorbachev removed Armenian-populated Karabakh from Azerbaijani governance by installing Volsky, he still left a couple of aspects of Karabakhi life in the control of Azerbaijan — mineral rights are said to be one, which doesn't concern us here, but air traffic control is another. Thus, our flight is being held up, neither by the tower in Yerevan nor the tower in Karabakh, one hundred miles away, but by the tower in Baku, three hundred miles away. "They say there's fog," says the minister's aide. "It's a very Turkish attitude," says the minister. An hour later we are released from the VIP lounge, bused to a far corner of the airport, and loaded into not a plane but a helicopter, a big, old-fashioned military contraption, which seems to be missing several pieces of its fuselage and carries a large drum of gasoline inside the cabin.

Our flight is quite marvelous and terrifying. First of all, it is now clear that Karabakh, though very near Armenia, is more or less inaccessible by any reasonable form of transport. For well over an hour we fly above a jagged expanse of snowcapped mountains, sometimes high, sometimes low, as when our pilot decides to drop down into a canyon to scare some sheep. Below us, periodically visible, is a road — *the* road — a primitive affair winding its way through the mountains by means of endless switchbacks.

We fly over an ancient monastery perched on a rocky promontory. Later, a cliffside filled with caves. Another deserted church, snow-covered. The pilot chews on a cheese sandwich and periodically skims the ground. Once we drop almost perpendicularly into a ravine and follow a twisting muddy river for a while — the scenic route.

Eventually, Stepanakert. There's lots of grass where we land. The wind is blowing. Wherever we are, it feels way up there, up in the sky, like Quito.

Several hundred people seem to be waiting at the tiny airport when we debark. Men in thick suits and women in black dresses. Serious country faces. A stillness everywhere. "Why the crowd?" asks Vartan. "I think to see you," says the minister.

We let Bud lead the way, since this is his deal, so to speak. It's true, the crowd is there for our arrival. Can Volsky really be that interested in faucets? "I don't see much industrial development around here," says Bud. Numerous cars have been provided to take us to Communist party headquarters, at least one for each of us, also a yellow police car that leads our odd cortege through the streets, blasting its siren whenever an oncoming vehicle approaches, and sometimes forcing it off the road.

Party headquarters are huge and underpopulated. Volsky awaits us in another of those conference chambers — a red car-

pet, long, shiny wood table, chairs of eccentric design, this time
no dust balls.

Volsky is about fifty, smooth of face, a little bulky, and wears
a tight blue suit with vest. He is attended by several Russian aides,
the Armenian mayor of Stepanakert, and two men in gray suits
whom he describes as engineers. "I've never been in a country
where so many people are described as engineers," says Bud under his breath.

Might we be about to start a meeting without cakes and cognac
and so on? Everyone is seated at the impressive shiny table, Bud
with his faucet box right in front of him, all the ministers and
engineers with grave expressions. But then in come the women
and the cakes and cognac and vodka and of course apples and
tangerines. Interminable toasts. Then we are summoned to our
feet to tour a factory.

"Is that the place where we could make the faucets?" says Bud.

"It's a possibility," says Volsky.

The factory is something from another era. Ancient machinery clinking and clanking, huffing and puffing, attended in only
the most nominal sense of the word by amiable, sleepy workers.
One such young woman is slowly feeding a strip of metal into a
gargantuan stamping machine, out of which emerges a leisurely
procession of imperfectly made little forks. "Can you believe it?"
Bud loudly whispers to Vartan. "This is worse than stone age.
It's third world."

Sadly, this seems true. But worse is to come. Since another
factory inspection looms on the schedule, Miriam asks instead to
visit the hospital. I go back with her into town, this sprawling,
strangely hushed Armenian town in the mountains, with its trees
and tiny gardens and a few pleasant buildings and an overall air
of time having stopped — and in a not very good way — some
while ago. The hospital is a disgrace or a disaster, depending on
how you choose to see these things. Far more backward than
anything in Armenia. The stench is overpowering. There's little
attempt at sanitation. No equipment. No medical supplies to speak
of. Linen gets changed every three weeks. Broken windows are
mended with cardboard. Morose and shivering patients lie about
in beds covered by a single filthy sheet. An Armenian doctor
says, "We've been under the Azerbaijani government all these

years. No money for our hospitals, no money for our schools. I'm so embarrassed you should see us like this, but it's how things are."

We rejoin the group in Volsky's office. Bud is still trying to talk about faucets, but Volsky has launched into a discussion of grapes, of which they have plenty in Karabakh, also wine, which they send somewhere else to be bottled. "What we need," he says, "is a bottling plant."

"We don't do bottling plants," says Bud.

"Not a plant for making the bottles," says Volsky. "We already have the bottles. A plant for putting wine into the bottles."

"We don't do that either," says Bud.

He opens up the faucet box and starts laying the stuff on the table. Volsky picks up one of the pieces. "Maybe we could make some of it here and do the aluminum parts some other place."

"We don't use aluminum," says Bud.

"Of course," says Volsky.

"Comrade Volsky is himself an engineer and so understands the problem as a specialist," says one of his aides.

Volsky picks up the faucet part again. "This is so complicated," he says. "What we need is something simple, for the people. Things for which you need only a stamping press."

"Operating a stamping press isn't so simple," says Bud.

"What about a bottling plant?" says Volsky.

"I told you, we don't make bottling plants."

"We could use it also for our honey and for our red currant jam." Volsky is standing. Glasses and plates lie everywhere around us. Bud has started to put the faucet parts back in the box.

"You also need hospital supplies," says Miriam.

"Oh, *yes*," Volsky says. He sits down again, puts his head in his hands. "We need everything."

Not altogether unexpectedly, our helicopter doesn't — can't or won't — leave that night. So we stay in Stepanakert. There is no hotel, so we are put up, very kindly, in apartments of the town's leading citizens. Bud and I are billeted with the manager of the power company and his wife, a doctor. We are given their small room. They sleep with the children. It's close quarters even for traveling men. Cold outside and in. Bud tosses and turns as if dreaming of faucets. In the middle of the night, he gets up

and stands at the window. "What are you looking at?" I ask.
"Nothing," he says. He goes back to bed. "I feel so fucking sorry
for these guys," he says.

Back in Yerevan, our Armenian friends are happy that we have
been to Karabakh. "Isn't it beautiful?" says Kevork. Ardashat
says, "Did you know that Soviet Marshal Bagramian came from
Karabakh, also twenty-four official heroes of the Soviet Union?"
    "It's very poor," says Vartan.
    "I know," says Kevork. "But it gets so green in the springtime.
So many apples and grapes. Anyway, what is it to be rich? Here
we are rich in stones and rocks and earthquake victims. Here, all
the young people want to go to Los Angeles. They call it 'Los.'
'When I get to Los,' they say, 'I will have a house and a red
BMW.' "

Bud has left. Miriam is busy drawing up a list of needed medical
equipment. Vartan and I visit the monument on one of the hills
above Yerevan. Actually, we had meant to go to the soccer stadium, but a Soviet tank was rerouting traffic and we got lost.
"Let's go to the monument," said Vartan. So we did. Two Armenian guys from America paying our respects, so to speak.
There's a Stonehenge-like circle of great black granite columns.
An eternal flame honoring the dead in the great genocide in
Turkey of 1915 and 1916. A wind is blowing. Spring seems to
have vanished for the time being. Vartan stands in front of the
eternal flame, clasping and unclasping his hands. "Do you think
we are an unlucky people?" he says.
    "I don't know," I say.
    "I just hate it when people talk that way," he says angrily. "My
brother, my mother, they're always saying to me, 'We're so unlucky, we're such an ill-fated people!' I tell them, 'What's the
matter with you? We're alive, aren't we, in a country only two
hundred years old, everybody already scared to death of their
own shadow, and here we are, a people that's been around three
thousand years, surviving — hell, doing better than surviving —
going strong.' "
    "That's a good thought, Vartan," I say. I like Vartan. I bet he
is a good architect in Chicago and doesn't put up buildings where

fourteen floors are going to crash to the ground simultaneously like a French pastry. I think of the girl without feet who drew the picture of the girl without feet, skipping rope, flying in the air.

We are walking away from the monument, back toward the steps going down — to our car, the hotel, home, the future. "I tell them that," says Vartan quietly, "and then I go back about my business, and then I spend half the energy of my life trying to believe it."

Three Soviet soldiers are standing together at the bottom of the steps. Young boys with dun-colored flak jackets. Two with tanned faces. Afghanistan sunburns? Vartan has fished into his pocket — for what? Cigarettes. He looks at the pack, then at the soldiers. Then he hands it to one of them. "It's a funny thing. I'd just started to smoke again," he says as we walk toward our car.

JACQUES BARZUN

The Paradoxes of Creativity

FROM THE AMERICAN SCHOLAR

THE FIRST PARADOX resides in the very idea of Creation. To most people, that idea means producing something where nothing was before — making a thing out of nothing. But the same people who take that meaning for granted also believe from common sense and the teachings of science that nothing can be made from nothing; every object or creature is only the transformation of some pre-existing thing. In scientific terms, this is the law of conservation governing matter and energy.

But by a further turn of thought the question arises: How did anything whatever come to be for later conservation and transformation? The idea of creation ex nihilo returns full force. Believers in the literal truth of the Bible are sure of an answer, which is that an all-powerful being performed what none of us can do. Unfortunately, the well-named book of Genesis is also of two minds; it contains not one but two stories of creation. In the first chapter, the world and its denizens come out of chaos, which is nothing. In the second, they are made out of the ground, which is already there, as in most primitive cosmogonies. Biblical scholars tell us that the more majestic creation-from-the-void was in fact a later, sophisticated version that got put ahead of the other, older one. The vast majority of the church fathers and Catholic believers, as well as all good Protestants, have believed in creation out of nothing. This conception is so strong that it influenced the King James translators, who in strict grammar should have said that God *gave form* to the earlier chaos.

These differences and distinctions occur again, as we shall see, in theories of artistic and scientific creation. The present-day conflict between creationists and evolutionists exemplifies this dualism: to create species, evolution needs material to work on. This situation is paradoxical because there seems no way to escape seesawing between the two ideas; it is virtually a form of human thought; we encounter it on the humblest level. Take the useful household book called *How to Make Something Out of Nothing*. The title is catchy but makes one suspicious. Hence the subtitle, which is: *Newel Posts into Candelabra*. With this double view we get creation *and* evolution; the one excites our love of miracles, the other reassures common sense — and also invites us to perform with the aid of a recipe.

But to return for a moment to creation on the large scale, what does the latest science say about the genesis of the cosmos? The so-called Big Bang theory of the astrophysicists states that it came out of the void in a sudden explosion. Is this creation from nothing? The answer is yes, or rather yes *but*, because if you ask "explosion of what?" you are told that a vacuum is not altogether empty. It contains sweet nothings called "quantum fluctuations," which can somehow coagulate into something. Nothing happens until, according to calculations, the nothings add up to twenty-two pounds. Then comes the Big Bang. It is clear that Paradox Number One has science in its grip too. What is more, the do-it-yourself book about candelabra has its scientific counterpart: a Dr. Guth at Stanford has declared that given the right equipment he could get a universe going in his laboratory. Here, surely, is a man who can call himself gifted with creativity.

In contemporary culture, no idea is so appealing, no word is put to more frequent and more varied use than "creativity." In a new reference book of contemporary quotations, there are fifteen entries for Creativity and only three for Conversation, two for Wisdom, one for Contemplation, and none for Serenity or Repose. The magic of the word "creative" is so broad that no distinct meaning need be attached to it; it fits all situations, pointing to nothing in particular. Its sway extends over all of art and science, naturally, and it takes us beyond these to the basic conditions of modern society, to education, to our view of the human mind and what we conceive to be the goal of life itself.

Creativity has become what divine grace and salvation were to former times. It is incessantly invoked, praised, urged, demanded, hoped for, declared achieved, or found lacking. I take this last complaint from the most recent presidential campaign, in which a leading Democrat called Mr. Dukakis "lacking in creativity" — no further details given, the charge apparently self-explanatory.

The assumption is that creativity is an inborn quality that colors everything one does. It is no longer a rare power found in few people and concentrated on one particular skill. Indeed, it is often attributed to whole groups, as when the head of a dating agency said, "I wanted to attract the professional, the creative." But it is in business and education, both formerly thought rather humdrum, that the thought of creation is most obsessive. Not only are there several best sellers that teach "creativity in business," but corporations include "creative departments" and "directors of creative services." Schools advertise "Creative Continuing Education" or define education itself as "helping to live creatively through changing times." Simultaneously, critics complain that schools "do nothing for creativity, because they are institutionalized."

What else they could be we are not told, but we get an inkling when we hear that "after kindergarten, schools do not draw on creative ability." Kindergarten gives the child a freedom in learning that is close to play and it comes to an end in later grades. This is a clue to what concerns us here. "Creation" and "creativity" have come to mean simply release from compulsion and regimentation. This inference is confirmed by the now familiar demand for a "creative job" — that is, one in which much is left to individual initiative. A remark by the notable baseball player Ozzie Smith is to the point: "The first time I played shortstop I felt there was no other place for me on the field. It gave me the freedom to create as I feel." Clearly, he enjoys not being tied down to any of the other infield positions; at shortstop he roams at will, makes his own decisions, he is indeed a free agent.

It is the sense of being hemmed in by the job and the world that has caused the general yearning for something labeled creativity. The word is a condemnation of modern life, especially of modern work, organized as it is in vast networks, themselves parts of still larger systems. Rigid interdependence has long been cited as the cause of alienation on the factory assembly line; the same controls now hobble the mental worker, whose education and self-esteem make him resent a faceless coercion, worse than an arbitrary boss. "Create," then, means to do one's own thing, to perform by choosing means and opportunity at will.

Systems imply another feature, equally galling. Like industry, business and the professions now cut what is to be done into pieces assigned to different hands. Nobody produces anything whole, having a beginning, a middle, and an end. Everybody being a specialist means repetition without completion, so that no object ever emerges as the fruit of one's labors; nothing feeds the sense of accomplishment. Teamwork is much touted — by the organizers — but its satisfaction is indirect and loses its savor when the "team" is an anonymous mass in the hundreds, as happens not only in corporations but also in broadcasting networks, publishing empires, research laboratories, large foundations, and other supposedly intellectual establishments.

To sum up, the cult of creativity springs from the hatred of abstractness, dependence, repetition, and incompletion in work. The blight cannot be called drudgery, for this has always existed; the independent craftsman endured it cheerfully as a tested means toward the goal: a finished product, *his* product. Even the serf on the soil could look forward to a result, the harvest. The very ditch digger has his reward: he has created a hole, and from start to finish, whereas the truck driver who collects the tools of the diggers has only an endless round.

In these conditions, it was perhaps natural to borrow the term "create" from the artists, who pre-eminently make objects — whole objects at their own pace and according to their own ideas. But widespread as the feeling of deprivation in modern work may be, it is not evenly distributed: some people in business, industry, and the professions must be what *they* call creative, or the evil that a psychologist has called "career malaise" would not be curable by what he also calls a "creative work dimension." So we are bound to glance at these "dimensions." As it happens, a "Study of Creativity in Daily Life" has recently been made, complete with an Index of Creativity by which to measure oneself and others. It ranges from Minor Creativity to Exceptional. Here is an example of Minor: "a secretary who sometimes edits books on the side." Exceptional is "the amateur botanist who strictly limits hours at his regular job and often spends 20-hour days to complete botanical experiments."

This study is said to "illuminate the creative life." I find that it illuminates just the opposite. It confirms what I have said about the distaste for modern work, and the antidotes it names imply no more than the desire for autonomy and continuity of effort. This is not zeal for creation. Even the botanist who skimps on his duty to his employer and exemplifies the decline of the work ethic only makes amateur science into an absorbing hobby.

People who go in for avocations to fill the void left by their jobs and then stick the label "creative" on these sidelines are quite ingenuously debasing the meaning of the term. One tells us that "the home is a document to one's individuality and creativity." Another speaks of the "bold creativity" displayed by the chairman of a Senate subcommittee. The low point of nonsignificance in the use of the word was probably reached by the woman who, in recommending ways of making friends with strangers in a supermarket, said, "The secret is to be a little creative — think before you speak."

You can measure the distance that "creativity" has drifted away from the idea of creation if you change the phrase "a creative life" to "the life of a creator." This last phrase makes one think at once of Michelangelo or Beethoven or Einstein. The other is a thought-cliché or else a label not to be taken literally, as when we say that an actor creates a role or a freshman takes "creative writing." In this academic usage, "creative" denotes poetry or fiction; nobody could tell you why the essays of Montaigne and the Gettysburg Address were not creative writing. In any case, a creative writing course, being instruction, calls mostly for imitative writing.

This conventional usage was harmless, but now that the adjective has been trivialized, the idea of creativity has actually turned into its opposite. Far from promising the extraordinary and unheard of, it has come to signify a feature of employment that everybody once had a right to expect.

This new paradox was noted by a writer who deflated the claims of an advertising executive. "Creative," he said, "is industry jargon for words and ideas that go into an ad." One welcomes the translation but must not conclude that the abuse of "creative" is only a verbal fault. Rather, it is rooted in our conception of the human being. Democratic theory favors individualism (even though democratic practice may repress it) and the theory posits that, being by definition different, individuals possess originality and the urge to show it. Self-expression is promoted throughout the culture from infancy onward: be yourself, have a mind of your own, despise convention, speak up and protest, develop your unique abilities. These injunctions are expected to yield social benefits in the form of new perceptions, ideas, or devices. The word "innovation" is on everybody's tongue almost as often as the word "creative." Rewards in prestige and promotion await the innovative person with a creative plan — or vice versa.

Looking back over the last five hundred years, one may question whether the true creators of our civilization have ever needed this urging and coaching in order to become their remarkable selves and to make something really new. Most often their work has been hampered or ignored by the very society that now keeps boosting innovation. *This* paradox takes the form of saying, in words or by actions, "We want what is new and wonderful, not the strange and repellent thing that you offer." The people who are thought original and get pampered are those who bring familiar things titivated by touches of novelty. Think of the tricks that gain attention today in any of the arts; look at those who express themselves by tampering with what others have made — scriptwriters, directors of plays and operas who cut and transpose and change settings, adapters of all kinds. Shakespeare, whom everybody supposedly worships, is thus regularly mutilated by creative minds that know how to improve him.

When we speak soberly of creation in art or science, we surely mean something quite different. We have in mind a conception of art and intellect that developed in Western civilization beginning in the Renaissance and reaching its present form only in the early 1800s. The workers and craftsmen of earlier ages did not worry about self-expression and did not talk of creativity. On the contrary, the best craftsman was the one who reproduced the traditional model most exactly. Innovation came in the form of a new technical process — for firing clay or designing an arch; or again it arose out of religious decisions to use or not to use certain motifs or imagery. The great independent creator, the genius whom we affect to revere today, is a new social type who became the central figure in the cult of art when the rise of science brought on the decline of religion.

According to Shelley, it was Tasso who in the late 1500s first said that only God and the poet deserve the name of creator. Voltaire probably picked up the idea from Tasso and made a single casual use of it in the mid-eighteenth century. But by that time, the words "create" and "creation" had filtered into critical writing, although with a very limited sense. A poet was said to create when he introduced into his work fanciful, unreal beings and events. Thus Shakespeare's *Tempest* was called his most creative work, because of Ariel, Caliban, and the enchanted isle. It would have surprised everybody to hear that *Hamlet* was a creation, for it only held the mirror up to nature. Johnson's *Dictionary* of 1755 gives no instance of the term in the modern sense, nor does the four-volume enlargement of 1818. The only uses cited are: the king's creation of a peer, death creating a vacancy (or similar sequences), and lastly, an illusion leading to a false belief, as when Shakespeare in *Macbeth* calls the dagger "a creation of the mind."

The application of "creation" to a work of art coincided with a parallel change in the use of the word "genius." In ancient and medieval times, a genius or demon was a person's guardian spirit, giving good or evil advice in daily affairs. Then "genius" came to mean a knack of doing a particular thing — a gifted person was said to "have a genius" for calculation or public speaking. It gradually acquired a more honorific sense. By the 1750s "genius" was defined by the poet Edward Young as "the power of accomplishing great things without the means generally reputed necessary to that end." This notion fitted Shakespeare's case, for he was thought lacking in discipline, learning, and art. He had a wild, untutored genius.

In the next generation came the subtle shift from "having" to "being" a genius, with no limitation such as Young included in his praise. A genius was now a fully conscious, competent, and original "creator," and only two classes of artists were recognized: the geniuses and the nongeniuses, the second group being dismissed as "talents." Unable to create, they followed the path blazed by the genius.

The artist being seen as a creator gave art a new meaning. It was no longer a careful imitation of nature or observance of established rules. It was discovery, revelation, invention in all realms — new aspects of nature, new insights into character and social life, new and astonishing technique. The genius fashioned masterpieces that startled by their form and substance, thereby proving all rules wrong or futile; they also shocked by telling truths previously hidden behind convention and stupidity.

All this bore hard on the public and the merely talented. The art lover must now continually learn new habits and steel himself against the shocks, while every aspiring artist must strive for novelty at any cost. Since the works of genius, being born of a unique imagination, do not resemble one another nor those made earlier, each seemed a world complete in itself. The analogy with God's creation became obvious and inevitable.

Equally obvious is the fact that this new conception of the genius-creator has become for the modern world the prime model of human existence. The students who rioted in Chicago twenty years ago included in their platform: "the abolition of money" and "everybody an artist." As for adults, many now find the former patterns of glory — the soldier, the statesman, the divine — no longer on a par with the artist and the scientist. These are the new heroes, because they seem the only selfless and beneficent members of society; indeed they exemplify the scorn for money as well as the life that ordinary work precludes: no thought of gain, no routine, no orders from above or below, no bourgeois conventions — continual creativity and eternal fame.

The popularizing of such ideas came with the spread of public education and the diffusion of culture through libraries, museums, and the mechanical means of reproducing books, art, and music. The result has been that more and more people are tempted — indeed encouraged — to write novels, poems, and plays, to paint pictures, compose, and perform. It has begun to look as if artistic ability were universal and only stunted or repressed in those who do not become artists. Creativity, in short, is everybody's birthright. It is this democratizing that has produced the glut of acceptable works of art and with it the perpetual shortage of money for the support of artists. This in turn fuels perpetual resentment in artists and their well-wishers, even though modern society is the most generous on record in its eager consumption of cultural products.

Pondering all these facts suggests that in the blanket term "creativity" there are at least four layers of meaning. At the bottom is the commonplace quality of initiative illustrated above from workaday sources. Next comes the ordinary, widespread knack of drawing, singing, dancing, and versifying, modestly kept for private use. Above this level we find the trained professional artist, including the commercial, who supplies the market with the products in vogue. At the top is the rare bird, the genius, whose works first suggested the idea that a human being could be called a creator.

It seems to me to make no difference whether this scale denotes one quality bestowed in increasing amounts or two, three, or four distinct powers. What is important is to maintain in private and public opinion the awareness that there is a scale; one might call that effort "quality control." It should prevent one from believing, as many reviewers and other good people do, that the masterpieces touted in the journals every week or every month are actually such, and — at the other end of the scale — that the painting done by Johnny or Susan and the picking up of driftwood on the beach and the spraying of graffiti on the wall are creative acts in any reasonable sense.

A very able journalist recently wrote of a woman's giving birth as "the ultimate act of creation." If that is an acceptable view, then we must find some other word to describe God's performance and that of the great artist or scientist. The appreciation of true creators (and their early recognition) depends on remembering that even if their abilities are simply large in amount, there is a point where quantity suddenly turns into a difference of quality. It behaves like the critical mass in physics, which sets off a chain reaction in otherwise placid material. Colloquial speech records that same surprising sort of event when it uses "create" to mean whipping up a tantrum out of little or nothing.

The leap of creation tantalizes curiosity and prompts close scrutiny in hopes of an explanation. Some of the distinguishing traits of genius have long been noted. Plato wrote two dialogues on the ways of poets to show that they work in a kind of frenzy they cannot account for. That is the reason why the philosopher wanted to exclude them from his ideal republic: they are not rational, responsible people. Like the prophetess at Delphi, they are mad — and bad poets if they are *not* mad. He made a pun on the subject — Μαντικε (prophecy) is much the same as Μανικε (the state of being manic).

This observation is linked with the belief in a resident genius or demon whose urgings may inspire great deeds or great wickedness. With the prominence of "the artist," the connection between genius and strange, abnormal behavior was often taken for granted and served as an explanation. Shakespeare was only half joking when he described the poet with eyes "in fine frenzy rolling," and Dryden meant seriously his line about "great wits to madness near allied." Yet another piece of theorizing in this vein was published only five years ago.

Indeed, the systematic study of genius has swung between this assumption of the crazy artist and the idea of common ability rising in regular gradation to uncommon heights. Intelligence testers actually give to high scorers the name of genius; it is a standard classification. Earlier, Darwin's cousin Francis Galton had gathered statistics on what he called human faculty that proved to his satisfaction how it was distributed. It seemed to him a law of nature that there should be geniuses at one end of the curve to balance the idiots at the other.

Those investigators who, as it were, put their money on madness, have gone about proving their case by studying the parentage and diseases of artists. Cesare Lombroso, who found a criminal type, also found a genius type of warped physical and mental constitution. But the man who made the greatest splash with that idea was Dr. Max Nordau with his book *Degeneration,* a best seller that alarmed and delighted readers at the turn of the century. It asserted that nearly all contemporary masters in every art were degenerate or diseased: Zola, Wagner, Ibsen, Tolstoy, the Impressionists, were all hospital or asylum cases.

In a stunning refutation called "The Sanity of Art," Bernard Shaw established the paradox that poets and other artists are called great only when their works show the rest of the world some new and profound truth about man or society: geniuses, said Shaw, are "masters of reality." So if they are mad as well, it follows that it takes the mad to teach the sane. But of course the madness theory is unfounded. Some geniuses have been mad: Tasso, van Gogh, and Sir Isaac Newton showed symptoms of mental aberration, as did Dr. Johnson. But (like Johnson himself) Byron, Goethe, Rubens, and Berlioz were among the sanest men who ever lived, able managers of complex worldly enterprises, models of elevated common sense.

What is true is that when Dr. Nordau was making his diagnoses by remote inspection, a number of poets and artists were dragging out lives of disease, alcoholism, drug addiction, and psychosis. W. B. Yeats, who was strong and healthy, was appalled at the extent of the evil and wondered what curse had befallen his generation. The social and economic conditions of the time suffice to explain the curse — that is, the pressures that sensitive and often destitute human beings failed to withstand.

There is moreover what might be termed the biographical fallacy. Books about the lives of the great fill our minds with anecdotes of their odd behavior, but these are oddities only because the comparable acts of ordinary people are never written up for the world to read. We shake our heads on reading that Dickens had to have certain ornaments in a certain pattern on his writing table. But nobody ever hears of the bank manager who has to doodle and must have a colored pencil to do it or he cannot think financially. Yet both are merely using a sensory stimulus to trigger a habit of work.

The specific traits of creative genius have never been ascertained, nor any correlation with genetic, medical, or environmental factors. I have read more English, German, Italian, and French studies of genius than I care to remember, and I think their findings would leave any reader unconvinced and uninstructed. For a sample, turn to the article "Creativity" in the *Encyclopedia of the Social Sciences*. It starts out with the usual confidence of people armed with method and faith in science; it winds up pathetically with a list of characteristics that covers the full range of human abilities — necessarily so, since the world's great performers have been of every kind and temperament.

It is wiser and more entertaining to read good biographies, and even better, memoirs, letters, and diaries. If one guards against the fallacy of "How odd!" they will be found to disprove every cliché, including the definition of genius as an infinite capacity for taking pains — or, as they say it in French, "a protracted patience." Ruskin, writing to Rossetti, repeatedly urged him not to draw and rub out and draw again, adding on one occasion, "I am not more sure of anything in this world than that the utmost a man can do is that which he can do without effort." Shaw put it succinctly when he said, "Great art is either easy or impossible." When Dickens was asked to account for the stroke of genius that changed *Pickwick Papers* in chapter six from a set of rural mishaps for comic illustration into a piece of world literature, all he said was, "Then I thought of Mr. Pickwick."

But no sooner do we conclude that inspiration is all, than we bump into Flaubert, who toiled at his desk like a digger in a coal mine. Of course, his full output was four novels and three short stories, not Dickens's fifteen novels, plus unnumerable tales, travel notes, and historical sketches, all this done while editing periodicals and giving public readings. To Flaubert great art was not impossible but it was not easy. Nor was it to Beethoven, whose notebooks testify to the very effort that Ruskin advised against — try and try again until the theme, the development, and the form satisfy. Many others have recorded their life-and-death struggle with the material of their art. Conrad was a great storyteller from the start, but Balzac had to write trash for ten years before his genius erupted. As Goethe said, "Blood sticks to the work."

As for men of science, they have touted unwearied persistence as the chief condition of their creativeness. But they have also spoken of sudden illumination — Gauss idly gazing at the hills outside his window, Poincaré finding the solution of intractable problems on arising from sleep, and so on. Chalk up another paradox.

And it is not the last. So far from creativity being a permanent trait that varies only in intensity, it can disappear totally — and sometimes reappear. Hugo Wolf and A. E. Housman are notorious cases in point. Both had two periods of creative energy separated by a long fallow interval. And the saying that poets die young may carry a double meaning in the word "die": the body survives but the genius has gone, as is frequently true of mathematicians and chess players. At the opposite extreme we find long-lived poets, such as Wordsworth and Victor Hugo, who keep on producing genuine poetry to the end. They go to work, as somebody has said, like bureaucrats, writing day in and day out. The quality fluctuates, but the power never vanishes.

Still more puzzling in its variations is the occurrence of creative historical periods. Why the crowd of great painters and thinkers in early Renaissance Italy, then the migration of the art to the Netherlands? Why the Elizabethan dramatists and musicians? France, Spain, Germany, Austria, and Russia also have their high moments in one or another art, which relapses into the worthy regularity of the talented, until the next outbreak of the creative epidemic. No correlation is to be found between these bursts of genius and peace or war, freedom or tyranny, prosperity or decline, let alone with climate or race. The only feature present every time is the crowding of the gifted on one spot. But this is a kind of tautology, since creative period *means* a cluster of creators, which soon attracts to its center other eager artists from all over. Here again, the critical mass changes the character of the pre-existing elements.

Baffled in the search for something like a genius type, modern psychologists and critics have pursued another entity, which they call the creative process. It is characteristic of a technological age to imagine that creation is a series of steps that can be discovered and analyzed, like digestion or photosynthesis. The public, too, accepts the idea when librarians exhibit writers' manuscripts and bid everybody observe the "process" by which the poet got to his final draft. Well, manuscript corrections may be interesting, but as explanation they are illusory. What impelled dissatisfaction with a bad line may be guessed, but not the leap from it to the perfect phrasing. Besides, great writers have often spoiled some of their work by late revisions — Dryden, Wordsworth, Henry James, to name a few. Is that a process of de-creation?

If creation were a process, by this time its operation would have been reduced to formulas, recipes, which intelligence and method could apply to produce great art and great science. Those who come nearest to seizing the secret are the immediate followers of the innovators; and followers, by common consent, rank second best. For what they have caught from the creators is technique, and technique is not enough. Something more is needed — and perhaps something less. Take the music of Saint-Saëns. Here was a precocious, enormously gifted musician; he could turn out pieces that seemed as if written by Mozart or Beethoven or anybody he wished. But as Berlioz, who was his mentor, regretfully remarked, the young man lacked *in*experience. Courses in fiction writing may number top-notch students, yet not turn out Chekhovs and Henry Jameses; though someone here and there may in time become — himself. Similarly, laboratories all over the globe are manned by scientists who probably deserve to be called brilliant without being of the breed of Newton, Faraday, Pasteur, and Einstein. In short, creation does not proceed, it occurs.

If so, what is the conceivable source of the creative power? Could one discover it, at least one paradox would be removed — I mean the apparent contradiction of great art achieved with ease or else with anxious toil. One could say that some artists must dig a deep well to tap the source, whereas others have a spring that bubbles up on its own. Or to put it differently, the creative moments are what matter and they come at different intervals during the work, which is always long and laborious. The ever-inventive Dickens spent long mornings in front of a series of false starts, and Balzac rewrote again and again on one set of proofs after another.

We are thus brought to the final paradox, the one inside the mind. For the past fifty years, the characteristics of creators have been attributed to the Unconscious, with a capital *U*. Depth psychology posits that the instincts drive the mind and that individual thought is shaped by the way in which those drives are handled. In human society, the vicissitudes of growing up, as well as the permanent forces of culture, create inhibitions or repressions. These modify the interplay between the parts of this machinery and hence determine its products. According to one interpretation, great artists are like children, who, unsocialized, heed the imagination and speak out freely. The conscious mind of the adult artist and his acquired techniques merely organize the spontaneous voices from the Unconscious. Geniuses keep in touch with this creative force while the rest of us bottle it up by conventions and neuroses. Through this unusual freedom, the creator is able to express fundamental reality and teach us to see it as it is.

It is true that some artists have likened themselves to outspoken children, but this diagram of the psychologists is open to objections. In the first place, it supposes the mind to be a sort of gearbox set in motion by an engine below. The analogy fails to explain: a powerful engine, unobstructed, will make wheels move faster or longer, but it cannot make them do one thing rather than another. The pattern of the mind must itself be different if it is to perform different things, some of them extraordinary. Alternatively, if creativeness comes from the Unconscious, this hypothetical organ must hold knowledge of life and art in solution for crystallization by the mind; but the theory assigns no such range or subtlety to the biological drives.

Besides, the Unconscious is a piece of equipment that by definition everybody possesses. If, as is said, it contains the archetypal forms of feeling and belief that underlie both common thought and works of art, it follows that something else must exist to diversify this common fund of fantasy and make the visions of the poet differ from the daydreams of the ordinary man. Finally, it is notorious that artists, like most civilized people, suffer from neuroses; indeed, they suffer perhaps more, if we may judge from their misadventures in practical life. This contradicts the assumption that their remarkable works betoken ready communication with their Unconscious, particular or collective.

What, if anything, do the creators themselves have to say about conscious and unconscious? I mentioned earlier Poincaré's report of his mode of discovery: he struggles with a problem for many days, then lets it go, and in the end the hint of a solution comes to him as he emerges from sleep. Milton's muse, the poet said, "dictates to him slumbering"; Mozart wrote that while composing he felt as if he were under the spell of a strong dream. Helmholtz, the German physicist, would take solitary walks for relief from concentration, and the sought-for idea would come unbidden into his mind. Berlioz in his memoirs contrasts the unwelcome task of writing prose with that of writing music, which he says happens of itself, as by "an inexplicable mechanism."

All these observations point to the workings of a nonconscious agency, but is it the Unconscious of theory? Clearly, the unseen agency is put to work by the conscious mind, which demands an object and prepares elaborately to handle the makings of it. Nor is nonconscious incubation reserved for creators. When you can't remember a name, you try hard at first to bring it back — and fail. Having given up, you find it a while later floating up of its own accord. Every professional writer knows that the exact word he wants but cannot summon up will soon present itself if he only keeps on writing. Surely the deep Unconscious is not a dictionary; so the word or name that pops up was not among the drives or archetypes but in the subliminal region from which, for example, we draw the ability to play the piano while also talking seriously to a friend. The subliminal is not an originating force, but our memories and habits stored away.

It would appear, then, that the mystery of creation defies analysis; it may do so forever, like the workings of mind itself. Yet one student of the mind has offered facts and ideas that seem to me to bring us if not an explanation of genius and creation at least a right conception of their workings. I refer to William James, who took up these questions several times in different connections.

The genius, according to James, has an enormous capacity for perceiving similarities among disparate things; his mind jumps across the grooves cut by common experience. His is also a sensitive mind; every stimulus starts multiple trains of thought, wildly free associations. "In such minds," says James, "subjects bud and sprout and grow. . . . Their ideas coruscate, every subject branches infinitely before their fertile minds." This explains why being too good a student can limit creativity — what Berlioz termed "the lack of inexperience" — for learning follows traveled roads. And James, with *his* characteristic genius, draws a comparison which is at once comic and illuminating. He says that the profusion of possible ideas in the creative mind resembles the confusion of the muddle-headed person; hence the *eminently* muddle-headed are in a sense close to genius.

But clearly there is a difference between the two, which Dr. Harry Wilmer pointed out when he said that the nongenius "lets the awareness slip by." The genius's goal rivets his attention and puts order among his ideas. In fact, his concentration upon the activity required — writing, painting, composing; and in the sciences, observing, calculating, conceptualizing — becomes an obsession. In this effort, not merely the mind and the will but the whole organism — muscles, blood, nerves, and glands — are involved. This mad passion or passionate madness is the reason why psychopathic personalities are often creators and why their productions are perfectly sane; the disturbance makes for the obsession, while the contents of the work are formed by the fertile, subtle, and vigilant intellect. This conception of genius would account for the paradox that it consists both of sudden inspiration and of patient, painstaking work. Hence also the versatility and often superhuman bulk of its output.

James's description has other corollaries. In essence, one act of creation is as amazing as a dozen, but in practice we reserve our fervent admiration for the artist who creates great works again and again. This amounts to a critical principle: magnitude and frequency of success are the proper measure of creativity. Exquisiteness and perfection may occasionally beguile us more, but they are lesser achievements. Again, the error of regarding children as artists is due to overlooking the paucity of their intellectual and emotional resources. Sensitive and uninhibited they may be, but their minds cannot encompass the vast array of thoughts, memories, and associations that the great artist fuses into a single shape. Every good listener has noticed this limitation in the child virtuoso who tries to interpret a masterpiece.

These considerations add force to the suggestion that the term "creativity" should not be loosely applied, squandered upon works and workers that are respectable enough on their own level but that do not stand comparison with genuine creation. Nowadays, originality, the cult of the new, and plain shock power have such a hold on our judgment that we pay humble attention to a great deal of nonsense and charlatanism. This gullibility spreads wide and provides a market for the users of the topsy-turvy as a formula. Present the familiar upside down and there's originality, nobody can deny that it's new. It is anybody's guess how much of contemporary art is the outcome of this recipe. One recent example turns up in an unimportant film, but it is typical. The maker of *Without a Clue* tells us, "It was that moment when you think, 'There's a good idea. What if Watson is actually the genius and Holmes is this ridiculous ham in front of Scotland Yard?' " Truly a splendid idea for defeating expectation, but a far cry from the idea that first created Holmes and Watson out of little or nothing.

It may seem an ultimate paradox to end with an example from a genre that can plead as excuse that it is not creative but commercial. Yet it is significant for the same reason that led me to distinguish creation from creativity. That reason lies in my conviction that a long period of creation is coming to an end. For some five hundred years Western civilization has enjoyed a profusion of high art, art "created by genius." Today, the conditions arising from machine industry and the democratic state have persuaded the world that creative power is within the reach of all by natural right, like political power. That belief has brought out many agreeable things that resemble true creation and are said to be the real thing.

But this extensive effort has had unexpected results. It has not only diluted the meaning of "creative"; it has also glutted the market with innumerable objects and performances arbitrarily called art, thereby making it even more arduous for true creation to find a public. Still more generally, "creative" foolery has been distorting, denaturing, destroying the fund of culture amassed since the Renaissance. That is the sense in which the filmmaker quoted above is typical. He found a pair of well-known creations and his creativity prompted him to confound their meaning, blur their appeal. This is in the tradition of Duchamp's putting a mustache on Mona Lisa and many other imitations of that famous de-creative act.

The impulse and the clever deeds are part of an irresistible historical sweep. Some of us might prefer to live in a time of construction, which has a different kind of excitement. But let no one repine. Rebuilding is bound to come, because true creative power is a phoenix, and the forces of destruction are clearing the space for its new flight, none can tell when or where. Meantime, if we are to recognize the bird when it appears, let us not forget that creation means making something new and making it out of little or nothing.

ANATOLE BROYARD

Intoxicated by My Illness

FROM THE NEW YORK TIMES MAGAZINE

SO MUCH of a writer's life consists of assumed suffering, rhetor-
ical suffering, that I felt something like relief, even elation, when
the doctor told me that I had cancer of the prostate. Suddenly
there was in the air a rich sense of crisis, real crisis, yet one that
also contained echoes of ideas like the crisis of language, the
crisis of literature, or of personality. It seemed to me that my
existence, whatever I thought, felt, or did, had taken on a kind
of meter, as in poetry, or in taxis.

When you learn that your life is threatened, you can turn toward
this knowledge or away from it. I turned toward it. It was not a
choice but an automatic shifting of gears, a tacit agreement between my body and my brain. I thought that time had tapped
me on the shoulder, that I had been given a real deadline at last.
It wasn't that I believed the cancer was going to kill me, even
though it had spread beyond the prostate — it could probably
be controlled, either by radiation or hormonal manipulation. No,
what struck me was the startled awareness that one day something, whatever it might be, was going to interrupt my leisurely
progress. It sounds trite, yet I can only say that I realized for the
first time that I don't have forever.

Time was no longer innocuous, nothing was casual anymore.
I understood that living itself had a deadline. Like the book I
had been working on — how sheepish I would feel if I couldn't
finish it. I had promised it to myself and to my friends. Though
I wouldn't say this out loud, I had promised it to the world. All
writers privately think this way.

When my friends heard I had cancer, they found me surprisingly cheerful and talked about my courage. But it has nothing to do with courage, at least not for me. As far as I can tell, it's a question of desire. I'm filled with desire — to live, to write, to do everything. Desire itself is a kind of immortality. While I've always had trouble concentrating, I now feel as concentrated as a diamond, or a microchip.

I remember a time in the 1950s when I tried to talk a friend of mine named Jules out of committing suicide. He had already made one attempt and when I went to see him he said, "Give me a good reason to go on living." He was thirty years old.

I saw what I had to do. I started to sell life to him, like a real estate agent. Just look at the world, I said. How can you not be curious about it? The streets, the houses, the trees, the shops, the people, the movement, and the stillness. Look at the women, so appealing, each in her own way. Think of all the things you can do with them, the places you can go together. Think of books, paintings, music. Think of your friends.

While I was talking I wondered, Am I telling Jules the truth? He didn't think so, because he put his head in the oven a week later. As for me, I don't know whether I believed what I said or not, because I just went on behaving like everybody else. But I believe it now. When my wife made me a hamburger the other day I thought it was the most fabulous hamburger in the history of the world.

With this illness one of my recurrent dreams has finally come true. Several times in the past I've dreamed that I had committed a crime — or perhaps I was only accused of a crime, it's not clear. When brought to trial I refused to have a lawyer — I got up instead and made an impassioned speech in my own defense. This speech was so moving that I could feel myself tingling with it. It was inconceivable that the jury would not acquit me — only each time I woke before the verdict. Now cancer is the crime I may or may not have committed and the eloquence of being alive, the fervor of the survivor, is my best defense.

The way my friends have rallied around me is wonderful. They remind me of a flock of birds rising from a body of water into the sunset. If that image seems a bit extravagant, or tinged with satire, it's because I can't help thinking there's something comi-

cal about my friends' behavior, all these witty men suddenly saying pious, inspirational things.

They are not intoxicated as I am by my illness, but sobered.
Since I refused to, they've taken on the responsibility of being
serious. They appear abashed, or chagrined, in their sobriety.
Stripped of their playfulness these pals of mine seem plainer,
homelier — even older. It's as if they had all gone bald overnight.

Yet one of the effects of their fussing over me is that I feel
vivid, multicolored, sharply drawn. On the other hand — and
this is ungrateful — I remain outside of their solicitude, their
love and best wishes. I'm isolated from them by the grandiose
conviction that I am the healthy person and they are the sick
ones. Like an existential hero, I have been cured by the truth
while they still suffer the nausea of the uninitiated.

I've had eight-inch needles thrust into my belly where I could
feel them tickling my metaphysics. I've worn Pampers. I've been
licked by the flames and my sense of self has been singed. Sartre
was right: you have to live each moment as if you're prepared to
die.

Now at last I understand the conditional nature of the human
condition. Yet, unlike Kierkegaard and Sartre, I'm not interested in the irony of my position. Cancer cures you of irony.
Perhaps my irony was all in my prostate. A dangerous illness fills
you with adrenaline and makes you feel very smart. I can afford
now, I said to myself, to draw conclusions. All those grand gen-
eralizations toward which I have been building for so many years
are finally taking shape. As I look back at how I used to be, it
seems to me that an intellectual is a person who thinks that the
classical clichés don't apply to him, that he is immune to homely
truths. I know better now. I see everything with a summarizing
eye. Nature is a terrific editor.

In the first stages of my illness I couldn't sleep, urinate, or
defecate — the word "ordeal" comes to mind. Then when my
doctor changed all this and everything worked again, what a vo-
luptuous pleasure it was. With a cry of joy I realized how marvelous it is simply to function. My body, which in the last decade
or two had become a familiar, no longer thrilling old flame, was
reborn as a brand-new infatuation.

I realize of course that this elation I feel is just a phase, just a rush of consciousness, a splash of perspective, a hot flash of ontological alertness. But I'll take it, I'll use it. I'll use everything I can while I wait for the next phase. Illness is primarily a drama and it should be possible to enjoy it as well as to suffer it. I see now why the romantics were so fond of illness — the sick man sees everything as metaphor. In this phase I'm infatuated with my cancer. It stinks of revelation.

As I look ahead, I feel like a man who has awakened from a long afternoon nap to find the evening stretched out before him. I'm reminded of D'Annunzio, the Italian poet, who said to a duchess he had just met at a party in Paris, "Come, we will have a profound evening." Why not? I see the balance of my life — everything comes in images now — as a beautiful paisley shawl thrown over a grand piano.

Why a paisley shawl, precisely? Why a grand piano? I have no idea. That's the way the situation presents itself to me. I have to take my imagery along with my medicine.

ALAN M. DERSHOWITZ

Shouting "Fire!"

FROM THE ATLANTIC MONTHLY

WHEN the Reverend Jerry Falwell learned that the Supreme Court had reversed his $200,000 judgment against *Hustler* magazine for the emotional distress that he had suffered from an outrageous parody, his response was typical of those who seek to censor speech: "Just as no person may scream 'Fire!' in a crowded theater when there is no fire, and find cover under the First Amendment, likewise, no sleazy merchant like Larry Flynt should be able to use the First Amendment as an excuse for maliciously and dishonestly attacking public figures, as he has so often done."

Justice Oliver Wendell Holmes's classic example of unprotected speech — falsely shouting "Fire!" in a crowded theater — has been invoked so often, by so many people, in such diverse contexts, that it has become part of our national folk language. It has even appeared — most appropriately — in the theater: in Tom Stoppard's play *Rosencrantz and Guildenstern Are Dead* a character shouts at the audience, "Fire!" He then quickly explains: "It's all right — I'm demonstrating the misuse of free speech." Shouting "Fire!" in the theater may well be the only jurisprudential analogy that has assumed the status of a folk argument. A prominent historian recently characterized it as "the most brilliantly persuasive expression that ever came from Holmes' pen." But in spite of its hallowed position in both the jurisprudence of the First Amendment and the arsenal of political discourse, it is and was an inapt analogy, even in the context in which it was originally offered. It has lately become — despite, perhaps even because of, the frequency and promiscuousness of its invocation — little more than a caricature of logical argumentation.

The case that gave rise to the "Fire!"-in-a-crowded-theater analogy, *Schenck* v. *United States,* involved the prosecution of Charles Schenck, who was the general secretary of the Socialist party in Philadelphia, and Elizabeth Baer, who was its recording secretary. In 1917 a jury found Schenck and Baer guilty of attempting to cause insubordination among soldiers who had been drafted to fight in the First World War. They and other party members had circulated leaflets urging draftees not to "submit to intimidation" by fighting in a war being conducted on behalf of "Wall Street's chosen few."

Schenck admitted, and the Court found, that the intent of the pamphlets' "impassioned language" was to "influence" draftees to resist the draft. Interestingly, however, Justice Holmes noted that nothing in the pamphlet suggested that the draftees should use unlawful or violent means to oppose conscription: "In form at least [the pamphlet] confined itself to peaceful measures, such as a petition for the repeal of the act" and an exhortation to exercise "your right to assert your opposition to the draft." Many of its most impassioned words were quoted directly from the Constitution.

Justice Holmes acknowledged that "in many places and in ordinary times the defendants, in saying all that was said in the circular, would have been within their constitutional rights." "But," he added, "the character of every act depends upon the circumstances in which it is done." And to illustrate that truism he went on to say:

> The most stringent protection of free speech would not protect a man in falsely shouting fire in a theater, and causing a panic. It does not even protect a man from an injunction against uttering words that may have all the effect of force.

Justice Holmes then upheld the convictions in the context of a wartime draft, holding that the pamphlet created "a clear and present danger" of hindering the war effort while our soldiers were fighting for their lives and our liberty.

The example of shouting "Fire!" obviously bore little relationship to the facts of the Schenck case. The Schenck pamphlet contained a substantive political message. It urged its draftee readers to *think* about the message and then — if they so chose — to act on it in a lawful and nonviolent way. The man who shouts "Fire!" in a crowded theater is neither sending a political message nor inviting his listener to think about what he has said and decide what to do in a rational, calculated manner. On the contrary, the message is designed to force action *without* contemplation. The message "Fire!" is directed not to the mind and the conscience of the listener but, rather, to his adrenaline and his feet. It is a stimulus to immediate *action*, not thoughtful reflection. It is — as Justice Holmes recognized in his follow-up sentence — the functional equivalent of "uttering words that may have all the effect of force."

Indeed, in that respect the shout of "Fire!" is not even speech, in any meaningful sense of that term. It is a *clang* sound, the equivalent of setting off a nonverbal alarm. Had Justice Holmes been more honest about his example, he would have said that freedom of speech does not protect a kid who pulls a fire alarm in the absence of a fire. But that obviously would have been irrelevant to the case at hand. The proposition that pulling an alarm is not protected speech certainly leads to the conclusion that shouting the word "fire" is also not protected. But the core analogy is the nonverbal alarm, and the derivative example is the verbal shout. By cleverly substituting the derivative shout for the core alarm, Holmes made it possible to analogize one set of words to another — as he could not have done if he had begun with the self-evident proposition that setting off an alarm bell is not free speech.

The analogy is thus not only inapt but also insulting. Most Americans do not respond to political rhetoric with the same kind of automatic acceptance expected of schoolchildren responding to a fire drill. Not a single recipient of the Schenck pamphlet is known to have changed his mind after reading it. Indeed, one draftee, who appeared as a prosecution witness, was asked whether reading a pamphlet asserting that the draft law was unjust would make him "immediately decide that you must erase that law." Not surprisingly, he replied, "I do my own thinking." A theatergoer would probably not respond similarly if asked how he would react to a shout of "Fire!"

Another important reason why the analogy is inapt is that Holmes emphasizes the factual falsity of the shout "Fire!" The Schenck pamphlet, however, was not factually false. It contained political opinions and ideas about the causes of the war and about appropriate and lawful responses to the draft. As the Supreme Court recently reaffirmed (in *Falwell* v. *Hustler*), "The First Amendment recognizes no such thing as a 'false' idea." Nor does it recognize false opinions about the causes of or cures for war.

A closer analogy to the facts of the Schenck case might have been provided by a person's standing outside a theater, offering the patrons a leaflet advising them that in his opinion the theater was structurally unsafe, and urging them not to enter but to complain to the building inspectors. That analogy, however, would not have served Holmes's argument for punishing Schenck. Holmes needed an analogy that would appear relevant to Schenck's political speech but that would invite the conclusion that censorship was appropriate.

Unsurprisingly, a war-weary nation — in the throes of a know-nothing hysteria over immigrant anarchists and socialists — welcomed the comparison between what was regarded as a seditious political pamphlet and a malicious shout of "Fire!" Ironically, the "Fire!" analogy is nearly all that survives from the Schenck case; the ruling itself is almost certainly not good law. Pamphlets of the kind that resulted in Schenck's imprisonment have been circulated with impunity during subsequent wars.

Over the past several years I have assembled a collection of instance — cases, speeches, arguments — in which proponents of censorship have maintained that the expression at issue is "just like" or "equivalent to" falsely shouting "Fire!" in a crowded theater and ought to be banned, "just as" shouting "Fire!" ought to be banned. The analogy is generally invoked, often with self-satisfaction, as an absolute argument-stopper. It does, after all, claim the high authority of the great Justice Oliver Wendell Holmes. I have rarely heard it invoked in a convincing, or even particularly relevant, way. But that, too, can claim lineage from the great Holmes.

Not unlike Falwell, with his silly comparison between shouting "Fire!" and publishing an offensive parody, courts and commentators have frequently invoked "Fire!" as an analogy to expression that is not an automatic stimulus to panic. A state supreme court held that "Holmes' aphorism . . . applies with equal force to pornography" — in particular to the exhibition of the movie *Carmen Baby* in a drive-in theater in close proximity to highways and homes. Another court analogized "picketing . . . in support of a secondary boycott" to shouting "Fire!" because in both instances "speech and conduct are brigaded." In the famous Skokie case one of the judges argued that allowing Nazis to march through a city where a large number of Holocaust survivors live "just might fall into the same category as one's 'right' to cry fire in a crowded theater."

Outside court the analogies become even more badly stretched. A spokesperson for the New Jersey Sports and Exposition Authority complained that newspaper reports to the effect that a large number of football players had contracted cancer after playing in the Meadowlands — a stadium atop a landfill — were the "journalistic equivalent of shouting fire in a crowded theater." An insect researcher acknowledged that his prediction that a certain amusement park might become roach-infested "may be tantamount to shouting fire in a crowded theater." The philosopher Sidney Hook, in a letter to the *New York Times* bemoaning a Supreme Court decision that required a plaintiff in a defamation action to prove that the offending statement was actually false, argued that the First Amendment does not give the press carte blanche to accuse innocent persons "any more than the First Amendment protects the right of someone falsely to shout fire in a crowded theater."

Some close analogies to shouting "Fire!" or setting off an alarm are, of course, available: calling in a false bomb threat; dialing 911 and falsely describing an emergency; making a loud, gunlike sound in the presence of the President; setting off a voice-activated sprinkler system by falsely shouting "Fire!" In one case in which the "Fire!" analogy was directly to the point, a creative defendant tried to get around it. The case involved a man who calmly advised an airline clerk that he was "only here to hijack the plane." He was charged, in effect, with shouting "Fire!" in a crowded theater, and his rejected defense — as quoted by the court — was as follows: "If we built fire-proof theaters and let people know about this, then the shouting of 'Fire!' would not cause panic."

Here are some more-distant but still related examples: the recent incident of the police slaying in which some members of an onlooking crowd urged a mentally ill vagrant who had taken an officer's gun to shoot the officer; the screaming of racial epithets during a tense confrontation; shouting down a speaker and preventing him from continuing his speech.

Analogies are, by their nature, matters of degree. Some are closer to the core example than others. But any attempt to analogize political ideas in a pamphlet, ugly parody in a magazine, offensive movies in a theater, controversial newspaper articles, or any of the other expressions and actions catalogued above to the very different act of shouting "Fire!" in a crowded theater is either self-deceptive or self-serving.

The government does, of course, have some arguably legitimate bases for suppressing speech which bear no relationship to shouting "Fire!" It may ban the publication of nuclear-weapon codes, of information about troop movements, and of the identity of undercover agents. It may criminalize extortion threats and conspiratorial agreements. These expressions may lead directly to serious harm, but the mechanisms of causation are very different from that at work when an alarm is sounded. One may also argue — less persuasively, in my view — against protecting certain forms of public obscenity and defamatory statements. Here, too, the mechanisms of causation are very different. None of these exceptions to the First Amendment's exhortation that the government "shall make no law . . . abridging the freedom of speech, or of the press" is anything like falsely shouting "Fire!" in a crowded theater; they all must be justified on other grounds.

A comedian once told his audience, during a stand-up routine, about the time he was standing around a fire with a crowd of people and got in trouble for yelling "Theater, theater!" That, I think, is about as clever and productive a use as anyone has ever made of Holmes's flawed analogy.

ANNIE DILLARD

The Stunt Pilot

FROM ESQUIRE

DAVE RAHM lived in Bellingham, Washington, north of Seattle.
Bellingham, a harbor town, lies between the alpine North Cascade Mountains and the San Juan Islands in Haro Strait above
Puget Sound. The latitude is that of Newfoundland. Dave Rahm
was a stunt pilot, the air's own genius.

In 1975, with a newcomer's willingness to try anything once, I
attended the Bellingham Air Show. The Bellingham airport was
a wide clearing in a forest of tall Douglas firs; its runways suited
small planes. It was June. People wearing blue or tan zipped
jackets stood loosely on the concrete walkways and runways outside the coffee shop. At that latitude in June, you stayed outside
because you could, even most of the night, if you could think up
something to do. The sky did not darken until ten o'clock or so,
and it never got very dark. Your life parted and opened in the
sunlight. You tossed your dark winter routines, thought up mad
projects, and improvised everything from hour to hour. Being a
stunt pilot seemed the most reasonable thing in the world; you
could wave your arms in the air all day and all night, and sleep
next winter.

I saw from the ground a dozen stunt pilots; the air show scheduled them one after the other, for an hour of aerobatics. Each
pilot took up his or her plane and performed a batch of tricks.
They were precise and impressive. They flew upside down, and
straightened out; they did barrel rolls, and straightened out; they
drilled through dives and spins, and landed gently on a far runway.

For the end of the day, separated from all other performances of every sort, the air show director had scheduled a program titled "Dave Rahm." The leaflet said that Rahm was a geologist who taught at Western Washington University. He had flown for King Hussein in Jordan. A tall man in the crowd told me Hussein had seen Rahm fly on a visit the king made to the United States; he had invited him to Jordan to perform at ceremonies. Hussein was a pilot, too. "Hussein thought he was the greatest thing in the world."

Idly, paying scant attention, I saw a medium-sized, rugged man dressed in brown leather, all begoggled, climb in a black biplane's open cockpit. The plane was a Bücker Jungman, built in the thirties. I saw a tall, dark-haired woman seize a propeller tip at the plane's nose and yank it down till the engine caught. He was off; he climbed high over the airport in his biplane, very high until he was barely visible as a mote, and then seemed to fall down the air, diving headlong, and streaming beauty in spirals behind him.

The black plane dropped spinning, and flattened out spinning the other way; it began to carve the air into forms that built wildly and musically on each other and never ended. Reluctantly, I started paying attention. Rahm drew high above the world an inexhaustibly glorious line; it piled over our heads in loops and arabesques. It was like a Saul Steinberg fantasy; the plane was the pen. Like Steinberg's contracting and billowing pen line, the line Rahm spun moved to form new, punning shapes from the edges of the old. Like a Klee line, it smattered the sky with landscapes and systems.

The air show announcer hushed. He had been squawking all day, and now he quit. The crowd stilled. Even the children watched dumbstruck as the slow, black biplane buzzed its way around the air. Rahm made beauty with his whole body; it was pure pattern, and you could watch it happen. The plane moved every way a line can move, and it controlled three dimensions, so the line carved massive and subtle slits in the air like sculptures. The plane looped the loop, seeming to arch its back like a gymnast; it stalled, dropped, and spun out of it climbing; it spiraled and knifed west on one side's wings and back east on another; it turned cartwheels, which must be physically impossible;

it played with its own line like a cat with yarn. How did the pilot know where in the air he was? If he got lost, the ground would swat him.

Rahm did everything his plane could do: tailspins, four-point rolls, flat spins, figure eights, snap rolls, and hammerheads. He did pirouettes on the plane's tail. The other pilots could do these stunts too, skillfully, one at a time. But Rahm used the plane inexhaustibly, like a brush marking thin air.

His was pure energy and naked spirit. I have thought about it for years. Rahm's line unrolled in time. Like music, it split the bulging rim of the future along its seam. It pried out the present. We watchers waited for the split-second curve of beauty in the present to reveal itself. The human pilot, Dave Rahm, worked in the cockpit right at the plane's nose; his very body tore into the future for us and reeled it down upon us like a curling peel.

Like any fine artist, he controlled the tension of the audience's longing. You desired, unwittingly, a certain kind of roll or climb, or a return to a certain portion of the air, and he fulfilled your hope slantingly, like a poet, or evaded it until you thought you would burst, and then fulfilled it surprisingly, so you gasped and cried out.

The oddest, most exhilarating and exhausting thing was this: he never quit. The music had no periods, no rests or endings; the poetry's beautiful sentence never ended; the line had no finish; the sculptured forms piled overhead, one into another without surcease. Who could breathe, in a world where rhythm itself had no periods?

It had taken me several minutes to understand what an extraordinary thing I was seeing. Rahm kept all that embellished space in mind at once. For another twenty minutes I watched the beauty unroll and grow more fantastic and unlikely before my eyes. Now Rahm brought the plane down slidingly, and just in time, for I thought I would snap from the effort to compass and remember the line's long intelligence; I could not add another curve. He brought the plane down on a far runway. After a pause, I saw him step out, an ordinary man, and make his way back to the terminal.

The show was over. It was late. Just as I turned from the runway, something caught my eye and made me laugh. It was a swallow, a blue-green swallow, having its own air show, apparently inspired by Rahm. The swallow climbed high over the runway, held its wings oddly, tipped them, and rolled down the air in loops. The inspired swallow. I always want to paint, too, after I see the Rembrandts. The blue-green swallow tumbled precisely, and caught itself and flew up again as if excited, and looped down again, the way swallows do, but tensely, holding its body carefully still. It was a stunt swallow.

I went home and thought about Rahm's performance that night, and the next day, and the next.

I had thought I knew my way around beauty a little bit. I knew I had devoted a good part of my life to it, memorizing poetry and focusing my attention on complexity of rhythm in particular, on force, movement, repetition, and surprise, in both poetry and prose. Now I had stood among dandelions between two asphalt runways in Bellingham, Washington, and begun learning about beauty. Even the Boston Museum of Fine Arts was never more inspiriting than this small northwestern airport on this time-killing Sunday afternoon in June. Nothing on earth is more gladdening than knowing we must roll up our sleeves and move back the boundaries of the humanly possible once more.

Later I flew with Dave Rahm; he took me up. A generous geographer, Dick Smith, at Western Washington University, arranged it, and came along. Rahm and Dick Smith were colleagues at the university. In geology, Rahm had published two books and many articles. Rahm was handsome in a dull sort of way, blunt-featured, wide-jawed, wind-burned, keen-eyed, and taciturn. As anyone would expect. He was forty. He wanted to show me the Cascade Mountains; these enormous peaks, only fifty miles from the coast, rise over nine thousand feet; they are heavily glaciated. Whatcom County has more glaciers than the lower forty-eight states combined; the Cascades make the Rocky Mountains look like hills. Mount Baker is volcanic, like most Cascade peaks. That year, Mount Baker was acting up. Even from my house at the shore I could see, early in the morning on clear days, volcanic vapor rise near its peak. Often the vapor made a cloud that swelled all morning and hid the snows. Every day the newspapers reported on Baker's activity: Would it blow? (A few years later, Mount St. Helens did blow.)

Rahm was not flying his trick biplane that day, but a faster, enclosed plane, a single-engine Cessna. We flew from a bumpy grass airstrip near my house, out over the coast and inland. There was coastal plain down there, but we could not see it for clouds. We were over the clouds at five hundred feet and inside them too, heading for an abrupt line of peaks we could not see. I gave up on everything, the way you do in airplanes; it was out of my hands. Every once in a while Rahm saw a peephole in the clouds and buzzed over for a look. "That's Larsen's pea farm," he said, or "That's Nooksack Road," and he changed our course with a heave.

When we got to the mountains, he slid us along Mount Baker's flanks sideways.

Our plane swiped at the mountain with a roar. I glimpsed a windshield view of dirty snow traveling fast. Our shaking, swooping belly seemed to graze the snow. The wings shuddered; we peeled away and the mountain fell back and the engines whined. We felt flung, because we were in fact flung; parts of our faces and internal organs trailed pressingly behind on the curves. We came back for another pass at the mountain, and another. We dove at the snow headlong like suicides; we jerked up, down, or away at the last second, so late we left our hearts, stomachs, and lungs behind. If I forced myself to hold my heavy head up against the G's, and to raise my eyelids, heavy as barbells, and to notice what I saw, I could see the wrinkled green crevasses cracking the glaciers' snow.

Pitching snow filled all the windows, and shapes of dark rock. I had no notion which way was up. Everything was black or gray or white except the fatal crevasses; everything made noise and shook. I felt my face smashed sideways and saw rushing abstractions of snow in the windshield. Patches of cloud obscured the snow fleetingly. We straightened out, turned, and dashed at the mountainside for another pass, which we made, apparently, on our ear, an inch or two away from the slope. Icefalls and cornices jumbled and fell away. If a commercial plane's black box, such as the FAA painstakingly recovers from crash sites, could store videotapes as well as pilots' last words, some videotapes would look like this: a mountainside coming up at the windows from all directions, ice and snow and rock filling the screen up close and screaming by.

Rahm was just being polite. His geographer colleague wanted to see the fissure on Mount Baker from which steam escaped. Everybody in Bellingham wanted to see that sooty fissure, as did every geologist in the country; no one on earth could fly so close to it as Rahm. He knew the mountain by familiar love and feel, like a face; he knew what the plane could do and what he dared to do.

When Mount Baker inexplicably let us go, he jammed us into cloud again and soon tilted. "The Sisters!" someone shouted, and I saw the windshield fill with red rock. This mountain looked infernal, a drear and sheer plane of lifeless rock. It was red and sharp; its gritty blades cut through the clouds at random. The mountain was quiet. It was in shade. Careening, we made side-ways passes at these brittle peaks too steep for snow. Their rock was full of iron, somebody shouted at me then or later; the iron had rusted, so they were red. Later, when I was back on the ground, I recalled that, from a distance, the two jagged peaks called the Twin Sisters looked translucent against the sky; they were sharp, tapered, and fragile as arrowheads.

I talked to Rahm. He was flying us out to the islands now. The islands were fifty or sixty miles away. Like many other people, I had picked Bellingham, Washington, by looking at an atlas. It was clear from the atlas that you could row in the salt water and see snow-covered mountains; you could scale a glaciated moun-tainside with an ice ax in August, skirting green crevasses two hundred feet deep, and look out on the islands in the sea. Now, in the air, the clouds had risen over us; dark forms lay on the glinting water. There was almost no color to the day, just black-ened green and some yellow. I knew the islands were forested in dark Douglas firs the size of skyscrapers. Bald eagles scav-enged on the beaches; robins the size of herring gulls sang in the clearings. We made our way out to the islands through the layer of air between the curving planet and its held, thick clouds.

"When I started trying to figure out what I was going to do with my life, I decided to become an expert on mountains. It wasn't much to be, it wasn't everything, but it was something. I was going to know everything about mountains from every point of view. So I started out in geography." Geography proved too pedestrian for Rahm, too concerned with "how many bushels of wheat an acre." So he ended up in geology. Smith had told me that geology departments throughout the country used Rahm's photographic slides — close-ups of geologic features from the air.

"I used to climb mountains. But you know, you can get a better feel for a mountain's power flying around it, flying all around it, than you can from climbing it tied to its side like a flea."

He talked about his flying performances. He thought of the air as a line, he said. "This end of the line, that end of the line — like a rope." He improvised. "I get a rhythm going and stick with it." While he was performing in a show, he paid attention, he said, to the lighting. He didn't play against the sun. That was all he said about what he did.

In aerobatic maneuvers, pilots pull about seven positive G's on some stunts and six negative G's on others. Some gyrations push; others pull. Pilots alternate the pressures carefully, so they do not gray out or black out.

Later I learned that some stunt pilots tune up by wearing gravity boots. These are boots made to hook over a doorway; wearing them, you hang in the doorway upside down. It must startle a pilot's children to run into their father or mother in the course of their home wanderings — the parents hanging wide-eyed, upside down in the doorway like a bat.

We were landing; here was the airstrip on Stuart Island — that island to which Ferrar Burn was dragged by the tide. We put down, climbed out of the plane, and walked. We wandered a dirt track through fields to a lee shore where yellow sandstone ledges slid into the sea. The salt chuck, people there called salt water. The sun came out. I caught a snake in the salt chuck; the snake, eighteen inches long, was swimming in the green shallows.

I had a survivor's elation. Rahm had found Mount Baker in the clouds before Mount Baker found the plane. He had wiped it with the fast plane like a cloth and we had lived. When we took off from Stuart Island and gained altitude, I asked if we could turn over — could we do a barrel roll? The plane was making a lot of noise, and Dick Smith did not hear any of this, I learned later. "Why not?" Rahm said, and added surprisingly, "It won't hurt the plane." Without ado he leaned on the wheel and the wing went down and we went somersaulting over it. We up-ended with a roar. We stuck to the plane's sides like flung paint. All the blood in my body bulged on my face; it piled between my skull and skin. Vaguely I could see the chrome sea twirling over Rahm's head like a baton, and the dark islands sliding down the skies like rain.

The G's slammed me into my seat like thugs and pinned me while my heart pounded and the plane turned over slowly and compacted each organ in turn. My eyeballs were newly spherical and full of heartbeats. I seemed to hear a crescendo; the wing rolled shuddering down the last 90 degrees and settled on the flat. There were the islands, admirably below us, and the clouds, admirably above. When I could breathe, I asked if we could do it again, and we did. He rolled the other way. The brilliant line of the sea slid up the side window bearing its heavy islands. Through the shriek of my blood and the plane's shakes I glimpsed the line of the sea over the windshield, thin as a spear. How in performance did Rahm keep track while his brain blurred and blood roared in his ears without ceasing? Every performance was a tour de force and a show of will, a *Machtspruch*. I had seen the other stunt pilots straighten out after a trick or two; their blood could drop back and the planet simmer down. An Olympic gymnast, at peak form, strings out a line of spins ten stunts long across a mat, and is hard put to keep his footing at the end. Rahm endured much greater pressure on his faster spins using the plane's power, and he could spin in three dimensions and keep twirling till he ran out of sky room or luck.

When we straightened out, and had flown straightforwardly for ten minutes toward home, Dick Smith, clearing his throat, brought himself to speak. "What was that we did out there?"

"The barrel rolls?" Rahm said. "They were barrel rolls." He said nothing else. I looked at the back of his head; I could see the serious line of his cheek and jaw. He was in shirtsleeves, tanned, strong-wristed. I could not imagine loving him under any circumstance; he was alien to me, unfazed. He looked like

GI Joe. He flew with that matter-of-fact, bored gesture pilots use. They click overhead switches and turn dials as if only their magnificent strength makes such dullness endurable. The half circle of wheel in their big hands looks like a toy they plan to crush in a minute; the wiggly stick the wheel mounts seems barely attached.

A crop-duster pilot in Wyoming told me the life expectancy of a crop-duster pilot is five years. They fly too low. They hit buildings and power lines. They have no space to fly out of trouble, and no space to recover from a stall. We were in Cody, Wyoming, out on the north fork of the Shoshone River. The crop duster had wakened me that morning flying over the ranch house and clearing my bedroom roof by half an inch. I saw the bolts on the wheel assembly a few feet from my face. He was spraying with pesticide the plain old grass. Over breakfast I asked him how long he had been dusting crops. "Four years," he said, and the figure stalled in the air between us for a moment. "You know you're going to die at it someday," he added. "We all know it. We accept that; it's part of it." I think now that, since the crop duster was in his twenties, he accepted only that he had to say such stuff; privately he counted on skewing the curve.

I suppose Rahm knew the fact too. I do not know how he felt about it. "It's worth it," said the early French aviator Mermoz. He was Antoine de Saint-Exupéry's friend. "It's worth the final smashup."

Rahm smashed up in front of King Hussein, in Jordan, during a performance. The plane spun down and never came out of it; it nosedived into the ground and exploded. He bought the farm. I was living then with my husband out on that remote island in the San Juans, cut off from everything. Battery radios picked up the Canadian Broadcasting Company out of Toronto, half a continent away; island people would, in theory, learn if the United States blew up, but not much else. There were no newspapers. One friend got the Sunday *New York Times* by mail boat on the following Friday. He saved it until Sunday and had a party, every week; we all read the Sunday *Times* and no one mentioned that it was last week's.

One day, Paul Glenn's brother flew out from Bellingham to

visit; he had a seaplane. He landed in the water in front of the cabin and tied up to our mooring. He came in for coffee, and he gave out news of this and that, and — Say, did we know that stunt pilot Dave Rahm had cracked up? In Jordan, during a performance: he never came out of a dive. He just dove right down into the ground, and his wife was there watching. "I saw it on CBS News last night." And then — with a sudden sharp look at my filling eyes — "What, did you know him?" But no, I did not know him. He took me up once. Several years ago. I admired his flying. I had thought that danger was the safest thing in the world, if you went about it right.

Later I found a newspaper. Rahm was living in Jordan that year; King Hussein invited him to train the aerobatics team, the Royal Jordanian Falcons. He was also visiting professor of geology at the University of Jordan. In Amman that day he had been flying a Pitt Special, a plane he knew well. Katy Rahm, his wife of six months, was sitting beside Hussein in the viewing stands, with her daughter. Rahm died performing a Lomcevak combined with a tail slide and hammerhead. In a Lomcevak, the pilot brings the plane up on a slant and pirouettes. I had seen Rahm do this: the falling plane twirled slowly like a leaf. Like a ballerina, the plane seemed to hold its head back stiff in concentration at the music's slow, painful beauty. It was one of Rahm's favorite routines. Next the pilot flies straight up, stalls the plane, and slides down the air on his tail. He brings the nose down — the hammerhead — kicks the engine, and finishes with a low loop.

It is a dangerous maneuver at any altitude, and Rahm was doing it low. He hit the round on the loop; the tail slide had left him no height. When Rahm went down, King Hussein dashed to the burning plane to pull him out, but he was already dead.

A few months after the air show, and a month after I had flown with Rahm, I was working at my desk near Bellingham, where I lived, when I heard a sound so odd it finally penetrated my concentration. It was the buzz of an airplane, but it rose and fell musically, and it never quit; the plane never flew out of earshot. I walked out on the porch and looked up: it was Rahm in the black and gold biplane, looping all over the air. I had been wondering about his performance flight: could it really have been so beautiful? It was, for here it was again. The little plane twisted all over the air like a vine. It trailed a line like a very long mathematical proof you could follow only so far, and then it lost you in its complexity. I saw Rahm flying high over the Douglas firs, and out over the water, and back over farms. The air was a fluid, and Rahm was an eel.

It was as if Mozart could move his body through his notes, and you could walk out on the porch, look up, and see him in periwig and breeches, flying around in the sky. You could hear the music as he dove through it; it streamed after him like a contrail.

I lost myself; standing on the firm porch, I lost my direction and reeled. My neck and spine rose and turned, so I followed the plane's line kinesthetically. In his open-cockpit black plane, Rahm demonstrated curved space. He slid down ramps of air, he vaulted and wheeled. He piled loops in heaps and praised height. He unrolled the scroll of the air, extended it, and bent it into Möbius strips; he furled line in a thousand new ways, as if he were inventing a script and writing it in one infinitely recurving utterance until I thought the bounds of beauty must break.

From inside, the looping plane had sounded tinny, like a kazoo. Outside, the buzz rose and fell to the Doppler effect as the plane looped near or away. Rahm cleaved the sky like a prow and tossed out time left and right in his wake. He performed for forty minutes; then he headed the plane, as small as a wasp, back to the airport inland. Later I learned Rahm often practiced acrobatic flights over this shore. His idea was that if he lost control and was going to go down, he could ditch in the salt chuck, where no one else would get hurt.

If I had not turned two barrel rolls in an airplane, I might have fancied Rahm felt good up there, and playful. Maybe Jackson Pollock felt a sort of playfulness, in addition to the artist's usual deliberate and intelligent care. In my limited experience, painting, unlike writing, pleases the senses while you do it, and more while you do it than after it is done. Drawing lines with an airplane, unfortunately, tortures the senses. Jet bomber pilots black out. I knew Rahm felt as if his brain were bursting his eardrums, felt that if he let his jaws close as tight as centrifugal force pressed them, he would bite through his lungs.

"All virtue is a form of acting," Yeats said. Rahm deliberately turned himself into a figure. Sitting invisible at the controls of a distant airplane, he became the agent and the instrument of art and invention. He did not tell me how he felt when we spoke of his performance flying; he told me instead that he paid attention to how his plane and its line looked to the audience against the lighted sky. If he had noticed how he felt, he could not have done the work. Robed in his airplane, he was as featureless as a priest. He was lost in his figural aspect like an actor or a king. Of his flying, he had said only, "I get a rhythm and stick with it." In its reticence, this statement reminded me of Veronese's "Given a large canvas, I enhanced it as I saw fit." But Veronese was ironic, and Rahm was not; he was as literal as an astronaut; the machine gave him tongue.

When Rahm flew, he sat down in the middle of art and strapped himself in. He spun it all around him. He could not see it himself. If he never saw it on film, he never saw it at all — as if Beethoven could not hear his final symphonies not because he was deaf but because he was inside the paper on which he wrote. Rahm must have felt it happen, that fusion of vision and metal, motion and idea. I think of this man as a figure, a college professor with a Ph.D. upside down in the loud band of beauty. What are we here for? *Propter chorum,* the monks say: for the sake of the choir.

"Purity does not lie in separation from but in deeper penetration into the universe," Teilhard de Chardin wrote. It is hard to imagine a deeper penetration into the universe than Rahm's last dive in his plane, or than his inexpressible wordless selfless line's inscribing the air and dissolving. Any other art may be permanent. I cannot recall one Rahm sequence. He improvised. If Christo wraps a building or dyes a harbor, we join his poignant and fierce awareness that the work will be gone in days. Rahm's plane shed a ribbon in space, a ribbon whose end unraveled in memory while its beginning unfurled as surprise. He may have acknowledged that what he did could be called art, but it would have been, I think, only in the common misusage, which holds art to be the last extreme of skill. Rahm rode the point of the line to the possible; he discovered it and wound it down to show. He made his dazzling probe on the run. "The world is filled, and filled with the Absolute," Teilhard de Chardin wrote. "To see this is to be made free."

STANLEY ELKIN

At the Academy Awards

FROM HARPER'S MAGAZINE

AT THE Academy Awards, the entrance to the Shrine Civic Auditorium is flanked by four giant Oscars quite, or so it seems to
me, like sullen, art deco Nazis. Set maybe a hundred feet back
from these, two temporary grandstands have been constructed
for three thousand or so fans — day-of-the-locust types, extras,
all the tribal, representative legions who come to these things,
drawn, it could almost be, by the limousines themselves, gleaming cream-colored packages of celebrity.

*Maybe because Galati never returned my calls or that I couldn't get into
Swifty Lazar's private party at Spago for a few hundred of his friends.
Or, first things first, putting, as it were, the horse before the cart, because
of my turf* (those few or so blocks of Washington University campus and the several more of proximal neighborhood where I've
lived almost thirty years now like something deposited in the
fossil record) *I am essentially cloutless, this pushing-sixty geriatric babe,
out of my element, in over my head.* I wait while Joan assembles the
wheelchair stashed in the trunk of the cab before I even try to
get out. But that's the point of these exercises, yes? The upstairs/
downstairs, city mouse/country mouse, cattleman/farmer liaisons — all the slicker/rube relationships. Why, it's practically science fiction, journalism is, or this *kind* of journalism anyway, the
refractive we-go-there or they-come-here displacements. Reac-
tive chemistry just one more bankable myth, or, no, not one more,
almost the only game in town, at the core, I bet, of half the plots
in all the pix I've come in person all this way from Heartland to

Coastland to watch being honored. More, probably. Isn't *The Ac-cidental Tourist* about an educated, affectless, upper-middle-class writer who becomes involved with a spunky, blue-collarish, Jean Arthur type who keeps a kennel and trains his dog? And doesn't *Dangerous Liaisons* have the experienced mix it up with the in-nocent? *Working Girl* transforms a girl from Staten Island into a kind of Cinderella when her scheming, upper-class boss injures herself in a skiing accident. And *Rain Man*, the ultimate rube/slicker story, is a tale of two brothers, one your sweet, helpless idiot savant, the other your callous, high-flying car salesman. (With the exception of *Mississippi Burning*, I'd seen all the candidates for Best Picture 1988. Do I have a life or what?)

All the movies are some variation of *The Prince and the Pauper;* drama, that is, through collided worlds. But plot is *about* mixing it up. Not *this*, then *that* so much as characters caught out, em-barrassed, in a dream. This is fiction's essence anyway, the the-matics of opposites. Cops and robbers, cowboys and Indians, are nothing if not versions of the class struggle.

And all stories are travelogues, finally, or why would I have said what I did about journalism? Us Marco Polos are wide of eye, bumpkins, rubes and rustics, hicks and insulars. We travel by turnip truck (as Joan and I, minding the pennies, made the trip west on a carrier almost, it made so many stops, like a street-car). Something surreal in the heart, something slapstick in the head, all the binary opposition of rigged polarity.

So, hardly your customary correspondent. More your plant, more your little old hand-wringer. There, in the clear California sunshine, beyond the California velvet roping off the red Cali-fornia carpet, below the three-thousand-plus plebes in the char-ity-built grandstands, your reporter taking the air in black tie and wheelchair, basking at ground level — get this picture — among the milling celebs, bucking in the bowels for celeb him-self, nonchalant, see, his face absent expression, unless indiffer-ence, carefully composed as the neutral poker puss of a high-stakes gambler, is the giveaway, my mean, squeezed mien, I mean: I give them nothing, *nothing*. My gimlet glare, my crabbed judg-mentals, the studied, Prussian composure of some old-timey stu-dio head. (I *ought* to be in pictures!) Projecting both to the cheap seats and to the stars themselves, all those famous, by-bone-

structure-fated lives ambling the red carpet, outgoing and chip-
per in the still photography as brides and grooms. Because it *is*
like a wedding, and they move past the press, straining toward
them with tape recorders and microphones, as if along a receiv-
ing line.

Here is Roy Rogers. Here is Dale Evans. Old Roy packs a six-
shooter on his spangled pants. Miss Dale is beaming and looking
demure in her late seventies as if, despite her stylized cowlady
duds, no woman was ever libbed.

Here is Dorothy Lamour, so much resembling my mother I
feel my face breaking ranks, like waving.

Here is Karl Malden, here's Vincent Price.

Here are Cyd Charisse and Tony Martin. Here's Alice Faye.
Here are the Bridgeses, Lloyd, Jeff, and what's-his-name. Here's
Jimmy Stewart in his pink old age.

Most of them — this is peculiar — I *don't* recognize. (Michelle
Pfeiffer, River Phoenix, Melanie Griffith, people whose movies
you wait till they come out in video.) It's just these that the fans
in the bleachers, sending some distant early warning of celebrity,
alert us to. They actually go "ooh," they actually go "ah," making
this raw, rough purr of awe.

And it really *is* like a wedding, it really is. We're looking at —
what? — a dozen million dollars' worth of duds here. Some of
the younger guys wear postmodern tuxedos. Blair Underwood,
a lawyer for the home firm on *L.A. Law,* has dark sequins hanging down the arms of his tuxedo jacket like a kind of glazed hair.
Several fellows wear black running shoes with their tuxedos —
formal Reeboks, dress Nikes. I see, no shit, a leather tuxedo.
And there's another man in a tux with a long rabbinical coat
over it. And another whose bow tie spills over his shirtfront like
a growth.

Security is trying to hustle the ticket holders — our comps, in
the thirty-third or thirty-fourth row, cost $150 each; that's the
incredibly inflated figure that's printed right on them in what I
can only conceive of as Weimar Republic numerals; the ones to
the Board of Governors Ball afterward claim to be worth $450
apiece — into the Shrine Auditorium, but I don't want to go in
just yet, and the wheelchair, like some flying carpet for gimps,
provides a sort of cover. A woman in a black floor-length skirt

and dark, sheerish blouse, her outfit vaguely reminiscent of a
circus performer's, the dog- or bird-trainer's snagged, stitched
fishnet, say, and who carries a walkie-talkie, gives me permission
to stay outside a while longer to watch the movie stars arrive.
(There's Tom Hanks, there's Olivia Newton-John, there's Michael Caine.)

Gradually I feel the features of my great stone face subside,
erode in the presence of all this fame, my ego not put down but
beside the point. If I could see my reflection now I would probably look windblown, punchy as the Sphinx. Someone in the
bleacher seats waves a sign that says JOHN 3:16, but it ain't *really*
any day of the locust here. The crowd's much too mellow, befit-
ting the time zone and circumstances. Though perhaps a bit
barmy. The things people say! There's John Cleese. Someone
shouts out at him, "Good luck tonight, good luck. Thank you for
all the comedy you've brought us over the years. Thank you,
sir!"

And still they keep coming, a parade of the physically elect,
the incredibly handsome, the fabulously beautiful. It suddenly
seems astonishing to me that presences like these could play *just*
human beings. It seems, I don't know, a sort of reverse hubris.
(There's Jeff Goldblum. There's Gregory Hines.) They better
watch themselves, is what I think. They better cool it, this weird
dressing down they do for a living like, oh, grown-ups squeezing
into the getups of children. They better look what they're doing
or they could freeze like that.

There's Kevin Kline.

*Maybe because I didn't say anything to Roger Ebert when I spotted him
standing with the other reporters. Maybe because I didn't identify myself
and remind him that we were both of us scheduled to speak in two weeks
at a memorial service for a mutual friend.*

To say I feel betrayed would be overstating it. But I do feel had.
A little. A little I do. It takes a while, maybe through the first
half hour of the Awards show, but pretty soon I realize that no
one is here who doesn't have to be. The two hundred or so nominees in the twenty-three categories. The fifty-some-odd presenters — there's Candice Bergen, there's Sean Connery, there's Kim

Novak — the hundred singers and dancers — there's Tita Omeza,
there's Regan Patno, there's Carla Earle — and all the not-to-be-
numbered members serving on the eleven Academy commit-
tees. Then, when spouses and friends are thrown in, well, there
you are, you've accounted for at least a couple of thousand people. I can't account for the rest of the folks in the hall — people
vaguely associated with the industry, I suppose, or society types,
perhaps, who come every year but who almost certainly no one
from my part of town would recognize. I would think many of
us occupy proffered seats, as, in a different season, we might be
the guests of corporate season-ticket holders at a ball game or
concert.

It's the same in my business, the same in yours. Most folks
have edge, some little piece of the action, first refusal, or the
privilege of wholesale, the travel agent's unlimited mileage, the
congressman's rank or salesman's discount, this one's backstage
access, that one's dibs on the float's leftover roses, the meat that
would only spoil otherwise.

What I mean is, there's no such thing as the gratuitously high-
profiled here. We're an audience of cliques and special interests.
The real players are home, watching on TV, or with Swifty at
Spago. Joan and I are tucked a bit to the right and toward the
back in a section two or three steps above orchestra level; in the
thirty-third or thirty-fourth row, as I say, just under the over-
hang of the balcony in what is probably a forty-row auditorium.

Why I'm steamed, to the extent I am, is that I've watched these
ceremonies for years. Always I'd come away not star-struck but
filled with some prize-in-every-box sense of a homogenized, evenly
distributed fame. Now, in my immediate area, except for a few
stars straggling into the hall and walking past our discrete little
acreage — there's Max von Sydow — to take their seats by the
5:30 P.M. deadline, I recognize only myself and my wife.

Clearly, the star-spangled demographics are off this evening.
Even money they always were. And suddenly I understand
something, that all the splash and flourish of all those advertised
lives I'd seen on all those Oscar shows had been nothing but
camera angles, a sort of trick photography, doctored like Chinese
news. And why not? Pros put this stuff together. There are tricks
to every trade — maybe there are actual filters that take out by-

standers like a kind of sunscreen. Or maybe Fame is only the fine-tuning of some driving, evolutionary will, natural selection doing its flaked and flashy thing. You think Zapruder shot his film by accident? He aimed that camera at that gunned-down President. Like Oswald himself, he was only following his heart, some abiding tropism that turned him toward history, that turns us all toward what seems important. If nothing's going on, you pass, you fold, you excuse yourself and get a sandwich.

So if this is the gala, where *is* everybody? is what I'm saying.

What can I tell you about an Oscar ceremony you don't already know? You've watched them for years. Taking in our pageants like our bonbons, the secret sinfuls — the Miss Universe, the Miss America, the Miss Teenage America, the Miss *Mrs.* America. The Tonys and Emmys and Grammys. The People's Choice, the Golden Globes, the Country Musics, the Clios and Peabodys. All those endeavors awards, all these little faits accomplis. Do *I* have to tell you?

This is how far we've come. This is the ascent of man, awards only the persistence of a presumed justice, the shortest distance between thumbs up and thumbs down; lions, Christians, and the development of the jury system. The Academy Desserts. Because it isn't competition or truth at the core of entertainment; it's judgment, it's criticism. It's having a say. It's having a say and getting to change it from year to year. Even the World Series starts up again the following year. As if we *demanded* qualitative distinctions, a world with heroics, champions.

My first celebrity, the worst thing I ever did, and some observations:

In 1955, about three or four weeks into basic training, we were doing bayonet drill. This was in a field in the Colorado Rockies. As I recall it now, and it's very fuzzy, we were either two lines of recruits lined up across from each other or a long, continuous line facing practice dummies, some stuffed, canvas enemy. It could even be that nothing was across from us, that we were only going through the motions, doing what wouldn't then have been called imaging, thrusting our bayonets, fixed to our M-1s, in some choreography of vacant engagement, the sergeant in charge of our charge calling out half a catechism: "WHAT'S THE SPIRIT OF THE BAYONET?" To our lunging, choric response: *"TO KILL!"* Shouting "TO KILL!" but thinking "chicken shit." Then something happened I'll never forget. Suddenly there was this officer on horseback, a one- or two-star general. I'm no more equestrian than soldier. I don't know the gaits. I can't tell the moment a walk becomes a trot, a trot a canter, a canter a gallop. What this was was none of those anyway. It may not even have been motion so much as some practiced, show-the-flag horse/man ballet, the mixed and ambled military leisurelies of mince and prance and strutting in place. I remember his long gleaming boots; I think he had a sidearm. If he'd broken into iambic pentameter or rallied us with speeches out of Shakespearean history plays, recited the chain of command, King to St. George, St. George to God, or tried to rouse us with the For-God-and-Countrys, I wouldn't have been more surprised. No — stunned! I'd never seen a general before. Mostly sergeants dealt with us, corporals, NCOs whose power came out of the barrel of their mouths, the sheer threatening noises they made. This man, if he even was a man, on that horse, if it even was a horse, was dead solid Power itself. He could have owned the field, the mountains. He could have *been* the field, the mountains, and if he wasn't my first celebrity, he was — to use Faulkner's word — my first avatar. The upshot was that I suddenly understood the spirit of the bayonet clear as crystal.

And here's the worst thing I ever did:

In the spring of 1975, I was a visiting professor at Yale living in a third-floor apartment at Timothy Dwight College. Timothy Dwight has in its endowment the Chubb Fellowships, grants that bring visiting politicians in for three-day visits. The semester I was there, Jimmy Carter, John Lindsay, Maynard Jackson, and Hubert Humphrey were all Chubb Fellows.

On the morning of the day of the worst thing I ever did I was coming downstairs with my laundry just as Hubert Humphrey was stepping out of the Chubb apartment. His hostess, Shelley Fishkin, saw me and introduced us. Humphrey and I shook hands and went about our business. That evening there were to be three functions in the senator's honor: a cocktail party at the master's house for everyone, a dinner to which I wasn't invited, and, later, a party at the Fishkins' to which I was. Two out of three ain't bad and I hold no grudges. When I showed up at the cocktail party, Humphrey spotted me, broke away from his group, and said, "*Saaay*, I didn't know you were *that* Stanley Elkin!"

Now, unless the senator was confusing me with the historian Stanley Elkins, I don't believe he thought I was any kind of Stanley Elkin at all. What probably happened was that after our brief introduction Shelley must have identified the guy with the laundry basket as the visiting writer. In any event, I was being patronized. I knew it, and it annoyed me. In the two-hour interval between the dinner I hadn't been invited to and the party I had, I'd had some drinks and arrived at the party a little late. The Whiffenpoofs were serenading the senator. They finished and left. Immediately, everyone in the room crowded around Humphrey and started asking him questions, about the upcoming conventions, about foreign affairs, whatever was on the agenda that spring. Really, it was more like a press conference than a party. And that's when I made my move.

"Excuse me, Senator," I said.

"*Yes?*"

"Could you get me a Coca-Cola?"

"You want me to get you a Coca-Cola?"

People were paying more attention than they had even to the Whiffenpoofs, baa baa baa.

"If you would, please. There's a whole tub of them behind you. Right there. Over against the wall."

I know it sounds dramatic, but Humphrey was watching me closely. Christ, everyone was. "All right," he said finally, and handed me a can.

"That's the way you hand somebody a Coca-Cola?" I reproached him.

"What," he said. It wasn't a question.

"Well, it's just that there's that little tin whoosie on top. I might cut myself. I better not try opening that. No sir," I told him, and gave the Coke back. Very deftly he did something deliberately to disable it.

"Gosh," said Hubert Humphrey, "I can't do it either," and put the useless can back in my hand. He'd won, the happy warrior, and by now he probably had all too clear an idea about the kind of Stanley Elkin I really was.

Or the time we lived in Virginia, maybe a hundred miles from

Washington, and every so often we'd go up for a weekend, poke
around the museums, do a monument or agency, maybe take in
a congressional hearing, then come in at six o'clock and eat the
big seafood. The thing of it is, Washington has always depressed
me. I have the feeling, as I have in Paris or anywhere glamorous,
I'm not only a tourist but a stranger, that big things are happening, important shifts, large goings-on in the social and cultural
tectonics, the great, carved intentions of the world, but not to
me. For all that the guides insist it's my White House, I know
better. I know it's worth my ass to sit down in one off-limits chair
or touch, unauthorized, one lousy velvet rope. I had a sense,
wherever I happened to be in those days, that the good stuff was
going on elsewhere. Georgetown was where the action was, the
Virginia hunt country, and this knowledge broke my heart.

There's a shop in Los Angeles on Melrose where the used
clothes of movie stars are sold to the public. The appeal of an
autograph, I think, is the homeopathic magic it contains, the
voodoo I-touched-yous — and not *just* the voodoo I-touched-yous,
however farfetched or removed (the hand that shook the hand
that shook the hand), but the voodoo you-touched-*mes,* too. Ain't
it feasible, I mean, that the inventory in that Melrose shop and
the rags, bones, and hanks of hair of the saints and martyrs should
have, at least from the consumer's point of view, something in
common — that religious feelings, the love of God even, may
only be a higher type of star-struck, awe and agape what there
was before TV and the talkies? We do some of our best business
in the atmosphere of angels. Be still, oh, be still, my bobby-soxer
heart!

It's hard, at the Academy Awards, to distinguish between those
stars I saw outside, in the flesh, and those I see on the stage.
Joan has the same difficulty. A couple of months later, watching
a video of the ceremonies, both of us will be unable to remember
having seen particular parts of the show. We sat through all but
the last ten minutes or so — missing Best Performance by an
Actress, missing Best Picture, to beat the crowds, to put dibs on
the rest rooms — but neither of us remembers having seen Cher,
or Richard Dreyfuss, or Carrie Fisher. Jane Fonda has dropped
through our short-term memory, Merv Griffin. Anjelica Huston

and Donald Sutherland are out of the loop. Indeed, both of us
have more vivid memories of the acceptance speeches of people
we'd never heard of, achievers in art direction, achievers in sound,
than we have of the coy presenter banter of the household names.
Television and movies at once create and obliterate fame. I recall what Dustin Hoffman said in his acceptance speech because
he said it clumsily, because, unless he was acting, there was this
unscripted slippage into the human register.

It's easy to knock these ceremonies, of course, which, on television at least, and even in person, seem an invitation to ar-
chaeologists, some artifacts from the Zircon Age. It's easy to knock
these ceremonies because here at the Academy Awards, where
glitz hands off to glitz and it's this Mardi Gras of diamonds larger
than rhinestones, structure surrenders to motion, to din, to appearance as arbitrary and frantic as a chase scene. Ironically, at
the Academy Awards, all sense of the theatrical gives way neither to wit nor spectacle but to stunt — how many presenters,
like so many clowns, can be crammed into the Volkswagen. (And
I'm failing the form here, am insufficiently a stand-in for the
little guy. The slicker/rube is inoperable. There is no awe, only
humiliation, stripped privilege like a scuttled form, and I've
slipped genres, my piece at one remove — *I blame Galati, I blame
S. Lazar, I blame Roger Ebert, I blame Molly, my daughter, who at
approximately the same time her father is being denied access to the Action is taking the Middle East by storm, is dining with the Rabins at their
home in Jerusalem through the good offices of a connected friend* —
from the freshman's classic theme about why he can't write one.)
The show — and I had almost said "services" — reminds one of
summer camp, of tacked-on, interminable verses, stanzas of
pointless, round-robin story told first by A and kept up by B, by
C and D and E and all, that do not so much advance the plot as
simply continue it.
    The president of the Academy of Motion Picture Arts and
Sciences introduces Tom Selleck, who brings on Melanie Griffith and Don Johnson, who banter reflexively, list the nominees
for Best Supporting Actress (always, somehow, all nominees and
the films for which they've been nominated will be announced
in the vaguely runway accents and unnatural sing-song of a fash-

ion show, almost, it would seem, in Don Pardo's descriptive RV and Turtle-Waxian tropes), open the envelope, and give Geena Davis an Oscar. Miss Davis thanks Anne Tyler, Ruth Myers, Larry Kasdan, Ray London, Bill Hurt, and Jeff Goldblum. And we go to commercial like a seventh-inning stretch.

Rhymeless and reasonless, this is how the evening happens.

Until gradually I'm proved wrong and the true structure of the ceremonies (neither car chase nor stunt, motion nor din, how many presenters on the head of a pin, nor even long summer's endless ninety-nine bottles of beer on the wall or its row, row, row your boats around the campfire) finally begins to emerge. Why, it's a *board game* is what it is! Certainly! Of course! Drama and suspense, action and irony, the Oscars according to Parker Brothers! The Academy Awards designed for the long, lazy laid-back of a rainy day. All the cul-de-sacs, skipped turns, jumped spaces, bonuses (a Special Achievement Award to Richard Williams for animation direction of *Who Framed Roger Rabbit;* an honorary Academy Award to the National Film Board of Canada), and even its graduated values (Achievement in Art Direction is less important than Best Actor exactly as Baltic Avenue is less valuable than Park Place) suggest all the drawn-out, delayed gratification and jittery interruption of the final winner-takes-all, Best Picture, like the kid holding the most houses, hotels, and cash.

At the Academy Awards, you can't get there from here. It's a de-Ezekielized world of detached and scattered bones. A Voice, like the disembodied sound of some Las Vegan casino god, produces Walter Matthau, Walter Matthau produces Bob Hope and Lucille Ball. At the Academy Awards, it's a pointless, incomplete vaudeville. Bob Hope and Lucille Ball present nineteen "Oscar Winners of Tomorrow" in an endless every-man-for-himself song and dance about ambition and narcissism philosophically distilled from *A Chorus Line* without the benefit of that show's melody, passion, talent, or wit. At the Academy Awards, it's a drawn-out, almost fastidious, customary kowtow. It's the obligatory standing ovation. You could put money down on who's going to get one, but who'd be sucker enough to take your bet? Bob Hope and Lucille Ball get one. Out of almost Chinese respect, only it's not so much ancestor worship as a gift for survival, for longevity, and, really, in a business where it ain't any Oscar winners of tomorrow who take the cake or stop the show, not even for talent so much as for the legendary, inoffensively bankable. We *love* Lucy. We're nuts about Hope. We eat up their routine. *They* eat up their routine.

> HOPE: What a night! I haven't seen so many gorgeous girls since I spent Father's Day with Steve Garvey. *(Lucy laughs heartily.)* But I've got the *most* gorgeous girl right by my side — Lucille Ball, right *there!*
>
> LUCY: Thank you. It really is wonderful to be here, and a particular thrill especially with you, Bob. It's a very secure feeling being up here with a man who's been on the Oscar show twenty-six times.
>
> HOPE: That's true.
>
> LUCY: And never won.
>
> HOPE: You had to mention it, huh?
>
> LUCY: Well . . .
>
> HOPE: It's not that I haven't begged. I've been on my knees more than Jimmy Swaggart. Anyway, a lot of people are wondering what Lucy and I are doing up here together. You know, we made four pictures together.
>
> LUCY: Yeah, talk about dangerous liaisons.
>
> HOPE: Even though we haven't been working in a while, we still keep in touch with everything. In fact, today the Ayatollah Khomeini called me and asked who wrote *Ishtar*.
>
> LUCY: And I heard they've offered you a role in the picture about Dan Quayle's visit to the White House.
>
> HOPE: Yeah, *The Accidental Tourist*. Actually, I was called back to Washington to paper-train the puppies.
>
> LUCY: Aww.
>
> HOPE: You know Millie, the White House dog, had three puppies. Actually she had five, but the Senate rejected two.
>
> LUCY: Bob, can we stop now? . . .
>
> HOPE: Yeah. *(in his but-seriously-folks voice)* You're about to see nineteen of the hottest young actors and actress in pictures. These are the people who will be winning Oscars way into the next century.
>
> LUCY *(in a but-seriously-folks voice of her own):* That's right. You've already seen them act in hit movies, but tonight you're going to see them sing and dance.

Because there's always the "but-seriously-folks" voice. Because there's always the silly double entendre of show business's mixed signals, its Trust Me idiomatics like some dead language. (Because I never heard of these "Oscar Winners of Tomorrow" and neither have you.) Because it *is* a sort of archaeology here, because in a real way, here, at the Academy Awards, we're on site, in the very future's very digs, at Routine's locale, perhaps the single place in all geography at the one moment in all time when so many could understand without recourse to footnotes the merely momentarily humorous argot of the Proper Noun, self-referential, egocentric, and obliterating the distinctions between Show Biz and State. The "Father's Day with Steve Garvey," "Jimmy Swaggart," "dangerous liaisons," and "Ayatollah Khomeini/*Ishtar*" lines (Salman Rushdie understood): the incredibly labored setup and syntax of Bob Hope's playing the lead in a movie about Dan Quayle's visit to the White House and calling the film *The Accidental Tourist;* the joke about the Senate rejecting two of Millie's puppies, are already like relics, like stuff pressed into geology.

And these anger me too — this banter, these "jokes." From my resentment pool, deep as some sea trench, rises a personal bile. It's the second time I've felt had, and this time "betrayed" *wouldn't* be overstating it. It ain't the papered house now but something on actual behalf of actual art. It's stupidity that has me down. Bob Hope's simplistic, condescending view of history and of ourselves, me. Because I take it personally, the good-natured contempt, the artificial scorn, the false assumption like a wink up in your face like a slap, or the car salesman's nudge like an elbow to your rib that we're all pals here, that we're in it together. Well — we ain't.

(Physically, it's been a hell of a year for me. In February my multiple sclerosis started to multiply. In March I got my wheelchair. In late June I went into the hospital for a course of Solumedrol and Cytoxin in the hope that those drugs would strengthen me, or at least freeze my disease at its current level, but before they were even started I had a strange experience. I was trying to tell Joan I had a terrible headache, but all I could say was "I have this awful haircut." I knew what I said was wrong, and understood everything Joan and the nurse were trying to tell me. I thought I was having a stroke. "I think," I told them, "I'm having an Australian crawl." I was taken for Doppler exams, for angiograms to the head, and it was discovered that only 2 percent of my right carotid artery was open. The left carotid artery had shut down completely. I was given an endarterectomy on the right side of my throat. They cleaned my plugs and points, but I suffered a mild heart attack from the anesthesia. This is the House that Jack built. After a time, they said, when I was strong enough, they said, I would need a heart angiogram to check out the damage. I would have, they said, depending on what the pictures showed, three options: I could be "managed medically"; I might be a candidate for an angioplasty — they send tiny balloons up your arteries and Roto-Rooter the schmutz from your system, all that old lox and cream cheese, all that ancient butter and eggs, all that red meat and smoke — or, they said, I would have to have open-heart surgery, a second heart bypass. "Out of the question," I told them. "Never again." But there is more to the quality of life than the quality of life, and when the angiogram showed I would either have to have the bypass or die, I chickened out and chose to live.)

Because there *is* more to the quality of life than the quality of life. Because one would to the woods no more with flibbertigibbets. Because camp is not enough, nor hype, nor kitsch, nor glamour, nor glitz, nor all pop culture's various altitudes, low to high like some kid's practice scales. Because *vita*'s too *brevis* and *ars* ain't *longa* enough by a country mile. And because here, at the Academy Awards, it isn't good enough finally to fabricate quality and celebration like some currency minted by hoopla, ads taken out in the trades — the clang and bang and claque of cash. And because it's a masque here, finally, some deal with the graced and favored, power in league with bone structure, haute couture, physiques as mannered and looked after as French gardens — Youth and Beauty like some topiary architecture of the only platonically human. (And it may just be something this side of sin in the actor's art, a stooping to conquer, a feeling I cannot shake all evening that pacts have been signed, the stronger pledges taken, temporal *quids* for immortal *quos*.) *Of course, if Galati had only returned my calls to the Four Seasons it might all have been different; Galati, up for an award himself for his screenplay for* The Accidental Tourist; *Galati, whom I'd put into pictures, the single person in all the world — save one's children — whose life I'd changed, whose*

name in those brief old days when I could have been a contender, Char-
lie, I had at once volunteered when asked if I could think of anyone who
could do the adaptation of a book I'd written and on which this teensy
little option had been taken out like an inexpensive hit. Who might have
gotten us a place, tourists at the Tourist *table, supping with Geena*
Davis, with Jeff Goldblum, with Lawrence Kasdan, with Charles Okun
and Michael Grillo, producers, with Bill Hurt if I really got lucky and
my theory proved wrong about no one coming to these do's unless some-
thing was in it for him. Perhaps then the grapes would not have been so
sour. — Or not. Maybe it was the time zone, hours behind my own, psy-
chological months even, the overlapping seasons of my humiliations be-
tween hospital and Hollywood, the bleak occasion of my below-stairs per-
spectives, the gut hard feelings between my mortality and their own blessed
lives like gifts from the Genes Fairies.

(I forgive Galati. I even understand him. He's up for an award,
there's lots on his mind; there are probably studio flowers in his
suite, baskets of fruit, congratulatory telegrams all over the place.
It's a simple question of who needs the aggravation, hospitality
to some guy you're into for your career, a pain in the ass on
unfamiliar turf, It's Swifty L., who doesn't even know me, I'll
never forgive.)

Though we get to go to a couple of parties anyway. (And, later,
I even have an opportunity to speak to Larry Kasdan personally.
Joan is calling for a cab from a bank of phones at the Shrine.
I'm right behind her, maybe five feet away, in my wheelchair. At
the next phone over there's this important-looking young man,
and I hear him say something like "Tell him Larry Kasdan. Yeah,
thanks." When he hangs up I say, "Excuse me, sir, but are you
Mr. Kasdan?" I don't think he sees me in the chair because he's
looking around to see where the voice is coming from. Then he
glances down and spots me. "Yes," he says. "Aren't you with Frank
Galati?" I ask, syntactically putting, as it were, the accent on the
wrong syllable. "He was at my table all evening," he tells me,
annoyed, and stalks off.)

The Shrine Exposition Hall looks like a soundstage. It's been
made over for the Board of Governors Ball, but it could be a set
for an immense wedding party or the most expensive prom in
human history. Or, indeed, the venue for almost any formal "af-

fair," from bar mitzvah to state dinner. There's a kind of carpeting, there are ice sculptures, a tiny dance floor around a round
raised platform for the band. Everywhere, as decoration, there
are battalions of those muscular art deco Oscars like some futur-
istic fascist coinage. Our table, in the two hundreds like a dangerously elevated blood pressure, in deep steerage, is maybe a
block and a half from the entrance as the wheelchair rolls. I pray
there isn't a fire.

I cast my eyes around the huge hall for a celeb but come up
empty. Of course, we are, in terms of the seating, somewhere in
space, about, if this were the universe, where *Voyager* 2 might
start to give out. It's all, as far as the eye can see, limbo here-a-
bouts. At our table there seem to be a bunch of folks down from
Sacramento — politicians, their spouses. There are no place cards.
No effort is made at introductions. The cat has got this reporter's tongue. Joan breaks the disinterested ice, and it turns out
there *is* a celebrity at the table. It's the daughter of Willie Brown,
the influential California Democrat. She's there on a date. The
presence of the others at the $450-per-person sit-down dinner
is, and remains, completely puzzling. I wonder aloud if *anyone*
in this immense room has actually put out cash money to be
here, and have again the sense that we're all beneficiaries of some
huge, pointless charity, a sort of Sunshine Fund for the already
tan. No one responds to my observations, but it could be the din.
We're on a soundstage indeed. I find I can talk (save Joan's grace)
only to the woman on my right, a political spouse (I think) and,
in her own right, a travel agent. We spend the evening, or she
does, discussing frequent-flier miles, letting me in on the almost
Hermes Trismegistean arcana — tricks of the trade, arrangements, how to crack the system, all the secret alchemicals of
turning paper credit into distance and upgrades. You must never
cash your miles in for a free flight, you buy your tickets at the
discount. I don't think I understand a word she says, but I recognize passion when I hear it. She's flown farther than the secretary of state, she tells me proudly. Sitting there in my tux, I'm
too ashamed to admit that we beat the system by coming out
here on this flying trolley car that keeps stopping to pick up
passengers along the way and gives you a transfer in Phoenix,
Arizona.

She is giving me the headache. To break her concentration, I study the menu to get some idea of what I've been eating. This is what 450 ghost bucks will get you these days:

POACHED SALMON AND ARUGULA ROULADE

With yellow and green french beans
and sliced mango on baby spring greens
with creamy honey-lime vinaigrette

BREADS

Homemade corn sticks,
whole wheat walnut rolls, and
garlic-herb knots with sweet butter rosettes

CHICKEN BREAST GRILLED OVER ALDERWOOD
Pommes soufflées in potato baskets
Grilled zucchini, baby white eggplant,
fresh baby corn

And that, Dear Diary, is all there was to it. Absolutely nothing else happened to us that night at the Governors Ball.

"You really think we should go to this party?" asks Joan.
    "I'm on assignment," I tell her. "I'm duty bound."
    "I'm a good sport, do you know that?"
    "You *are* a good sport," I admit, which is just about when she goes off to break the dollar to get the change to call the cab to take us to the El Rescate 2nd Annual Academy Awards Benefit at Vertigo in downtown L.A. It's supposed to be one of the "alternative parties" the younger, more serious movie people are said to favor these days.
    The $150-per-head admission at the door, like the $1,200 we've already cost our phantom benefactors for the privilege of going to the Academy Awards and watching the big TV show in person and, later, eating the garlic-herb knots and baby white eggplant — all that bread and veggies to the Stars — has been mysteriously waived. I don't get to identify myself — as per instructions — to Patrick Lippert in "Joe sent me," speakeasy inflections, or even flash the tickets Nanci Ryder (whom I don't know and have never seen and only spoken to on the telephone twice, on which she calls me Stanley — *me, Stanley,* a crippled-up

old man who in just over three months is doomed to have his throat cut and his chest cracked open for the second time in four years; *Stanley*, not Your Mortalityship or Your Woundship or even Mr. Elkin — *Stanley*, as if, as if, well, as if I were one of them, the larky freewheeling, high rolling of Earth) has sent over by special messenger to our hotel in Koreatown. Indeed, it's as if they've been waiting for us, keeping an eye out. As soon as Joan starts to assemble the wheelchair, two young men, too polite to be anything but bouncers, come to assist us. They take us through a special entrance and into the room.

Into an astonishing scene, one that I, Stanley, bad health's good sport, would never have expected ever to have witnessed. Not only too old but out of an altogether different, whatchamacallit, ethos, a different conation and even phylum maybe — my faint, poor pale human to their strident, unself-conscious, powerful, but entirely alien life force.

Black tie, according to the invitation, is optional, but that ain't it, that I'm the only man in the club in a tux, probably, for that matter, the only one in a jacket, or even in pants not artfully, sexually ripped into designer-torn, teasing jigsaw, fig-leaf puzzle patterns, or, as far as that goes, a buttoned shirt. They look vaguely like Oscars themselves, these guys. The women, oddly enough, are more formally dressed, many in gowns slightly reminiscent of hoop skirts. A girl near my wheelchair has to lean forward and flip up the back of her dress each time she sits down. Somehow she reminds me of a cartoon hen settling herself onto a Sunday-funnies egg. And that ain't it either.

What it is.

There used to be scenes in movies. Cut to an all-but-deserted nightclub. It's (metaphorically) quarter to three, there's no one in the place, Joe, except you and me. Most of the chairs have already been turned upside down on their tables. Only one couple, oblivious, obviously in love, is still dancing, gliding in the dim, romantically lighted room along the floor to some bluesy, dreamy tune in reeds, soft sax, muted brass, a tinkling piano in the next apartment. Waiters, impatient to go home, fidget, glance balefully at their watches, each other, sigh, toss "What can you do? They're in love. No one told me to go into my profession" occupational-hazard-type shrugs.

Now forget about the time (it's barely midnight) and the waiters (cocktail waitresses do the heavy lifting here) and the one lone couple (Vertigo isn't crowded, but there can't be more than eight or ten people dancing). Throw out the dreamy tune, the reeds and sax and muted brass. Forget the tinkling piano in the next apartment. You couldn't hear it with a radio telescope. Turn off the lowered, romantic lights. In their place substitute strobes popping and flashing like a bright barrage of incoming. On the club's small stage a heavy-metal band (of an element *so* heavy, *so* dense and base that whatever metal it represents has yet to be measured or even identified — black hole, perhaps) issues sounds so loud they would be heard by posts. Every instrument is electrically amplified, even the drums. For the second time that night I pray there isn't a fire.

The El Rescate 2nd Annual Academy Awards Benefit is a war zone.

A cocktail waitress shouts would we like a drink from the cash bar. A hundred and fifty bucks apiece at the door and it's a cash bar.

El Rescate was set up to assist a half million Central American refugees in the Los Angeles area with a variety of social services. It seems to me to be charity with a somehow coastal spin, though what is most striking is the pure surrealism of the event, the insufficiency of dancers in the big room, the hyperbolic music. Everywhere there are TV sets running videos of real war zones, their soundtracks silent against the explosive din and bang of the band. Earlier, of course, the sets had been tuned to the Awards, but we weren't here earlier and it isn't easy to imagine the scene. One thinks of sports — the World Series, Super Bowls, important away games, home games blacked out in their own cities, of all the taverns in all the towns with their enthusiastic, youthful clientele, whooping it up, making "We're number one, we're number one!" gestures with their fingers, crowding about the reporter, mugging for the TV cameras, the CBS local news at ten. It's impossible to imagine any of these people up for that sort of thing. For all their energy, the come-on of their driving, up-front dress, they seem detached to me, cynical. Like royals, they give off a faint stink of imperial airs. They're young, but somehow they seem as if they never had a youth. But what do *I* know, a guy redlined years ago by the underwriters? Probably

it's just more sour grapes, the prejudiced *pensées* of an embit-
tered ex-contender manqué.

(And there's the match-up right there, the carefully arranged
marriage of my stipulate, *shadchen* journalism, not rube/slicker
at all, but alive/dead — your reporter all gee-whizzed out in the
wheelchair.)

At any rate, this ain't, for us, where the action is anyway and,
like pols or priests at a party, we do maybe twenty-five minutes,
then metaphorically walk back to the hotel in the metaphorical
rain.

Joan's gone back to the room and left me in the lobby to wait for
Steve to join us for breakfast. He's a few minutes late, but I know
he'll be here soon, is on his way, is even now parking his car.
Meanwhile I take my ease in one of the hotel's deep, comfortable
chairs. It's a cold comfort, but one of the things I've learned
since losing my ability to get around is, well, patience isn't it exactly, but a sort of passive curiosity, a compensatory faculty like
the sharpened acuity of hearing in the blind, say, their increased
tactility. Anyway, I'm peculiarly suited to my disease, content,
up to a point, as a baby, absorbed by motes in the light, dis-
tracted by the parts of his toy mobile riding the currents of the
air. This is the close attention I pay to the world now, my crip-
ple's nosy scrutiny. I watch people checking out, their clear plastic garment bags holding evening gowns, tuxedos, and although
I recognize no one, I figure them, like me, for stringers, singers,
boys in the band, on the fringes, that is, of last night's ceremonies. I hear them double-checking, questioning the desk regarding their bills, the patient, difficult Oriental accents of the clerks.
Many of the guests are Korean. These chat up the clerks care-
lessly, cheerfully, *paisans* in this foreign hotel. Then I notice
something strange, startling even, comic, even moving.

Across from me is a well-dressed married couple. They are
Korean, probably in their forties. Arranged at their feet are bags
from significant shops and stores, their logos, chic, flagrant as
modern times. They have been on a shopping spree, and this is
somehow oddly touching to me. Then I see that they're joined
by a young man in his late teens. He has shopping bags, too.
He's in blue jeans, wears a light sweater. He laughs and puts his

arm familiarly around the man's shoulder. He hugs the woman. Only the kid is white, American. I can't quite make out what they're saying, or even the language they say it in. Why, he's adopted, I think. *They've gone and adopted an American kid!* And I'm stirred by the improbable ecumenicism of the world, the odd, turned tables of things, and feel suddenly hopeful, better than I have since I've been here.

Then the boy shakes hands with the two Koreans, waves so long, and leaves the hotel just as Steve comes into it.

Steve Zwicker is the outgoing chairman of our English department at Washington University. I like him because he's sane, a decent man bereft of neurosis and shtick. Unless you count, as I don't, his fear of, or maybe just his distaste for, flying. (A native Californian, he makes his frequent trips home on an Amtrak sleeper.) I'm fond of the Zwickers. During my sabbatical year in London, we rented our house to them. They didn't break anything. Steve and I agree about books, movies, have mostly the same opinions of our mutual friends. I go to all his kids' bar mitzvahs. He visits me in all my hospitals. He's an immaculate man, wry, sharp as good grapefruit. But chiefly, chiefly his sanity, his even-keel heart, which has less to do with any level, steady-as-she-goes fixity of purpose or unflappability of temperament than with his pitch-pipe instincts, some almost musical correctness of the emotions. Indeed, he has the benevolent, intelligent look of a musician in a symphony orchestra.

He's glad to see me. I'm glad to see him. And I have a familiar dividend of well-being, this jolt of bonding I feel whenever I'm with a friend I know from one place in another place essentially foreign to me. Though we share the turf here. It's my hotel, it's his hometown.

Then Joan steps out of the elevator, and we all go in to breakfast.

I'm not in my wheelchair, have elected to go the distance to the restaurant on my cane — and on Joan's arm. He's never seen me in my wheelchair. None of my friends has. My new, exacerbating disabilities are not out of the closest yet, but I'm stumbling badly, have to move along the wall for stability, leverage, playing the percentages with gravity, my waning strength. I notice Steve noticing. But once we're shown to our booth and seated, we're all equals again.

He asks how it went at the Awards, but I haven't sorted it all out yet and I can only tell him that for all the backstage and gossip I got out of it we could have stayed home and watched on TV. And I tell him about Galati, and Swifty Lazar — all my fish that got away.

Then we order. We order melons and berries, plates of lox, bagels, baskets of bread. Joan will have half a grapefruit, a poached egg, whole wheat toast. Coffee, we stipulate, is to be brought later. I love breakfast. I always have. In my book, it's the only meal — the long, luxurious leisurelies, at once normal and as ceremonial as high tea.

We talk. We talk about Molly's junior year abroad at Wadham College, Oxford University, my daughter the boater, how she earned her oar, her invitations to country houses on weekends, her trips between terms to Italy for the paintings, to Austria for the slopes. She's between terms now. Hilary term ended in March and we went to see her. We tell how she talked the manager at Durrants Hotel into upgrading our accommodations. We talk about our week in Paris together, her pals in the discos, from Oxford, Madison, Sarah Lawrence. As we speak, she's still in Israel with her connected friend. They'll be going on to Greece before they return to Oxford for Trinity term. Hilary term, Trinity. We discuss the morality of envying one's children.

Breakfast begins coming. The melon is swell, the berries and grapefruit. The lox, piled higher than corned beef in a sandwich in a deli, is more than we bargained for but not more than we can handle, its sheer weight incremental to our appetites. We try out different rolls, share pony pots of jam.

And talk easily, as comfortable with each other as the closed circle of movie stars at the Academy Awards. Wickedly, we discuss colleagues. I tease Steve about his money. He needles me about the long airplane ride ahead of us.

"TWA must have dozens of nonstops to St. Louis. Change carriers. Why lay over in Phoenix so long? Why do you have to stop in Houston? *Houston.* Isn't Houston on the Gulf of Mexico?"

"The magazine isn't paying for it. I am."

"That's not a good argument. I'm unimpressed."

"It's a difference of about $700."

"Suppose there's weather? In terms of time, you'd almost be better off with Amtrak."

In July, Steve will no longer be chairman of the English department. Wayne Fields will replace him. Steve was our first Jewish chairman, and when I see him in the halls I'll no longer have the opportunity to greet him as I used to do. "Good morning, Reb Chairman," or "Good evening, Reb Chairman." But we've finished our coffee. The breakfast, which has lasted longer than our dinner at the Governors Ball, and has been, for Joan, for me, much more fun, is just about over. I sign the check. "We have a plane to catch, Reb Chairman," I tell him, and rise carefully. Clumsily, I walk back into the lobby. I shake hands with my friend and say I'll see him back in St. Louis.

While Joan returns to the room to collect the wheelchair and arrange with a bellman about our bags, I prop myself against the cashier's counter and see to the bill.

By the time she comes down with the chair, I'm more than ready to sit in it. The bellman takes our bags and Joan pushes me toward the hotel's driveway, where we wait for the cab that will take us to the airport where we'll go to the gate to catch the plane that will bring us back to the town where we live in a house that stands on a street not far from the world that Jack built.

JOSEPH EPSTEIN

A Few Kind Words for Envy

FROM THE AMERICAN SCHOLAR

> Well, though many an arraigned mortal has in hopes of mitigated
> penalty pleaded guilty to horrible actions, did ever anybody seriously
> confess to envy? Something there is in it universally felt to be more
> shameful than even felonious crime.
> — Herman Melville

YOU MAY AS WELL know the worst about me, Doctor: I have not
coveted my neighbor's wife in years, and I certainly do not want
his Rolls-Royce, his duplex, or his shiny new fax machine. The
young walk by, with their lithe limbs and clear minds, the years
and years stretching out leisurely before them, and I feel no
longing to change places with them. Neither do I desire to be a
United States senator, a university president, the benevolent dic-
tator of a small, mineral-rich country nestled in a lush setting in
a lovely mild climate. I have no longing to enjoy the emoluments
of the editor of the *New York Times,* the president of L'Académie
Française, or Magic Johnson. Please do not understand me too
quickly here, Doctor. I am not, I assure you, expressing compla-
cency, smug (isn't "smug" the inevitable adjective here?) self-satisfaction with my own lot in life. No, something deeper, more
mysterious, is going on. I am, not to put too fine a point on it,
losing my capacity for envy, and I wonder, Doc, what can it mean?

I suppose none of this would worry me if, for so many years,
I hadn't envied so widely, so thoroughly, so energetically. Many
were the mornings I woke envying and many the nights I retired
to envy, with time off for several little breaks for envy during
the day. I read somewhere that one of the few benefits of grow-

ing older is that, in one's psychic economy, envy is replaced by admiration. I am not sure what I currently do with the time I once lavished upon envy, but I am quite sure that I do not pay it out in admiration. Can it be, too, that, now that I envy less, I shall grow fatter, for Horace, in the *Epistles,* remarks that "those who envy others grow thin despite vast wealth" (of envy, he adds, "Sicilian tyrants could never have contrived a better torture"). Is my loss of envy, then, likely to result in substantial weight gain? Am I, by envying insufficiently, endangering my health, Doc?

To begin my life not quite with the beginning of my life, the first thing I can remember envying was the parents of two boys I grew up with named Sammy and Billy Cowling. I loved my parents a very great deal, you understand, but on paper they just didn't stack up next to the Cowlings' parents. For openers, their father, Sam Cowling, Sr., was on the radio; he was the comedian on a then immensely popular radio show called *The Breakfast Club,* where, among other things, he did a bit entitled "Fiction and Fact from Sam's Almanac." Even at five years old, I knew that being on the radio was pretty hot stuff. He also happened to be a friendly man, kindly and thoughtful to children, and a good athlete. Sam Cowling, Sr., owned baseball spikes. I knew of no other father but the Cowlings' who owned spikes. Mrs. Cowling was feminine, beautifully so, and named (are you quite ready for this?) Dale, which was the name of Roy Rogers's wife. The Cowlings seemed so wondrous to me as a child that, in those days, I shouldn't have been surprised to learn that they kept a flowing-maned palomino in the dining room of their two-bedroom apartment. I don't want anyone to think that I envied the Cowling kids their parents so much that I would have traded my own for them. I would never finally have done that, but before deciding not to do it, I believe I would have had to give it considerable thought.

The second thing I remember envying was Catholics. For a time, from roughly age four to seven, I thought the United States was a Catholic country. This was owing partly to there being a preponderance of Catholic families on our block and partly to the movies of those years, a large number of which seemed to feature Bing Crosby, Barry Fitzgerald, Spencer Tracy, and Pat O'Brien playing priests. I envied the rigmarole of the Catholic

church, at least as it came across to me in the movies and in the
bits and pieces of it I was able to pick up from families such as
the Cowlings. Nothing theological or even religious about this,
for I was in fact rather like Valéry, who felt that the Protestants
had made a big mistake and should have gotten rid of God and
kept the pope. I liked the lighting of candles, the confessional
box, the prohibition against meat on Fridays, the clothes of priests
and the extraordinary get-ups of nuns. "May I offer you my
seat, Sister?" I used to say whenever the opportunity presented
itself on Chicago streetcars or el trains. "Excuse me, Father, but
would you care to have my seat?" I would announce with just a
slight hint of an Irish brogue. Any fisher of souls who knew his
business could have had me in the net in those days in fewer
than thirty seconds.

I keenly envied friends who had hair of a kind that could be
combed to resemble the hairdos of Gary Cooper, Cary Grant,
Clark Gable, John Wayne, Errol Flynn, and other movie stars of
the day. My own hair was thick, curly, thoroughly disobedient.
It resisted pompadours, widow's peaks, and wouldn't even tolerate a simple part. "My goodness," I remember my mother once
saying to me, "that part in your hair looks like Milwaukee Avenue," a reference to a lengthy diagonal street in Chicago that
every so often juts sharply to the left or right or takes a surprising turn. I longed for precisely the kind of hair I didn't have —
for lank hair that bopped up and down rhythmically when I ran
and that I would frequently have to brush back out of my eyes
with my hand. When crew cuts became the haircut of choice for
midwestern boys between twelve and eighteen, my hair wouldn't
allow a serious flat-top crew cut either. All my attempts to obtain
a crew cut ended in my coming away with an extremely short
haircut that, mocking the power of prayer and pomade, would
not stand up. Wishing to look like a brutish Big Ten athlete, I
merely looked, as I am told an immigrant woman in Princeton
once put it, like "a nice boy clean and cut from the Ivory League."

None of this, I realize, quite sounds like the envy that has had
such a poor historical press. I refer to the envy that Balzac, in
Lost Illusions, described as "an ignoble accumulation of disap-
pointed hope, frustrated talents, failures, and wounded preten-
sions"; that Orwell called "a horrible thing," which "is unlike all

other kinds of suffering in that there is no disguising it"; that the Austrian novelist Marie von Ebner-Eschenbach rated beneath hatred, noting that "hatred is a fertile, envy a sterile vice"; and that Gore Vidal, a writer scarcely known for specializing in the goodness of humankind, cites as "the only credible emotion, isn't it?" Pretty clearly the motive for Cain's slaying of Abel was envy. Melville's splendid *Billy Budd* shows the horror that envy acted upon can achieve. "The vilest affection," Francis Bacon called envy, "and the most depraved," and in cataloging by type those frequently obsessed by envy, he writes: "Deformed persons, and eunuches, and old men, and bastards, are envious." Not, as I say, a good historical press.

Envy is apparently more easily felt than defined. Semantically, the word provides a thicket out of which only a philologist in a pith helmet and carrying a magnifying glass is likely to emerge with his spirits intact. Envy and jealously, envy and emulation, envy and invidiousness, envy and ambition, envy and desire, the distinctions, the connections, the shades of meaning, the contextual nuances, all these things, if tracked down and carefully considered, could keep a fellow off the streets till well after the turn of the century. As there are some faces only a mother could love, so are there some books only a German scholar could write, and just such a book entitled *Envy: A Theory of Social Behaviour* has been written by a Professor Helmut Schoeck, but it, on the matter of definition, plunges one back into the thicket. The standard dictionaries, I fear, are not very helpful on this troublesome word either. I have, therefore, decided to supply my own definition: envy, I say, is desiring what someone else has — a desire usually heightened by the knowledge that one is unlikely to attain it. This definition nicely accommodates my feelings about Sam and Billy Cowling's parents, the Catholic church, and tractable hair.

My homemade definition leaves out the dark elements of spite, hostility, ill will, and begrudgment that most definitions of envy usually include. These elements cause the Parson in *The Canterbury Tales* to call envy "that foul sin . . . the worst sin there is"; these elements give envy its unenviable status as one of the seven deadly sins. Yet there is also a milder, even approbative sense of envy that is free from all malice, as when the Reverend Sydney

Smith, writing to Francis Jeffrey, remarks: "I envy your sense, your style, and the good temper with which you attack prejudices that drive me almost to the limits of sanity." I don't think that Sydney Smith, who chose his words punctiliously, misused "envy" here and that he really meant "admire" — he not only admired these qualities in McIntosh but wished he had them himself.

Along the same line, I recall several years ago, awaiting a table in a restaurant, sitting in a bar in which a man was hired to play, on a small electric organ, such sappy songs as "I Left My Heart in San Francisco," "The Way We Were," and "Raindrops Keep Falling on My Head." The unspoken consensus in the bar was that plainly this man loved his work too much, for he was banging away at his instrument with a fervor almost religious in intensity, making conversation just about impossible. Then, during a brief pause between numbers, a smallish, well-dressed man, a customer sitting only a few seats away from my own, walked over to him, handed him a hundred-dollar bill, and told him to take the rest of the night off. How I not only admired but envied that gesture, the rightness and not least the largeness of it! The fellow seemed pleased with the money, which was probably more than his regular night's wages; the room settled down into calm talk; and I felt a tinge of envy for what I had just witnessed, knowing that, had the notion even occurred to me, I probably would have offered the man a mere twenty bucks to knock off for an hour or so.

Not that I haven't felt my share of rich purple envy, the kind mixed with lots of malice and generally grudging feeling. But I don't recall feeling much envy of this kind when young. Such envy as I did feel was instead rather impersonal. I envied the freedom and wider experience of kids older than I; I envied boys who had the knack of winning the affection of beautiful girls; finally I envied those who had the unfailing ability to make themselves enviable. Being born to parents of middling wealth and being oneself of middling talent is surely to know envy more comprehensively than otherwise, for it permits envy of those both above and beneath you. From my earliest adolescence, I recognized that there were families who lived better than mine — in larger houses, with more expensive cars, and more capacious habits generally — and felt them, somehow, luckier than I. But I also felt envy for those born without my advantages, and the constraints that went along with them, and I remember reading, in high school, a series of novels with slum settings — *A Stone for Danny Fisher, The Amboy Dukes, The Hoods* — that made me feel that people who grew up in slums grew up more interestingly, sexier, luckier than I. Envy perhaps begins with the attribution of luck to the next fellow, for it seems that people with a real flair for envy — of whom I am clearly one — almost always see the next fellow as, somehow, luckier than themselves.

Very little about my youthful envy was subtle, and this, I believe, was owing to my having grown up in a family in which snobbery was almost nonexistent. Delicate, and even rather bulky, calibrations in status were of no concern to my parents, who did not bother to make many social distinctions beyond noting that some people were pleasant and some nasty, some rich and some poor, some gentile and some Jewish. Not at our dinner table were you likely to hear discussions about the fine distinctions between Williams and Amherst colleges, a Brooks Brothers and a J. Press suit, the Budapest and the Juilliard string quartets. The Midwest was my milieu, and middle western the outer limits of my view. In both my own high school graduating class and in the class that preceded mine, only two students went to Ivy League schools — both, as it happened, to Harvard — and neither was a boy it would have occurred to me to envy. For envy to take on interesting twists, shadings, and dark refinements, a little knowledge — always, as the old maxim has it, a dangerous thing — is required.

Three writers who did, I think, know a good deal about envy, young and at first hand, were F. Scott Fitzgerald, John O'Hara, and the journalist George Frazier. Fitzgerald, who lived in the poorest house on a very good block in St. Paul, Minnesota, learned about envy as a boy and had this knowledge honed as a young man who ran the gauntlet of snobbery at Princeton. The great event of John O'Hara's life turned out to be a nonevent, his not going to Yale, which, wise though O'Hara was in so many other ways, he appears never to have gotten over. George Frazier, who came from the Irish neighborhood in Boston known as Southie, went to Harvard but with the certainty that, as an Irishman in the early 1930s, he could never hope to make the best clubs or quite cut it with students who came from the best families and prep schools. Frazier was an admirer of the fiction of Fitzgerald and O'Hara, and all three men were immensely, intensely interested not only in style but in stylishness. Frazier even wrote a column in *Esquire* under the rubric "Style," which tended to be about people who had it and people who didn't. The three men also shared Irishness, at a time in our history when being Irish did not carry the comfortable, vaguely comical connotations it does today. I think they never got over the feeling of being boys and young men with their noses pressed to the glass, outsiders looking enviously in. Too keen an interest in style, I have come to suspect, betrays an early life of longing and envy.

The best-known method for combating envy is to arrange to acquire everything you want in life. Unfortunately, it often takes the better part of a lifetime to decide what, precisely, it is that you do want, which leaves damnably little time to acquire it. "I suppose you must be well," wrote Virgil Thomson to Paul Bowles, "you had everything there was when you were young; nothing left to have, I suppose." An odd error in so worldly-wise a man as Virgil Thomson, to think that wanting ever ceases. So long as avarice, lust, the appetite for glory, and snobbery continue to play as main attractions in the human heart, there is unlikely to be a serious shortage of wanting.

The sorting out of one's wants, especially when one is young, can be nearly a full-time job. I believe it was so for me, for, as I look back upon my young manhood, there was scarcely anything I didn't want and hence didn't vaguely find myself resenting in those who had it. I had only to see a beautiful woman with another man for my mind to jump to the question — the injustice, really — of why she was not instead with me. I would drive by suburban estates, walk past plush Park Avenue apartment buildings, and readily imagine myself happily ensconced therein. A Rolls-Royce convertible would tool by and, the resentment string in my heart plucking discordantly, I would not wish its owner well. (Not long ago, driving in heavy traffic in a flashy raspberry-colored Cadillac Seville, I suggested to the car's owner, an intelligent woman who takes the world as it is, that she put out her arm to request a break in the traffic so that she could get into the next lane. "I'm afraid," she said, "that in a car like this people tend not to give you many breaks.") When I was young all I really wanted from the world was money, power, and fame — and, naturally, the little perks that went along with them.

The problem, I have long since concluded, is that I spread my desire too thin. I merely wanted everything — but nothing, evidently, greatly enough. I also hit a lengthy detour in my desirousness — I am, apparently, still on it — when I developed this strange passion for acquiring the knack of writing interesting sentences. Although this passion freed me from the comprehensive generality of my desires, it concentrated my envy. For the first time, my envy lost its character of general longing and took a turn toward the particular, where envy usually gets unpleasant. What I now envied, with some intensity, was people of my own generation — I was then in my early twenties — who wrote better than I. Since I did not write all that well, my envy was given a wide berth and a fine chance for regular workouts. Around this time I can recall reading, in a biographical note, that a contributor to *Poetry,* a magazine I much admired, was born in 1940, which was three years later than I, a fact that registered like a rabbit punch to the kidneys. I didn't write poetry, you understand; nevertheless it seemed to me offensive for this young woman, three years my junior, to publish in a place in which I should have loved to publish had I written poetry. If this sounds a little crazy to you, not to worry; it only sounds crazy because it is.

The first of my contemporaries of whom I felt envious was a fellow undergraduate at the University of Chicago who had published a short story at the unconscionable age of sixteen. He had published it, moreover, not in some vulgar popular rag such as *The Saturday Evening Post* or *Redbook,* but in a then immitigably highbrow journal called *New World Writing,* where it appeared alongside work by the likes of Federico García Lorca and Wallace Stevens. I, who dreamed of publication, of seeing my name not in lights but in very small type (sans serifs), and who knew that publication, with luck, was still several years off, looked upon this boy and felt the sting of the world's terrible injustice. I also felt toward him a simple desire to exchange lives. I do not say that I despised him — he was very amiable, without the least air of superiority — but I should have preferred he matriculate elsewhere, so that his presence not remind me of my own drearily slow progress. Strangely, so far as I know he never published another thing. Did some personal tragedy intervene, I wonder, or was his petering out owing to his own lack of sufficient envy?

Writers and musicians tend to be rivalrous, which means, inevitably, envious and jealous. (Jealousy, Professor Schoeck holds, "remains the passionate endeavor to keep something that is one's own by right," whereas envy has to do with wanting something belonging to another.) Painters, for some reason, seem less envious of one another, or at least I, with limited knowledge, can think of more genuinely comradely behavior among painters than among musicians and writers. (All exceptions granted: John Morley, for example, said that Matthew Arnold "had not a spark of envy or jealousy.") Envy figures to be deepest at the top. Isaac Stern is famously generous to young musicians, but is he, I wonder, sound on the subject of Jascha Heifetz? At a dinner party in heaven, I think it probably a good idea not to invite, on the same evening, Shakespeare, Goethe, and Tolstoy; nor would I recommend seating Leonardo and Michelangelo next to each other. Having achieved great fame, having garnered all the world's great prizes, does not necessarily slake envy. Nor are scientists free from envy. "Don't call X this morning," a friend once advised of a scientific acquaintance of ours. "The Nobel Prize was announced, and since he didn't win it again this year, he's likely to be in a foul mood." The joke here is that, a few years earlier, X had already won it.

But then artists and scientists have no monopoly on envy; it is merely that their often monstrous egotism tends to display it in high comic relief. Academics are very good at envy, too, and it takes so little to get their envy into gear: the slightest advantage or advancement gained by a colleague will usually turn the trick. Modern corporations, sociologists and journalists have been claiming for years, are scarcely more than envy organized. Freud contended that all women, to lesser or greater degree, were envious, because of the absence in their own anatomy of a certain male appendage — as sweeping a generalization as our century has to offer. And as long as we're talking appendages, Melanie Klein, the Freudian psychoanalyst, maintained that envy is learned, literally, at the breast, and in a paper entitled "Envy and Gratitude" she rattles on at depressing length about "the primary envy of the mother's breast." As a member of a generation whose parents felt breastfeeding was bad form — we, so to speak, ordered out — I feel disqualified from commenting on the persuasiveness of Dr. Klein's argument. I suppose, as the saying is, you had to be there.

Such theories — and I, for one, do not envy anyone who subscribes to them — gain currency chiefly because envy appears to be so universal a phenomenon that an equally universal theory seems to be required to account for it. No known society, from simple tribes organized around a belief in magic to large industrial nations organized around a belief in communist equality, has ever been entirely free from envy, and in many societies — those that are fearful of the evil eye of envy, those that through competition encourage envy — it has been dominant. Envy has long been considered a theological problem, with its power of sowing discord, especially where it abuts its sister sin of pride, for even among saints it is possible to imagine one envying the other's greater spirituality. Spiritual envy is often the subject of the novels and stories of J. F. Powers. The great political (Churchill, de Gaulle), spiritual (Gandhi, Martin Luther King, Jr.), and scientific (Freud, Einstein) figures of our century were none of them without envy in their lives. The pope, I am prepared to believe, is without envy, but was he before he became pope? Mother Teresa of Calcutta is the only person alive today that I can think of who appears to be utterly free from envy. Doubtless there are others, but if they were to meet in a convention I don't think one would need to reserve all the rooms in the Helmsley Palace to accommodate them.

I hope no one thinks that, because I began this essay by saying I was running out of envy, I imagine myself approaching the spiritual trim of Mother Teresa. "I have never known life without desire," remarks the hero of Italo Svevo's *Confessions of Zeno,* and neither, I must report, have I. And where there is desire, be assured, nearby envy lurks. I thought, for example, that I had long ago made my peace with money and material possessions. The terms of the treaty, set by me, were entirely in my favor. I liked having money, respected money, had not the least doubt

of the importance of money in human affairs. Yet I long ago
decided that I would never knowingly truckle for money, or, if
I could help it, expend great energy on projects whose sole result was pecuniary gain. Insofar as possible, I felt, everything I
did should either amuse me or contribute to my intellectual
progress — preferably both. My mind, in this scheme, would dwell
in the clouds, my bottom never rest for long on the bottom
line.

In exchange, I agreed to surrender all fantasies of real wealth:
the country estate, the Paris apartment, the limousine, the staff
of unobtrusive but absolutely reliable servants. Such fantasies
ought to have been easily enough surrendered, for fairly early
in life it became evident to me that I should never be rich. Part
of my problem is less an antipathy than an inability to concen-
trate for long on money. It isn't that my mind is too fine to be
violated by money matters, but instead that I haven't the attention span to learn the fundamentals of the stock, commodities,
options, and other markets or even to learn how to get the best
out of the smallish sums I am able to save. Part of the problem,
too, is that I could never quite imagine myself rich, with all the
world's objects within my grasp. You are rich, says Henry James
in *Portrait of a Lady*, when you can meet the demands of your
imagination. My imagination, that nag, would never allow surcease in its demands, so that even with billions I could not, by
Jamesian prescription, qualify as rich anyhow.

Do I, I ask myself, envy the very wealthy their riches and what
they have brought them? I like to think not, and yet I do find
myself taking a perhaps uncommon delight in hearing stories
about burglar alarm systems going off in homes with serious art
collections and spoiling otherwise gracious meals. Why does my
spirit jump a notch when I see a large Mercedes being towed
ignominiously off to Rolfe's Auto Repair? Can it be that we have
a case here of *Schadenfreude*, that little subdivision of envy that
Webster's allows itself the rare luxury of going alliterative to define as "malicious merriment at someone else's misfortune"? La
Rochefoucauld gives *Schadenfreude* a genuinely hideous twist when
he turns it very personal and remarks that "we always find something which is not displeasing to us in the misfortunes of our
best friends." That is not envy, though — it is merely pure hu-

man viciousness. But there is, I think, a national *Schadenfreude* that is excited by revelations about the ostensibly very fortunate — the rich, the beautiful, the immensely talented — living in great emotional squalor. Howard Hughes supplied the country with Schadenfreudic titillation that lasted for months when it came out that his having a fortune in the billions of dollars did not prevent his living, poor devil, at the emotional level of a rodent. On its dark side, a democracy enjoys few things more than the spectacle of the rich undone, the beautiful besmirched, the talented penalized. See any issue of the *National Enquirer, People,* or *Vanity Fair* for confirmation.

Whatever their other deprivations, academics, intellectuals, and artists find no shortage of occasions for *Schadenfreude* or straightforward envy. The promotion denied, the manuscript rejected, or the dead-on devastating review can put the ugly little curl into the sympathetic smile of the colleague one had thought, until now, civil enough and not displeased with your success. "The Book of My Enemy Has Been Remaindered" is the title of a poem by Clive James whose refrain lines run: "And I am pleased." "And I rejoice." "And I am glad."

In intellectual life, awards and prizes are no longer the efficient swizzle sticks for stirring envy that they once were. Pulitzers, Guggenheims, NEHs, NEAs, honorary degrees — too many of all of these have by now been given out, and to too many mediocre people, for them any longer to carry much prestige, and hence to excite much envy. One award, though, can still do the job — narrow the eyes, quicken the pulse, dry the palms, send a little black cloud across the heart — and this is a MacArthur Fellowship. "It isn't the principle," my father used to say when attempting to collect bad business debts, "it's the money." And so with "Big Macs," as they are known in the trade, it isn't the prestige — too many not very impressive MacArthur Fellows already walk the earth — it, too, is the money. To win a MacArthur Fellowship is to go on a five-year ride at as much as $75,000 a year, for a total score of nearly four hundred grand. Nowhere near the kind of money a switch-hitting second baseman can bring down, true, but still a nice piece of change.

My own carefully considered view of the MacArthur Fellowships was, I believe, similar to that held by most intellectuals,

artists, scientists, performers, and inventors: sheer resentment
for just about every nickel that did not go to me. I could understand the foundation's need to come across for a Navajo under-
water architect or a woman weightlifter who is making a series
of documentary films based on the Talmud; there are, after all,
political reasons for such awards. But I failed entirely to understand the reasoning behind all the awards to literary men and
women, none of whom, when you came right down to it (which
I did rather quickly), seemed nearly so fit for a MacArthur as I.
I won't go into my qualifications here, except to say that they
seemed to me damn near perfect: my work was unusual and
various; from the outside I must appear overworked; and, like
99 percent of my countrymen, I could use the dough. What was
more, a MacArthur Fellowship was one of the few such awards
I had any hope of winning, for I had long ago determined never
to apply for a grant or prize. If people wished to give me these
things, splendid, but I was raised to believe that you didn't ask
strangers for money.

So I went along from year to year, happy enough in my mild
resentment, gaily mocking each year's fresh crop of MacArthur
Fellows, until it was revealed to me that I had myself been nominated for a MacArthur. Good friends even sent me thoughtfully inflated letters of recommendation they had been asked to
send in on my behalf. The envy in my soul now had to make
room for its first cousin, greed. I thought a goodly amount in an
unconcentrated way about what I might do with the money such
a fellowship would bring in. If I had long ago agreed to forgo
the large luxurious things, I had a decided taste for the small
luxurious things: the German fountain pen, the Italian loafers,
the dish of raspberries in midwinter. With my MacArthur Fellowship, there would be more of these things, much more. And,
while at it, I ought to acquire some really good luggage. Most of
the money, I thought, I would pocket away in some high-yield
bank account, perhaps with an eye, at the end of the fellowship's
five years, to plunking it all down on a modest house on Fiesole
overlooking the red roofs of the city of Florence. The Big Macs
were announced, I knew, sometime in the summer, and so about
June first I began opening my mailbox in anticipation of finding
that envelope from the John D. and Catherine T. MacArthur

Foundation informing me that I had won a fellowship and might now, baby, let the good times roll. I thought, too, with some glee, how discouraging my winning a MacArthur Fellowship would be to my enemies. Alas, no letter arrived; it was not to be; and now, with the printing of these last few paragraphs, it isn't ever likely to be.

Had I won a MacArthur Fellowship, of course, I should have stepped across from the shady to the sunny side of the street — from being an envier to being envied. Even without a Mac-Arthur, I might, it occurs to me, already have crossed that street. In the eyes of many, I am among the world's lucky people. And so — I knock wood here, lest the evil eye fall upon me — do I generally think myself. I have all the essential things: work that amuses me, excellent health, freedom, the love of a good-hearted and intelligent woman. Ought not that be sufficient? It ought, except that, human nature being human nature — or is it instead my nature being my nature? — it hasn't been sufficient to diminish envy; or at least it hasn't been until recently.

Within the past few years, two acquaintances, roughly my contemporaries, have written books that have made them millions of dollars. Despite the fact that my most recent royalty check was for $2.49, I found that I did not feel the least wisp of envy for either of these fellows; nor do I now. Not long ago I went to dinner with a political columnist who appears regularly on television, and our meal was interrupted by a request for his autograph; on the way out of the restaurant he was twice stopped by strangers and congratulated for recent work. I thought this fascinating, but my envy gland, usually so sensitive, gave not a twitch. True, for my own writing, posterity and not prosperity is the name of my (slightly embarrassing to admit) desire; and rather than widespread fame, I prefer to have a good name among a select audience of the genuinely thoughtful. But none of this is a convincing reason not to have felt envious. What good is longing, after all, if you can't long for contradictory things: the pleasures that riches bring and a life of simplicity, fame and privacy both? If you are going to force envy to be consistent, you're likely to put it out of business.

Many people would, of course, prefer to see envy go permanently out of business. Arthur Rubinstein, in his memoirs, remarked that at bottom anti-Semitism was owed chiefly to envy, and that the anti-Semite's "real hatred is concentrated on the Jews who possess the highest standards of ethics, intelligence, and talents, on those who, whenever allowed to compete, become prominent in all possible fields like science, art, or economy." On the other side of the ledger, envy is a foe of drab leveling. L. P. Hartley has written an anti-utopian novel entitled *Facial Justice* in which equality is known as Good E and envy as Bad E; what makes envy Bad E is that it arouses people's passions for discrimination, degree, difference, all the things that give life variety and make it interesting. Without these differences, Hartley's novel argues, life is scarcely worth living.

Perhaps the problem lies in the word "envy" itself. There is a good envy, of the kind that encourages dreams and aspiration, and a bad envy, based on disappointment and hatred. Perhaps a new word is needed, one that falls between envy and admiration, to describe the positive qualities of the former and strip it of traditional pejorative meanings. But the language, as Flaubert remarked in a very different connection — he was trying to convince his mistress of his love for her by describing its intensity — the language, as Flaubert remarked, is inept.

Meanwhile, my own problem, I begin to realize, is that I am becoming more discriminating in my envy. What I am discriminating against is the world's larger, more obvious prizes: wealth, fame, power. Glittering though these prizes are, and as they once were to me, I now find them mainly glaring, and in my own life even a little beside the point. I still envy large things, among them genuine achievement, true religious faith, real erudition. I justify envy of these things on the ground that surely there is no point in envying things you can actually have and that it is only the unattainable that is worth a serious person's envy.

The only expensive item I continue to envy is a small, well-made house with a fine view of water and of a naturally elegant landscape. For the rest, I envy things on which a price tag cannot be put, many but not all of them fairly trivial. Permit me to list them. I envy anyone who can do a backward somersault in mid-air from a standing position. I envy men who have fought a war and survived it. I envy people who speak foreign languages easily. I envy performing artists who have the power to move and amuse audiences to the point where the audience wants the performance never to end. I envy people who can travel abroad with a single piece of carry-on luggage. I envy people who have good posture. Above all, I envy those few people who truly understand that life is a fragile bargain, rescindable at any time by the other party, and live their lives accordingly.

STEPHEN JAY GOULD

The Creation Myths
of Cooperstown

FROM NATURAL HISTORY

YOU MAY EITHER look upon the bright side and say that hope springs eternal or, taking the cynic's part, you may mark P. T. Barnum as an astute psychologist for his proclamation that suckers are born every minute. The end result is the same: you can, Honest Abe notwithstanding, fool most of the people all of the time. How else to explain the long and continuing compendium of hoaxes — from the medieval shroud of Turin to Edwardian Piltdown Man to an ultramodern array of flying saucers and astral powers — eagerly embraced for their consonance with our hopes or their resonance with our fears?

Some hoaxes make a sufficient mark upon history that their products acquire the very status initially claimed by fakery — legitimacy (although as an object of human or folkloric, rather than natural, history. I once held the bones of Piltdown Man and felt that I was handling an important item of Western culture).

The Cardiff Giant, the best American entry for the title of paleontological hoax turned into cultural history, now lies on display in a shed behind a barn at the Farmer's Museum in Cooperstown, New York. This gypsum man, more than ten feet tall, was "discovered" by workmen digging a well on a farm near Cardiff, New York, in October 1869. Eagerly embraced by a gullible public, and ardently displayed by its creators at fifty cents a pop, the Cardiff Giant caused quite a brouhaha around Syracuse, and then nationally, for the few months of its active life between exhumation and exposure.

The Cardiff Giant was the brainchild of George Hull, a cigar manufacturer (and general rogue) from Binghamton, New York. He quarried a large block of gypsum from Fort Dodge, Iowa, and shipped it to Chicago, where two marble cutters fashioned the rough likeness of a naked man. Hull made some crude and minimal attempts to give his statue an aged appearance. He chipped off the carved hair and beard because experts told him that such items would not petrify. He drove darning needles into a wooden block and hammered the statue, hoping to simulate skin pores. Finally, he dumped a gallon of sulfuric acid all over his creation to simulate extended erosion. Hull then shipped his giant in a large box back to Cardiff.

Hull, as an accomplished rogue, sensed that his story could not hold for long and, in that venerable and alliterative motto, got out while the getting was good. He sold a three-quarter interest in the Cardiff Giant to a consortium of highly respectable businessmen, including two former mayors of Syracuse. These men raised the statue from its original pit on November 5 and carted it off to Syracuse for display.

The hoax held on for a few more weeks, and Cardiff Giant fever swept the land. Debate raged in newspapers and broadsheets between those who viewed the giant as a petrified fossil and those who regarded it as a statue wrought by an unknown and wondrous prehistoric race. But Hull had left too many tracks — at the gypsum quarries in Fort Dodge, at the carver's studio in Chicago, along the roadways to Cardiff (several people remembered seeing an awfully large box passing on a cart just days before the supposed discovery). By December, Hull was ready to recant, but held his tongue a while longer. Three months later, the two Chicago sculptors came forward, and the Cardiff Giant's brief rendezvous with fame and fortune ended.

The common analogy of the Cardiff Giant with Piltdown Man works only to a point (both were frauds passed off as human fossils) and fails in one crucial respect. Piltdown was cleverly wrought and fooled professionals for forty years, while the Cardiff Giant was preposterous from the start. How could a man turn to solid gypsum while preserving all his soft anatomy, from cheeks to toes to penis? Geologists and paleontologists never accepted Hull's statue. O. C. Marsh, later to achieve great fame as a discoverer of dinosaurs, echoed a professional consensus in his unambiguous pronouncement: "It is of very recent origin and a decided humbug."

Why, then, was the Cardiff Giant so popular, inspiring a wave of interest and discussion as high as any tide in the affairs of men during its short time in the sun? If the fraud had been well executed, we might attribute this great concern to the dexterity of the hoaxers (just as we grant grudging attention to a few of the most accomplished art fakers for their skills as copyists). But since the Cardiff Giant was so crudely done, we can only attribute its fame to the deep issue, the raw nerve, touched by the subject of its fakery — human origins. Link an absurd concoction to a noble and mysterious subject and you may prevail, at least for a while. My opening reference to P. T. Barnum was not meant sarcastically; he was one of the great practical psychologists of the nineteenth century — and his motto applies with special force to the Cardiff Giant: "No humbug is great without truth at bottom." (Barnum made a copy of the Cardiff Giant and exhibited it in New York City. His mastery of hype and publicity assured that his model far outdrew the "real" fake when the original went on display at a rival establishment in the same city.)

For some reason (to be explored but not resolved in this essay), we are powerfully drawn to the subject of beginnings. We yearn to know about origins, and we readily construct myths when we do not have data (or we suppress data in favor of legend when a truth strikes us as too commonplace). The hankering after an origin myth has always been especially strong for the closest subject of all — the human race. But we extend the same psychic need to our accomplishments and institutions — and we have origin myths and stories for the beginning of hunting, of language, of art, of kindness, of war, of boxing, bowties, and brassieres. Most of us know that the Great Seal of the United States pictures an eagle holding a ribbon reading *e pluribus unum.* Fewer would recognize the motto on the other side (check it out on the back of a dollar bill): *annuit coeptis* — "he smiles on our beginnings."

Cooperstown may house the Cardiff Giant, but the fame of this small village in central New York does not rest upon its celebrated namesake, author James Fenimore, or its lovely Lake

Otsego or the Farmer's Museum. Cooperstown is "on the map" by virtue of a different origin myth — one more parochial but no less powerful for many Americans than the tales of human beginnings that gave life to the Cardiff Giant. Cooperstown is the sacred founding place in the official myth about the origin of baseball.

Origin myths, since they are so powerful, can engender enormous practical problems. Abner Doubleday, as we shall soon see, most emphatically did not invent baseball at Cooperstown in 1839 as the official tale proclaims; in fact, no one invented baseball at any moment or in any spot. Nonetheless, this creation myth made Cooperstown the official home of baseball, and the Hall of Fame, with its associated museum and library, set its roots in this small village, inconveniently located near nothing in the way of airports or accommodations. We all revel in bucolic imagery on the field of dreams, but what a hassle when tens of thousands line the roads, restaurants, and port-a-potties during the annual Hall of Fame weekend, when new members are enshrined and two major league teams arrive to play an exhibition game at Abner Doubleday Field, a sweet little ten-thousand-seater in the middle of town. Put your compass point at Cooperstown, make your radius at Albany — and you'd better reserve a year in advance if you want any accommodation within the enormous resulting circle.

After a lifetime of curiosity, I finally got the opportunity to witness this annual version of forty students in a telephone booth or twenty circus clowns in a Volkswagen. Since Yaz (former Boston star Carl Yastrzemski to the uninitiated) was slated to receive baseball's Nobel in 1989, and his old team was playing in the Hall of Fame game, and since I'm a transplanted Bostonian (although still a New Yorker and not-so-secret Yankee fan at heart), Tom Heitz, chief of the wonderful baseball library at the Hall of Fame, kindly invited me to join the sardines in this most lovely of all cans.

The silliest and most tendentious of baseball writing tries to wrest profundity from the spectacle of grown men hitting a ball with a stick by suggesting linkages between the sport and deep issues of morality, parenthood, history, lost innocence, gentleness, and so on, seemingly ad infinitum. (The effort reeks of silliness because baseball is profound all by itself and needs no excuses; people who don't know this are not fans and are therefore unreachable anyway.) When people ask me how baseball imitates life, I can only respond with what the more genteel newspapers used to call a "barnyard epithet," but now, with growing bravery, usually render as "bullbleep." Nonetheless, baseball is a major item of our culture, and it does have a long and interesting history. Any item or institution with these two properties must generate a set of myths and stories (perhaps even some truths) about its beginnings. And the subject of beginnings is the bread and butter of this column on evolution in the broadest sense. I shall make no woolly analogies between baseball and life; this is an essay on the origins of baseball, with some musings on why beginnings of all sorts hold such fascination for us. (I thank Tom Heitz not only for the invitation to Cooperstown at its yearly acme but also for drawing the contrast between creation and evolution stories of baseball, and for supplying much useful information from his unparalleled storehouse.)

Stories about beginnings come in only two basic modes. An entity either has an explicit point of origin, a specific time and place of creation, or else it evolves and has no definable moment of entry into the world. Baseball provides an interesting example of this contrast because we know the answer and can judge received wisdom by the two chief criteria, often opposed, of external fact and internal hope. Baseball evolved from a plethora of previous stick-and-ball games. It has no true Cooperstown and no Doubleday. Yet we seem to prefer the alternative model of origin by a moment of creation — for then we can have heroes and sacred places. By contrasting the myth of Cooperstown with the fact of evolution, we can learn something about our cultural practices and their frequent disrespect for truth.

The official story about the beginning of baseball is a creation myth, and a review of the reasons and circumstances of its fabrication may give us insight into the cultural appeal of stories in this mode. A. G. Spalding, baseball's first great pitcher during his early career, later founded the sporting goods company that still bears his name and became one of the great commercial moguls of America's gilded age. As publisher of the annual

Spalding's Official Base Ball Guide, he held maximal power in shaping both public and institutional opinion on all facets of baseball and its history. As the sport grew in popularity, and the pattern of two stable major leagues coalesced early in our century, Spalding and others felt the need for clarification (or merely for codification) of opinion on the hitherto unrecorded origins of an activity that truly merited its common designation as America's "national pastime."

In 1907, Spalding set up a blue ribbon committee to investigate and resolve the origins of baseball. The committee, chaired by A. G. Mills and including several prominent businessmen and two senators who had also served as presidents of the National League, took much testimony but found no smoking gun for a beginning. Then, in July 1907, Spalding himself transmitted to the committee a letter from an Abner Graves, then a mining engineer in Denver, who reported that Abner Doubleday had, in 1839, interrupted a marbles game behind the tailor's shop in Cooperstown, New York, to draw a diagram of a baseball field, explain the rules of the game, and designate the activity by its modern name of "base ball" (then spelled as two words).

Such "evidence" scarcely inspired universal confidence, but the commission came up with nothing better — and the Doubleday myth, as we shall soon see, was eminently functional. Therefore, in 1908, the Mills Commission reported its two chief findings: first, "that base ball had its origins in the United States"; and second, "that the first scheme for playing it, according to the best evidence available to date, was devised by Abner Doubleday, at Cooperstown, New York, in 1839." This "best evidence" consisted only of "a circumstantial statement by a reputable gentleman" — namely Graves's testimony as reported by Spalding himself.

When cited evidence is so laughably insufficient, one must seek motivations other than concern for truth value. The key to underlying reasons stands in the first conclusion of Mills's committee: hoopla and patriotism (cardboard version) decreed that a national pastime must have an indigenous origin. The idea that baseball had evolved from a wide variety of English stick-and-ball games — although true — did not suit the mythology of a phenomenon that had become so quintessentially American. In fact, Spalding had long been arguing, in an amiable fashion, with Henry Chadwick, another pioneer and entrepreneur of base-ball's early years. Chadwick, born in England, had insisted for years that baseball had developed from the British stick-and-ball game called rounders; Spalding had vociferously advocated a purely American origin, citing the Colonial game of "one old cat" as a distant precursor, but holding that baseball itself rep-resented something so new and advanced that a pinpoint of or-igin — a creation myth — must be sought.

Chadwick considered the matter of no particular importance, arguing (with eminent justice) that an English origin did not "detract one iota from the merit of its now being unquestionably a thoroughly American field sport, and a game too, which is fully adapted to the American character." (I must say that I have grown quite fond of Mr. Chadwick, who certainly understood evolu-tionary change and its chief principle that historical origin need not match contemporary function.) Chadwick also viewed the committee's whitewash as a victory for his side. He labeled the Mills report as "a masterful piece of special pleading which lets my dear old friend Albert [Spalding] escape a bad defeat. The whole matter was a joke between Albert and myself."

We may accept the psychic need for an indigenous creation myth, but why Abner Doubleday, a man with no recorded tie to the game and who, in the words of Donald Honig, probably "didn't know a baseball from a kumquat"? I had wondered about this for years, but only ran into the answer serendipitously dur-ing a visit to Fort Sumter in the harbor of Charleston, South Carolina. There, an exhibit on the first skirmish of the Civil War points out that Abner Doubleday, as captain of the Union artil-lery, had personally sighted and given orders for firing the first responsive volley following the initial Confederate attack on the fort. Doubleday later commanded divisions at Antietam and Fredericksburg, became at least a minor hero at Gettysburg, and retired as a brevet major general. In fact, A. G. Mills, head of the commission, had served as part of an honor guard when Doubleday's body lay in state in New York City, following his death in 1893.

If you have to have an American hero, could anyone be better than the man who fired the first shot (in defense) of the Civil

War? Needless to say, this point was not lost on the members of Mills's committee. Spalding, never one to mince words, wrote to the committee when submitting Graves's dubious testimony: "It certainly appeals to an American pride to have had the great national game of base ball created and named by a Major General in the United States Army." Mills then concluded in his report: "Perhaps in the years to come, in view of the hundreds of thousands of people who are devoted to base ball, and the millions who will be, Abner Doubleday's fame will rest evenly, if not quite as much, upon the fact that he was its inventor . . . as upon his brilliant and distinguished career as an officer in the Federal Army."

And so, spurred by a patently false creation myth, the Hall of Fame stands in the most incongruous and inappropriate locale of a charming little town in central New York. Incongruous and inappropriate, but somehow wonderful. Who needs another museum in the cultural maelstroms (and summer doldrums) of New York, Boston, or Washington? Why not a major museum in a beautiful and bucolic setting? And what could be more fitting than the spatial conjunction of two great American origin myths — the Cardiff Giant and the Doubleday Fable? Thus, I too am quite content to treat the myth gently, while honesty requires fessing up. The exhibit on Doubleday in the Hall of Fame Museum sets just the right tone in its caption: "In the hearts of those who love baseball, he is remembered as the lad in the pasture where the game was invented. Only cynics would need to know more." Only in the hearts; not in the minds.

Baseball evolved. Since the evidence is so clear (as epitomized below), we must ask why these facts have been so little appreciated for so long, and why a creation myth like the Doubleday story ever gained a foothold. Two major reasons have conspired: first, the positive block of our attraction to creation stories; second, the negative impediment of unfamiliar sources outside the usual purview of historians. English stick-and-ball games of the nineteenth century can be roughly classified into two categories along social lines. The upper and educated classes played cricket, and the history of this sport is copiously documented because the literati write about their own interests, and because the activities of men in power are well recorded (and constitute virtually all of history, in the schoolboy version). But the ordinary pastimes of rural and urban working people can be well nigh invisible in conventional sources of explicit commentary. Working people played a different kind of stick-and-ball game, existing in various forms and designated by many names, including "rounders" in western England, "feeder" in London, and "base ball" in southern England. For a large number of reasons, forming the essential difference between cricket and baseball, cricket matches can last up to several days (a batsman, for example, need not run after he hits the ball and need not expose himself to the possibility of being put out every time he makes contact). The leisure time of working people does not come in such generous gobs, and the lower-class stick-and-ball games could not run more than a few hours.

Several years ago, at the Victoria and Albert Museum in London, I learned an important lesson from an excellent exhibit on the late-nineteenth-century history of the British music hall. This is my favorite period (Darwin's century, after all), and I consider myself tolerably well informed on cultural trends of the time. I can sing any line from any of the Gilbert and Sullivan operas (a largely middle-class entertainment), and I know the general drift of high cultural interests in literature and music. But here was a whole world of entertainment for millions, a world with its heroes, its stars, its top forty songs, its gaudy theaters — and I knew nothing, absolutely nothing, about it. I felt chagrined, but my ignorance had an explanation beyond personal insensitivity (and the exhibit had been mounted explicitly to counteract the selective invisibility of certain important trends in history). The music hall was the chief entertainment of Victorian working classes, and the history of working people is often invisible in conventional written sources. It must be rescued and reconstituted from different sorts of data; in this case, from posters, playbills, theater accounts, persistence of some songs in the oral tradition (most were never published as sheet music), recollections of old-timers who knew the person who knew the person . . .

The early history of baseball — the stick-and-ball game of working people — presents the same problem of conventional invisibility — and the same promise of rescue by exploration of unusual sources. Work continues and intensifies as the history of sport becomes more and more academically respectable, but the broad outlines (and much fascinating detail) are not well established. As the upper classes played a codified and well-documented cricket, working people played a largely unrecorded and much more diversified set of stick-and-ball games ancestral to baseball. Many sources, including primers and boys' manuals, depict games recognizable as precursors to baseball well into the early eighteenth century. Occasional references even spill over into high culture. In *Northanger Abbey,* written at the close of the eighteenth century, Jane Austen remarks: "It was not very wonderful that Catherine . . . should prefer cricket, base ball, riding on horseback, and running about the country, at the age of fourteen, to books." As this quotation illustrates, the name of the game is no more Doubleday's than the form of play.

These ancestral styles of baseball came to America with early settlers and were clearly well established by Colonial times. But they were driven ever further underground by Puritan proscriptions of sport for adults. They survived largely as children's games and suffered the double invisibility of location among the poor and the young. But two major reasons brought these games into wider repute and led to a codification of standard forms quite close to modern baseball between the 1820s and the 1850s. First, a set of social reasons, from the decline of Puritanism to increased concern about health and hygiene in crowded cities, made sport an acceptable activity for adults. Second, middle-class and professional people began to take up these early forms of baseball, and with this upward social drift came teams, leagues, written rules, uniforms, stadiums, guidebooks: in short, all the paraphernalia of conventional history.

I am not arguing that these early games could be called baseball with a few trivial differences (evolution means substantial change, after all), but only that they stand in a complex lineage, better called a nexus, from which modern baseball emerged, eventually in a codified and canonical form. In those days before instant communication, every region had its own version, just as every set of outdoor steps in New York City generated a different form of stoopball in my youth, without threatening the basic identity of the game. These games, most commonly called town ball, differed from modern baseball in substantial ways. In the

Massachusetts Game, a codification of the late 1850s drawn up
by ballplayers in New England towns, four bases and three strikes
identify the genus, but many specifics are strange by modern
standards. The bases were made of wooden stakes projecting
four feet from the ground. The batter (called the striker) stood
between first and fourth base. Sides changed after a single out.
One hundred runs (called tallies), not higher score after a spec-
ified number of innings, spelled victory. The field contained no
foul lines, and balls hit in any direction were in play. Most im-
portantly, runners were not tagged out but were retired by
"plugging," that is, being hit with a thrown ball while running
between bases. Consequently, since baseball has never been a
game for masochists, balls were soft — little more than rags stuffed
into leather covers — and could not be hit far. (Tom Heitz has
put together a team of Cooperstown worthies to re-create town
ball for interested parties and prospective opponents. Since few
other groups are well schooled in this lost art, Tom's team hasn't
been defeated in ages, if ever. "We are the New York Yankees
of town ball," he told me. His team is called, quite appropriately
in general but especially for this essay, the Cardiff Giants.)

Evolution is continual change, but not insensibly gradual transition; in any continuum, some points are always more interesting than others. The conventional nomination for most salient
point in this particular continuum goes to Alexander Joy Cartwright, leader of a New York team that started to play in lower
Manhattan, eventually rented some changing rooms and a field
in Hoboken (just a quick ferry ride across the Hudson), and
finally drew up a set of rules in 1845, later known as the New
York Game. Cartwright's version of town ball is much closer to
modern baseball, and many clubs followed his rules — for stan-
dardization became ever more vital as the popularity of early
baseball grew and opportunity for play between regions increased. In particular, Cartwright introduced two key innova-
tions that shaped the disparate forms of town ball into a semblance of modern baseball. First, he eliminated plugging and
introduced tagging in the modern sense; the ball could now be
made harder, and hitting for distance became an option. Second, he introduced foul lines, again in the modern sense, as his
batter stood at a home plate and had to hit the ball within lines

defined from home through first and third bases. The game could now become a spectator sport because areas close to the field but out of action could, for the first time, be set aside for onlookers.

The New York Game may be the highlight of a continuum, but it provides no origin myth for baseball. Cartwright's rules were followed in various forms of town ball. His New York Game still included many curiosities by modern standards (twenty-one runs, called aces, won the game, and balls caught on one bounce were outs). Moreover, our modern version is an amalgam of the New York Game plus other town ball traditions, not Cartwright's baby grown up by itself. Several features of the Massachusetts Game entered the modern version in preference to Cartwright's rules. Balls had to be caught on the fly in Boston, and pitchers threw overhand, not underhand as in the New York Game (and in professional baseball until the 1880s).

Scientists often lament that so few people understand Darwin and the principles of biological evolution. But the problem goes deeper. Too few people are comfortable with evolutionary modes of explanation in any form. I do not know why we tend to think so fuzzily in this area, but one reason must reside in our social and psychic attraction to creation myths in preference to evolutionary stories — for creation myths, as noted before, identify heroes and sacred places, while evolutionary stories provide no palpable, particular thing as a symbol for reverence, worship, or patriotism. Still, we must remember — and an intellectual's most persistent and nagging responsibility lies in making this simple point over and over again, however noxious and bothersome we render ourselves thereby — that truth and desire, fact and comfort, have no necessary, or even preferred, correlation (so rejoice when they do coincide).

To state the most obvious example in our current political turmoil. Human growth is a continuum, and no creation myth can define an instant for the origin of an individual life. Attempts by anti-abortionists to designate the moment of fertilization as the beginning of personhood make no sense in scientific terms (and also violate a long history of social definitions that traditionally focused on the quickening, or detected movement, of the fetus in the womb). I will admit — indeed, I emphasized as a key argument of this essay — that not all points on a continuum are equal. Fertilization is a more interesting moment than most, but it no more provides a clean definition of origin than the most interesting moment of baseball's continuum — Cartwright's codification of the New York Game — defines the beginning of our national pastime. Baseball evolved and people grow; both are continua without definable points of origin. Probe too far back and you reach absurdity, for you will see Nolan Ryan on the hill when the first ape hit a bird with a stone; or you will define both masturbation and menstruation as murder — and who will then cast the first stone? Look for something in the middle, and you find nothing but continuity — always a meaningful "before," and always a more modern "after." (Please note that I am not stating an opinion on the vexatious question of abortion — an ethical issue that can only be decided in ethical terms. I only point out that one side has rooted its case in an argument from science that is not only entirely irrelevant to the proper realm of resolution but also happens to be flat-out false in trying to devise a creation myth within a continuum.)

And besides, why do we prefer creation myths to evolutionary stories? I find all the usual reasons hollow. Yes, heroes and shrines are all very well, but is there not grandeur in the sweep of continuity? Shall we revel in a story for all humanity that may include the sacred ball courts of the Aztecs, and perhaps, for all we know, a group of *Homo erectus* hitting rocks or skulls with a stick or a femur? Or shall we halt beside the mythical Abner Doubleday, standing behind the tailor's shop in Cooperstown, and say "behold the man" — thereby violating truth and, perhaps even worse, extinguishing both thought and wonder?

ANN HODGMAN

No Wonder They Call Me a Bitch

FROM SPY

I'VE ALWAYS WONDERED about dog food. Is a Gaines-burger really like a hamburger? Can you fry it? Does dog food "cheese" taste like real cheese? Does Gravy Train actually make gravy in the dog's bowl, or is that brown liquid just dissolved crumbs? And exactly what *are* by-products?

Having spent the better part of a week eating dog food, I'm sorry to say that I now know the answers to these questions. While my dachshund, Shortie, watched in agonies of yearning, I gagged my way through can after can of stinky, white-flecked mush and bag after bag of stinky, fat-drenched nuggets. And now I understand exactly why Shortie's breath is so bad.

Of course, Gaines-burgers are neither mush nor nuggets. They are, rather, a miracle of beauty and packaging — or at least that's what I thought when I was little. I used to beg my mother to get them for our dogs, but she always said they were too expensive. When I finally bought a box of cheese-flavored Gaines-burgers — after twenty years of longing — I felt deliciously wicked.

"Dogs love real beef," the back of the box proclaimed proudly. "That's why Gaines-burgers is the only beef burger for dogs with real beef and no meat by-products!" The copy was accurate: meat by-products did not appear in the list of ingredients. Poultry by-products did, though — right there next to preserved animal fat.

One Purina spokesman told me that poultry by-products consist of necks, intestines, undeveloped eggs and other "carcass remnants," but not feathers, heads, or feet. When I told him I'd been eating dog food, he said, "Oh, you're kidding! Oh, *no!*" (I came to share his alarm when, weeks later, a second Purina spokesman said that Gaines-burgers *do* contain poultry heads and feet — but *not* undeveloped eggs.)

Up close my Gaines-burger didn't much resemble chopped beef. Rather, it looked — and felt — like a single long, extruded piece of redness that had been chopped into segments and formed into a patty. You could make one at home if you had a Play-Doh Fun Factory.

I turned on the skillet. While I waited for it to heat up I pulled out a shred of cheese-colored material and palpated it. Again, like Play-Doh, it was quite malleable. I made a little cheese bird out of it; then I counted to three and ate the bird.

There was a horrifying rush of cheddar taste, followed immediately by the dull tang of soybean flour — the main ingredient in Gaines-burgers. Next I tried a piece of red extrusion. The main difference between the meat-flavored and cheese-flavored extrusions is one of texture. The "cheese" chews like fresh Play-Doh, whereas the "meat" chews like Play-Doh that's been sitting out on a rug for a couple of hours.

Frying only turned the Gaines-burger black. There was no melting, no sizzling, no warm meat smells. A cherished childhood illusion was gone. I flipped the patty into the sink, where it immediately began leaking rivulets of red dye.

As alarming as the Gaines-burgers were, their soy meal began to seem like an old friend when the time came to try some *canned* dog foods. I decided to try the Cycle foods first. When I opened them, I thought about how rarely I use can openers these days, and I was suddenly visited by a long-forgotten sensation of can-opener distaste. *This* is the kind of unsavory place can openers spend their time when you're not watching! Every time you open a can of, say, Italian plum tomatoes, you infect them with invisible particles of by-product.

I had been expecting to see the usual homogeneous scrapple inside, but each can of Cycle was packed with smooth, round, oily nuggets. As if someone at Gaines had been tipped off that a human would be tasting the stuff, the four Cycles really were different from one another. Cycle-1, for puppies, is wet and soy-

ish. Cycle-2, for adults, glistens nastily with fat, but it's passably
edible — a lot like some canned Swedish meatballs I once got in
a Care package at college. Cycle-3, the "lite" one, for fatties, had
no specific flavor; it just tasted like dog food. But at least it didn't
make me fat.

Cycle-4, for senior dogs, had the smallest nuggets. Maybe old
dogs can't open their mouths as wide. This kind was far sweeter
than the other three Cycles — almost like baked beans. It was
also the only one to contain "dried beef digest," a mysterious
substance that the Purina spokesman defined as "enzymes" and
my dictionary defined as "the products of digestion."

Next on the menu was a can of Kal Kan Pedigree with Chunky
Chicken. Chunky *chicken?* There were chunks in the can, certainly — big, purplish-brown chunks. I forked one chunk out
(by now I was becoming more callous) and found that while it
had no discernible chicken flavor, it wasn't bad except for its
texture — like meat loaf with ground-up chicken bones.

In the world of canned dog food, a smooth consistency is a
sign of low quality — lots of cereal. A lumpy, frightening, bloody,
stringy horror is a sign of high quality — lots of meat. Nowhere
in the world of wet dog foods was this demonstrated better than
in the fanciest I tried — Kal Kan's Pedigree Select Dinners. These
came not in a can but in a tiny foil packet with a picture of an
imperious Yorkie. When I pulled open the container, juice spurted
all over my hand, and the first chunk I speared was trailing a
long gray vein. I shrieked and went instead for a plain chunk,
which I was able to swallow only after taking a break to read
some suddenly fascinating office equipment catalogues. Once
again, though, it tasted no more alarming than, say, canned hash.

Still, how pleasant it was to turn to *dry* dog food! Gravy Train
was the first I tried, and I'm happy to report that it really does
make a "thick, rich, real beef gravy" when you mix it with water.
Thick and rich, anyway. Except for a lingering rancid-fat flavor,
the gravy wasn't beefy, but since it tasted primarily like tap water,
it wasn't nauseating either.

My poor dachshund just gets plain old Purina Dog Chow, but
Purina also makes a dry food called Butcher's Blend that comes
in Beef, Bacon & Chicken flavor. Here we see dog food's arcane
semiotics at its best: a red triangle with a *T* stamped into it is

supposed to suggest beef; a tan curl, chicken; and a brown *S,* a piece of bacon. Only dogs understand these messages. But Butcher's Blend does have an endearing slogan: "Great Meaty Tastes — without bothering the Butcher!" *You know, I wanted to buy some meat, but I just couldn't bring myself to bother the butcher . . .*

Purina O.N.E. ("Optimum Nutritional Effectiveness") is targeted at people who are unlikely ever to worry about bothering a tradesperson. "We chose chicken as a primary ingredient in Purina O.N.E. for several reasonings," the long, long essay on the back of the bag announces. Chief among these reasonings, I'd guess, is the fact that chicken appeals to people who are — you know — *like us.* Although our dogs do nothing but spend eighteen-hour days alone in the apartment, we still want them to be *premium* dogs. We want them to cut down on red meat, too. We also want dog food that comes in a bag with an attractive design, a subtle typeface, and no kitschy pictures of slobbering golden retrievers.

Besides that, we want a list of the Nutritional Benefits of our dog food — and we get it on O.N.E. One thing I especially like about this list is its constant references to a dog's "hair coat," as in "Beef tallow is good for the dog's skin and hair coat." (On the other hand, beef tallow merely provides palatability, while the dried beef digest in Cycle provides palatability *enhancement.*)

I hate to say it, but O.N.E was pretty palatable. Maybe that's because it has about 100 percent more fat than, say, Butcher's Blend. Or maybe I'd been duped by the packaging; that's been known to happen before.

As with people food, dog snacks taste much better than dog meals. They're better looking too. Take Milk-Bone Flavor Snacks. The loving-hands-at-home prose describing each flavor is colorful; the writers practically choke on their own exuberance. Of bacon they say, "It's so good, your dog will think it's hot off the frying pan." Of liver: "The only taste your dog wants more than liver — is even more liver!" Of poultry: "All those farm fresh flavors deliciously mixed in one biscuit. Your dog will bark with delight!" And of vegetable: "Gardens of taste! Specially blended to give your dog that vegetable flavor he wants — but can rarely get!"

Well, I may be a sucker, but advertising *this* emphatic just doesn't convince me. I lined up all seven flavors of Milk-Bone Flavor Snacks on the floor. Unless my dog's palate is a lot more sensitive than mine — and considering that she steals dirty diapers out of the trash and eats them, I'm loath to think it is — she doesn't detect any more difference in the seven flavors than I did when I tried them.

I much preferred Bonz, the hard-baked, bone-shaped snack stuffed with simulated marrow. I liked the bone part, that is; it tasted almost exactly like the cornmeal it was made of. The mock marrow inside was a bit more problematic: in addition to looking like the sludge that collects in the treads of my running shoes, it was bursting with tiny hairs.

I'm sure you have a few dog food questions of your own. To save us time, I've answered them in advance.

Q. Are those little cans of Mighty Dog actually branded with the sizzling word BEEF, *the way they show in the commercials?*

A. You should know by now that that kind of thing never happens.

Q. Does chicken-flavored dog food taste like chicken-flavored cat food?

A. To my surprise, chicken cat food was actually a little better — more chickeny. It tasted like inferior canned pâté.

Q. Was there any dog food that you just couldn't bring yourself to try?

A. Alas, it was a can of Mighty Dog called Prime Entree with Bone Marrow. The meat was dark, dark brown, and it was surrounded by gelatin that was almost black. I knew I would die if I tasted it, so I put it outside for the raccoons.

SUE HUBBELL

The Vicksburg Ghost

FROM THE NEW YORKER

> The human predicament is typically so complex that it is not alto-
> gether clear which lies are vital and what truths beg for discovery.
> — "Vital Lies, Simple Truths: The Psychology of Self-Deception,"
> by Daniel Goleman

I GUESS MOST people found it hard to believe that Elvis Presley
didn't die after all but instead is alive and well and shopping at
Felpausch's Supermarket, in Vicksburg, Michigan. I know I did
when I read about it in the *New York Times* last fall. The *Times*
wasn't on record as saying, "The King Lives," or anything like
that, but it did report that a Vicksburg woman named Louise
Welling had said she'd seen him the year before, in the supermarket's checkout line. Her sighting encouraged Elvins everywhere, many of whom believe that Presley faked his death. It
also added an extra fillip to Elvismania, which is part nostalgia
and part industry, the industry part consisting of the production
of Elvis memorabilia, books, articles, tours, and prime-time TV
"docudramas." Fans have made periodic demands for an Elvis
postage stamp, and a multimedia musical, *Elvis: A Rockin' Remembrance,* had an off-Broadway run this summer.

Promotion was what made Elvis Presley. In 1977, the year of
his death, his likeness was more widely reproduced than any other
save that of Mickey Mouse, and it has been reported that the
news of his demise was greeted by one cynic with the words "Good
career move!" According to Albert Goldman, the biographer who
tells this story, Presley was by then a porky, aging, drug-befud-
dled Las Vegas entertainer and was getting to be a hard person-

ality to promote. The Presley image shorn of the troublesome
real man was easier to market. For example, after the King's
death, Presley's manager, Colonel Thomas A. Parker, contracted with a vineyard in Paw Paw, Michigan — a town not far
from Vicksburg — to produce a wine called Always Elvis. Its label bears a head shot of the entertainer, in a high-collared spangled white shirt, singing into a hand-held microphone. Colonel
Parker's own four-stanza poem appears on the back of the bottle. Goldman has computed that the poem earned Parker $28,000
in royalties, "making him, line for line, the best-paid poet in the
world." Although the wine is no longer produced, I was able to
find a dusty old bottle in my local liquor store. In the interests
of journalism, I sampled it. It was an adequate companion to the
poem, which closes with the couplet

> We will play your songs from day to day
> For you really never went away.

In its year-end double issue, *People* ran a story featuring recent photographs of Elvis purportedly taken by readers around
the country, each picture as vague and tantalizing as snapshots
of the Loch Ness monster. While debate mounted over whether
or not Elvis Presley was still alive, I got stuck back there in the
part of the *Times* story which said that he was shopping at Felpausch's. By the latter part of the 1950s, when Elvis arrived to
sweep away the dreariness of the Eisenhower years, I was too
old to respond to the Dionysian sexual appeal that he had for
his teenage maenads; consequently, I was also unmoved by
retro-Elvis. But I did grow up near Vicksburg. My family lived
in Kalamazoo, a bigger town (in which Elvis was also said to have
appeared) twelve miles to the north, and we spent our summers
at a lake near Vicksburg. My widowed mother now lives at the
lake the year round, and when I visit her I often shop at Felpausch's myself. I know Vicksburg tolerably well, so when I read
the account in the *Times* I strongly suspected that the reporter
had been snookered by a group of the guys over at Mar-Jo's
Café on Main Street, half a block from Felpausch's, which is on
Prairie Street, the town's other commercial thoroughfare. Last
June, while I was visiting my mother, I decided to drive into
Vicksburg and find out what I could about the Elvis Presley story.

*

Vicksburg is a pretty village of two thousand people, more or less. A hundred and fifty years ago, when it was first settled by white people, the land was prairie and oak forest. James Fenimore Cooper, who lived for a time in the nearby town of Schoolcraft, wrote about the area in his book *Oak Openings*. It is in southern Michigan, where the winters are long and gray, and even the earliest settlers complained of the ferocity of the summertime mosquitoes. Vicksburg's one-block commercial section has been spruced up in recent years. There are beds of petunias at the curb edges, and new façades on the nineteenth-century buildings. The carefully maintained Victorian houses on the side streets are shaded by maples big enough to make you think elm. A paper mill, built near a dam that the eponymous John Vickers constructed on Portage Creek for his flour mill, has long provided employment for the local people, but today the village has become something of a bedroom community for commuters to Kalamazoo. Still, it seems very like the place I knew when I used to come to band concerts on Wednesday evenings at the corner of Main and Prairie during the summers of the 1930s and 1940s. The band concerts are a thing of the past, but there are other homegrown entertainments, such as one going on the week I was there — the annual Vicksburg Old Car Festival, which is run by Skip Knowles, a local insurance man. The festival has a fifties theme, and last year, inspired by the commotion that Louise Welling's sighting of Elvis had produced, Knowles added an Elvis-look-alike contest to the roster of events. Knowles has his office in a storefront on Main Street that used to be Matz's Confectionery, where I first discovered lime phosphates (known locally as "green rivers").

And the teenagers are still bored. While I was in the library going through back issues of local newspapers, two high school girls introduced themselves to me, saying that they had lived in Vicksburg all their lives and would be happy to talk to me about it. I asked them what they thought about Elvis Presley. They smiled patronizingly and informed me that no one they knew paid any attention to him. "But *everything* just stands still in Vicksburg," one of them confided. "We go to Kalamazoo on Saturday nights. I can't wait to get out of here and go to college."

Mar-Jo's has stayed the same, too. It has been in the same

place for forty years. It was named after Marge Leitner and her partner, Josephine, whose last name no one at the café can remember. It is your basic tan place: tan floor, tan walls, tan tables, tan counter. The sign taped to the cash register was new to me. It said:

THIS IS NOT
BURGER KING
YOU GET IT
MY WAY
OR YOU DON'T
GET IT
AT ALL

But the men having coffee together at the big round table near the front windows could have been the same ones sitting there the last time I was in, which was a couple of years ago.

"How's you-know-who?" gray crew cut asks feed-store cap. "Don't see her anymore."

The others guffaw, and one says, "He's taken her clothes."

"What clothes?" feed-store cap shoots back. A ripple of caffeine-fueled laughter circles the table.

Shirley White, a small, wiry woman, has been a waitress at Mar-Jo's for eleven years. Her hair is dark and tightly curled. She is efficient and cheerful. She knows virtually all her customers by name and how they like their coffee, and she banters with all of them. She gets to work at 4:45 every morning, so she is usually way ahead of the best of the town wits, giving as good as she gets. The coffee-club boys once arranged the kind of prank on her that made me suspect them of the Elvis Presley caper. One of the regulars was a big man whom she could deftly unsettle with a clever phrase or two. His invariable riposte was a mumbled "Paybacks are hell." A few years ago, he was on vacation in Florida when her birthday came around, and she had nearly forgotten about him. Mar-Jo's was jammed that day, and no one would tell her why. "Just as I was busiest, this really big monkey walked in," she told me. "At least, it was a big guy dressed in a monkey costume, and he kept following me around, getting in my way. I was real embarrassed, and everyone kept laughing.

Then a messenger handed me something called an Ape-O-Gram. It had just three words: 'Paybacks are hell.' "

Nearly all the coffee drinkers thought that the Elvis Presley sighting was as funny as the Ape-O-Gram, but no one would own up to having had a hand in making up the story. Louise Welling, it seemed, was a real person, and well known in town. She lived to the east, a few miles outside the village, they told me. "She's different, that's for sure," one of the coffee drinkers said. "No one believes her about Elvis Presley, but we all enjoyed it. Kind of put Vicksburg on the map. Isn't it funny? Elvis Presley wasn't even a very good singer. But I don't think Louise thinks it's funny." They referred me to a woman in town who knew Louise Welling better than they did and lived not far from her.

I went over to see the woman, who had an office in town, and talked to her with the understanding that her name would not be used. "Yes," she said. "I guess you could say that Louise is different. Her whole family is different, except for her husband, who works at General Motors. He's real quiet. But she's not crazy or anything. In fact, I think she's real bright. I don't know what to make of her claim that she saw Elvis Presley. She was a big Elvis fan from way back, but she doesn't bring him up or talk about this stuff unless someone asks her. She's a kind woman. She's reliable, too, and I wouldn't hesitate to call her if I had trouble. I'm afraid that after the story came out a lot of people played jokes on her. Made Elvis phone calls. Sent her Elvis letters. I'm pretty sure she's not in it for money. She just seems to think it's an interesting story, and it makes her mad when people don't believe her. Of course, none of us do. I don't know anyone in this town who thinks she really saw Elvis Presley. She was furious with the Vicksburg newspaper because they wouldn't run her story."

It seemed odd to me that the *Vicksburg Commercial* had not used Louise Welling's story — a story that had made the *New York Times* — so I called up Jackie Lawrence, the owner of the *Commercial,* and asked her to meet me for lunch at Mar-Jo's. Jackie Lawrence, a former nurse, is a big woman with curly brown hair, and she smiles a lot when she talks about Vicksburg, her adopted town. There are, she said, perhaps a dozen loyal Elvis fans in town — people who make pilgrimages to Graceland and would *like* to believe Louise Welling even if they don't.

We studied the daily specials, which were posted on the wall, and I decided to order Ken's Homemade Goulash. Next to the list of specials were snapshots of Ken Fowler, a cheerful young man with a fine brushy mustache, who bought Mar-Jo's two years ago and does a lot of the café's cooking. Shortly after he bought the place, he had a birthday, and the regulars, the waitresses, and Ken's wife conspired to bring in a belly dancer. The event was captured on film, and the posted snapshots show Ken, in apparent embarrassment, on a chair in one corner of the café, surrounded by laughing customers as a woman in gold draperies writhes in front of him.

Jackie Lawrence told me that she remembered Louise Welling coming into the newspaper office, which is a few doors down from Mar-Jo's, in March 1988, six months after the sighting at Felpausch's. At the time of her visit, Mrs. Welling knew that her story would soon be printed nationally, in the *Weekly World News* — and so it was, three months later. (According to Jim Leggett, who is the dean of freelance tabloid photojournalists and once schemed to drill a hole in Howard Hughes's coffin in order to photograph his face, the *Weekly World News* is not exactly esteemed in the trade. "It prints the flotsam left by the better tabloids," he told me.) Mrs. Welling had wanted the *Commercial* to run her story first, Lawrence said. "She stood right by my desk, trying to tell me all about it. I said to her, 'I'm sorry, I don't have time for this,' and showed her out the door. And if she came in again, I'd say the same thing."

There was only one mention in the *Commercial* of the stir caused by Louise Welling's encounter with Elvis. The winner of Skip Knowles's 1988 Elvis-look-alike contest, a truck driver named Ray Kajkowski, came into the newspaper office a few days after the event to ask for prints of any pictures that might have been taken. While he was there, he kissed Jean Delahanty, one of the *Commercial*'s reporters, and she wrote a column about it, which concluded, "Some days are better than others!"

There is no chamber of commerce, as such, in Vicksburg. The town doesn't need one; it has Skip Knowles. I had telephoned Knowles before coming to Vicksburg. "Give me a jingle when

you get in," he said. "Maybe we can do lunch." He is a handsome, trim, dark-haired man, and at our lunch a gold chain
showed through the open collar of his shirt. There was another
gold chain around his wrist. He was born in Atchison, Kansas,
he told me, but spent his teenage years — from 1962 to 1968 —
near Detroit, where he developed a passion for cars and for
cruising, that cool, arm-on-the-window, slow patrolling of city
streets which was favored by the young in those days. His dark
eyes sparkled at the memory.

"We had what we called the Woodward Timing Association,"
he said. "It was made up of the guys that cruised Woodward
Avenue. The Elias Big Boy at Thirteen Mile Road and Woodward was the place we'd go. But you know how the grass is always greener somewhere else? Well, my ultimate dream was to
cruise the Sunset Strip. It wasn't until I got married, in 1969,
and went out to California that I got to do that. And I talked to
those guys cruising the Strip, and you know what they told me?
It was *their* dream to cruise Woodward." He shook his head and
laughed. "My wife and I still cruise when we go to a city." He
hoped the local people had got cruising down pat for this year's
festival, he said, handing me a packet of publicity material and
a schedule of festival events. "I had to *teach* them how to cruise
last year, which was the first time we closed off the streets for it."

The second annual Elvis-look-alike contest would be held at
9 P.M. Saturday over on Prairie Street, in the parking lot of the
Filling Station, a fast-food restaurant across the street from Felpausch's. Skip Knowles knew a good thing when he had it. Before last summer, he said, the festival had been drawing several
thousand people, but each year he had had more trouble getting
good publicity. "I can't understand the way they handled the
Elvis business over at Felpausch's," he told me. "They even refused an interview with the *New York Times*. But I decided to play
it for whatever it was worth."

After the first Elvis-look-alike contest, Knowles received a lot
of calls from Louise Welling, who wanted to talk about Elvis
Presley with him. "I put her off," he said. "She's *really* different.
I think she really believes Presley never died." He also received
other phone calls and visits. When his secretary told him last fall
that a reporter from the *Times* was in his outer office waiting to

talk to him, he thought it was just a hoax — a joke like the ones dreamed up at Mar-Jo's. But when he came out the man introduced himself as the paper's Chicago bureau chief and interviewed him about the Elvis contest. Then a producer from Charles Kuralt's show, *Sunday Morning,* called and said he was interested in doing a segment for the show on the impact of the Elvis sighting in Vicksburg, and would anything be going on in Vicksburg around Thanksgiving time? "I told him, 'Look, I'll do *anything* to get you here,' " Knowles recalled. " 'If you want me to rent Cadillac limos and parade them up and down Main Street for you to film, I'll get them.' But the TV people never came."

I decided that it was time to talk to Louise Welling herself. I couldn't make an appointment with her by telephone because she had recently obtained an unlisted number, but one midweek morning I took a chance on finding her at home and drove out to see her. The Wellings live in the country, in a modest split-level house on non-split-level terrain; this is the sandy, flat part of Michigan, too far south for the ice-age glaciers to have sculpted it. Mrs. Welling sometimes works as a babysitter, but this morning she was home, along with four of her five children — all of them grown — and Nathan, her four-year-old grandson. Mrs. Welling is a heavyset woman with closely cropped dark hair and a pleasant face. Her eyes stay sad when she smiles. She touched my arm frequently as we talked, and often interrupted herself to digress as she told me her story. She said that she grew up in Kalamazoo and for a time attended St. Mary's, a Catholic grammar school there. When she turned sixteen, she was given a special present — a ticket to a Presley concert in Detroit. "Somehow, the fellow who took tickets didn't take mine, so after the first show I was able to move up, and I sat in front during the second," she said. "And then, toward the end, Elvis got down on his knee right in front of me and spread his arms wide open. Well, you can imagine what *that* would be like for a sixteen-year-old girl." Her voice trailed off, and she fell silent, smiling.

I asked her if she had continued to follow his career.

"When I got married, I started having children, and I never thought much about Elvis," she said. "After all, I had problems of my own." But then, in 1973, she saw a notice in a throwaway shopping newspaper from Galesburg, a nearby town, saying that Presley would be in Kalamazoo and, although he would not be performing, would stay at the Columbia Hotel there.

"I didn't try to get in touch with him," Mrs. Welling said, adding, with a womanly smile, "I had a husband, and you know how that is." Three years later, however, Presley appeared in concert in Kalamazoo, and she sent flowers to him at the Columbia Hotel, because she assumed that he would be staying there again. She went to the concert, too, and as she remembers it, Elvis announced in the course of it that he had a relative living in Vicksburg. "He said he liked this area," she recalled. "Kalamazoo is a peaceful place. He'd like that. And I think he's living at the Columbia right now, under another name. But they won't admit it there. Every time I call, I get a runaround. You know what I think? I think he has become an undercover agent. He was interested in that sort of thing."

"What year was it that you saw him in concert in Detroit?" I asked. I had read somewhere that Presley had not started touring outside the South until 1956.

"Oh, I don't remember," Mrs. Welling said. "I'm fifty-one now, and I had just turned sixteen — you figure it out."

The arithmetic doesn't work out — nor, for someone who grew up in Kalamazoo, does the Columbia Hotel. The Columbia had its days of glory between the First World War and Prohibition, and it was growing seedy by the forties, when I used to ride by it on my way to school. Its decline continued after I left Kalamazoo, until — according to Dan Carter, one of the partners in a development company that remodeled the hotel to create an office complex called Columbia Plaza — it became "a fleabag flophouse and, for a while, a brothel." Carter also told me that in the mid-eighties a rumor arose that Elvis Presley was living there, behind the grand pink double doors on the mezzanine, which open into what was once a ballroom. The doors have been locked for years — the empty ballroom, its paint peeling, belongs to the man who owns Bimbo's Pizza on the floor below — but that didn't deter Elvins here and abroad from making pilgrimages to Columbia Plaza. "You'd hear foreign voices out in the hallway almost every day," he said. "Then there was a visit from some people from Graceland — at least, they told us they were from Graceland, and they looked the part — who came by to see if we were making any money off this." They weren't, he said, and today the building's management denies that Elvis Presley, under any name, lives anywhere on the premises.

Mrs. Welling's next good look at Elvis Presley came at Felpausch's in September 1987. There had been, she told me, earlier hints. In 1979, she had seen a man in the back of the county sheriff's car when the police came to her house to check on the family's dog, which had nipped a jogger. "The man in the back seat was all slouched down, and he didn't look well," she said. "I'm sure it was Elvis." A few years later, black limousines began to appear occasionally on the road where she lives. "Now, who around here would have a limo?" she asked. Then she began seeing a man she believes was Elvis in disguise. "He looked real fake," she recalled. "He was wearing new bib overalls, an Amish hat, and a beard that didn't look real. I talked to a woman who had seen the same man, and she said he sometimes wore a false nose. Now, why does he have to bother with disguises? Why couldn't he have said that he needed a rest, and gone off to some island to get better?"

A note of exasperation had crept into Mrs. Welling's voice. She showed me a cassette that she said contained a tape that Presley made after he was supposed to have died; in it, she said, he explained why he had faked his death. But when she played it the sound was blurred and rumbly, and I couldn't make out the words. The tape had been issued in 1988, to accompany a book by a woman — with whom Mrs. Welling has corresponded — who put forward the theory that the body buried as Presley's was not his own. The book and another by the same author, which Welling said was a fictional account of a rock star who fakes his death, were lovingly inscribed ("It's hard to take the heat") to Mrs. Welling.

Here is what Mrs. Welling said happened to her in September 1987. She had just been to eleven o'clock Sunday Mass at St. Martin's Church. With grandson Nathan, she stopped at Felpausch's to pick up a few groceries. Having just celebrated one publicly accepted miracle, she saw nothing strange in the private miracle at the supermarket.

"The store was just about deserted," she said. "There wasn't

even anyone at the checkout register when I went in. But back
in the aisles I felt and heard someone behind me. It must have
been Elvis. I didn't turn around, though. And then, when I got
up to the checkout, a girl was there waiting on Elvis. He seemed
kind of nervous. He was wearing a white motorcycle suit and
carrying a helmet. He bought something little — fuses, I think,
not groceries. I was so startled I just looked at him. I knew it was
Elvis. When you see someone, you know who he is. I didn't say
anything, because I'm kind of shy and I don't speak to people
unless they speak first. After I paid for the groceries, I went out
to the parking lot, but no one was there."

I asked Mrs. Welling if she had told anyone at the time what
she had seen. She replied that she had told no one except the
author of the Elvis-isn't-dead book, who was "very supportive."
After that, she and her daughter Linda started seeing Elvis in
Kalamazoo — once at a Burger King, once at the Crossroads
Shopping Mall, and once driving a red Ferrari. And she said
that just recently, while she was babysitting and filling her time
by listening to the police scanner, she heard a man's voice ask,
"Can you give me a time for the return of Elvis?" and heard
Presley reply, "I'm here now."

I asked her what her family thought about her experiences.
Linda, a pale, blond woman who was sitting off to one side in a
dining alcove smoking cigarettes while I talked to her mother,
was obviously a believer, and occasionally she interjected reports
of various Elvis contacts of her own. "But *my* mother thinks it's
all nutty," Mrs. Welling said, laughing. "She says I should forget
about it. My husband doesn't say much — he's real quiet — but
he knows I'm not crazy."

It wasn't until the spring of 1988, Mrs. Welling said, that she
started getting in touch with the media. She claims that she didn't
bother talking to the people at the Vicksburg newspaper (although Jackie Lawrence remembers otherwise), because "it wasn't
an important newspaper." Instead, she tried to tell her story to
the *Kalamazoo Gazette* and people at the television station there.
No one would take her seriously — except, of course, the author
of the Elvis book. After Mrs. Welling had written to her and
talked to her on the telephone, a writer for the *Weekly World
News* phoned for an interview. Mrs. Welling asked him how he

knew about her, but he declined to reveal his sources. In early May, the tabloid prepared the ground for Mrs. Welling's story by running one that took note of the rumor that Presley was living in Columbia Plaza, and gave Mrs. Welling's friend a nice plug for her book. Shortly after that, the syndicated columnist Bob Greene gave the rumor a push. By that time, the *Kalamazoo Gazette* realized that it could no longer ignore Mrs. Welling's phone calls, and in its May 15 issue Tom Haroldson, a staff writer, wrote a front-page story headlined " 'Elvis Alive' in Kalamazoo, Say Area Woman and News Tabloid." That was the beginning of Mrs. Welling's fame, but it was not until June 28 that the *Weekly World News* told her whole story. In thousands of supermarkets, the issue appeared with a big front-page picture of Mrs. Welling and a headline in type an inch and a half high proclaiming, "I've Seen Elvis in the Flesh!" The story began to be picked up by newspapers around the country as a brightener to the increasingly monotonous accounts of the preconvention presidential campaigns. CBS investigated it for possible production on *60 Minutes*. Radio stations from coast to coast and as far away as Australia called to interview Louise Welling and anyone else they could find. Kalamazoo's mayor, Edward Annen, reacted to all this by announcing to a *Gazette* reporter, "I've told them that everyone knows this is where he lives and that they should send their residents here to spend tourist dollars to find him."

Funny signs sprouted throughout Kalamazoo and Vicksburg in places of commerce. A rival market of Felpausch's posted one that said, "Jimmy Hoffa Shops Here." A dentist boasted, "Elvis Has His Teeth Cleaned Here." At Mar-Jo's, the sign read, "Elvis Eats Our Meatloaf." The folks at Felpausch's, however, were not amused. Cecil Bagwell, then the store's manager, told the *Gazette*, "The cashier who supposedly checked out Elvis that day cannot remember anything about it," and characterized Mrs. Welling as "an Elvis fanatic." Bagwell no longer works at Felpausch's, but I spoke with Jack Mayhew, the assistant manager, who scowled when I brought up the subject. "I won't comment," he said, adding, nonetheless, "We've never given the story to anyone, and we're not going to. All I'll say is that the woman is totally —" and he rotated an extended finger beside his head.

Before I left Mrs. Welling that morning, I asked her why she thought it was that *she* had seen Elvis, when others had not — did not even believe her.

"I don't know, but the Lord does," she answered. "I'm a religious woman, and when things like this happen — that we don't understand — it just proves that the Lord has a plan."

The next day, a friend who had heard about my investigations telephoned to tell me that there had been an Elvis sighting just a week or so earlier, in Kalamazoo, at the delivery bay of the Fader Construction Company, which is owned by her family. She hadn't seen the man herself, she said, but the women in the office had insisted that the truck driver making the delivery was Elvis Presley. I suspected that it might have been Ray Kajkowski, winner of the Elvis-look-alike contest and kisser of Jean Delahanty. This turned out to be true. On Friday evening, at a run-through for the Old Car Festival's cruising event, I was introduced to Kajkowski by Skip Knowles, and Kajkowski confirmed that he had made quite a stir while delivering a shipment of concrete forms to Fader. He gave me his card — he has apparently made a second career for himself as an Elvis impersonator at parties and night clubs — and then he whipped out a pair of mirrored sunglasses, put them on, and kissed me, too. "Young, old, fat, skinny, black, white, good looking, not so good looking, I kiss them all," he said. "I'm a pretty affectionate fellow. I was raised in a family that hugged a lot."

Ray Kajkowski lives in Gobles, not far from Vicksburg. At forty-one, he is thick-featured, a bit on the heavy side, and looks like — well, he looks like Elvis Presley. He has big sideburns and dyed black hair, which he wears in a pompadour. He went down to Graceland recently with his wife and his two teenage sons to study the Presley scene and recalls that while he was in the mansion's poolroom a couple came in and the wife took one look at him and collapsed on the floor in a faint.

"When I was growing up, I felt like an outsider," he told me. "I didn't think I was as good as other people, because my dad wasn't a doctor or a lawyer. We were just common folks. I knew about Elvis even when I was a little kid. I didn't pay much attention, though, except that some of my buddies had pictures of

Elvis, so we'd trade those to our older sisters and their friends for baseball cards." He laughed.

"I felt like we were invaded when the Beatles came over," he continued. By that time — 1963 — he was at Central High School in Kalamazoo, and had begun to appreciate Presley's music and to defend it against foreign stars. "I mean, Elvis was a small-town boy who made good. He was just ordinary, and, sure, he made some mistakes, just like me or you or any of us. But he went from zero to sixty. He had charisma with a capital *C*, and somehow people still know it."

After Presley's death, Kajkowski said, he felt sad and started reading about Elvis and studying his old movies. "Then, in September or October 1987, right around then, I was at a 1950s dance in Gobles. My hair was different then, and I had a beard, but there was a fifty-dollar prize for the best Elvis imitator. Fifty bucks sounded pretty good to me, and I watched this one guy do an imitation, and he didn't move or anything, and I thought to myself, I can do better than that, so I got up and entered and won, beard and all. After that, I shaved off my beard, dyed my hair, and started building my act. I do lip-synch to Elvis tapes. I've got three suits now, one black, one white, one blue. My wife does my setups for me and runs the strobe lights. Evenings when we don't have anything else to do, we sit around and make scarves for me to give away. I cut them, and she hems them. When I'm performing, I sweat real easy, and I mop off the sweat with the scarves and throw them out to the gals. They go crazy over them. And the gals proposition me. They don't make it easy. Sometimes they rub up against me, and when I kiss them they stick their tongues halfway down my throat. Once, I went over to shake the guys' hands, because I figured it was better to have them on my side. But one big guy wouldn't shake my hand, and later he came over and grabbed me like a grizzly bear and told me to quit it. 'You don't sound like Elvis Presley. You don't look like Elvis Presley. Stop it.' I told him, 'Hey, it's all lip-synch! It's just an act! It's entertainment!' But I try to keep it under control. My wife's the woman I have to go home with after the act."

I asked Kajkowski if he had ever been in Felpausch's. As a truck driver, he said, he had made deliveries there; occasionally, he even shopped there. But although he owned a motorcycle, he said, he rarely drove it, and he never wore a white motorcycle suit.

I asked him what he made of Mrs. Welling's story.

"Well," he said thoughtfully, "when someone puts another person at the center of their life, they read about him, they think about him, I'm not surprised that he becomes real for that person."

Saturday night at nine o'clock Louise Welling is standing next to me in the Filling Station's parking lot — it is built on the site of John Vickers's flour mill — in a crowd that has just seen prizes awarded in the fifties dance concert and is waiting for the beginning of the second annual Elvis-look-alike contest. She is neatly dressed in a blue-and-white-checked overblouse and dark pants. Her hair is fluffed up, and she is wearing pretty pink lipstick. She invited me to come to the contest, and told me that although many of the entrants in such affairs didn't come close to Elvis she was hoping that this one would draw the real Elvis Presley out from hiding. "If he came to me in the past, I believe he'll come again," she said. "I hope it will be before I die. If he comes, I'm going to grab him and hold on to him and ask him why he couldn't just be honest about needing to get away for a rest. Why couldn't he just tell the truth? Look at all the trouble he's caused those who love him."

Earlier in the day, I stopped in at Mar-Jo's for coffee. There were lots of extra visitors in the café. Ken Fowler had turned on the radio to WHEZ, a Kalamazoo station, which was broadcasting live from out on the street, acting as the festival's musical host. Rock music filled the café. Patrons were beating time on their knees, and the waitresses had begun to boogie up and down behind the counter. I asked one of them — a girl named Laurie, who was decked out fifties style with a white floaty scarf around her ponytail — what she made of Mrs. Welling's story. "I think it's kind of fun," she said. "I haven't met the lady, but, you know, maybe she's right. After all, if Elvis Presley never died he has to be someplace."

Mrs. Welling is subdued as she stands next to me, but all attention — scanning the people, anticipatory. We are at the very back of the good-natured crowd, which has enjoyed the nostalgia, the slick cars, the dances, the poodle skirts, and the ponytails. She spots Kajkowski and says to me that he's not Elvis but "so far he's the only one here who even looks anything like him."

Skip Knowles is up on the stage, in charge of what has turned out to be a successful event. There have been record-breaking crowds. Six hundred and fifty cars were entered. He has had plenty of media coverage, and he seems to be having a very good time. He calls for the Elvis contest to begin. Ray Kajkowski's act is so good now that he has no competition — he is the only one to enter. I watch him play the crowd. He had told me, "When I first started, I really liked the attention, but now it's just fun to do the show, and, yeah, I do get caught up in it. I like the holding power I have over people. I know how it is to feel left out, so I play to everyone. But I like people in their mid-thirties or older best. I don't like to entertain for these kids in their twenties. The gals back off when I try to drape a scarf around them. I think that's an insult." Now he is dancing around the edge of the crowd, reaching out to kiss the women, who respond to him with delight and good humor, and then he launches into what Mrs. Welling tells me is "You're a Devil in Disguise." I look at her, and she seems near tears. Her shoulders slump. "I don't like to watch," she says softly, and walks away to gather her family together for the trip home.

On my own way home, on the morning after the festival, I made one final stop in Vicksburg, on the south side of town, at what is left of Fraser's Grove. For about forty years — up until the early 1920s — Fraser's Grove was one of this country's premier spiritualist centers. In 1883, Mrs. John Fraser, the wife of a well-to-do Vicksburg merchant, turned the twenty-acre woodland into a camp and gathering place for mediums, believers in mediums, and the curious. She had been inspired by a lecture on spiritualism given in a hall on Prairie Street by one Mrs. R. S. Lily, of Cassadaga, New York, a town in the spiritually fervent "burned-over" district of that state. In the years that followed, Mrs. Fraser became a national figure in séance circles, and another resident of Vicksburg, C. E. Dent, was elected president of something called the Mediums' Protection Union. A group calling itself the Vicksburg Spiritualists was formed shortly after Mrs. Lily's visit, and it met each Sunday. Its Ladies' Auxiliary held monthly chicken dinners (fifteen cents a plate, two for a quarter). On summer Sunday afternoons, people from around this country and abroad packed the campground at Fraser's Grove to talk of materialization and reincarnation and watch mediums go into trances to contact the dead. According to a 1909 issue of the *Vicksburg Commercial*, they debated subjects such as "Is the planet on which we live approaching final destruction, or is it becoming more permanent?" (A follow-up article reports that the Spiritualists opted for permanency.)

Trees still stand in much of Fraser's Grove, although some of them have been cut down to make room for a small housing development. The campground itself has been taken over by the Christian Tabernacle, which makes use of the old camp buildings. Tazzie, my German shepherd, was with me, and I parked at the edge of the grove to let her out for a run before we drove onto the interstate highway. We headed down a dim path, where events passing strange are said to have taken place. The grove produced no Elvis, no John Vickers, not even a phantom band concert or the apparition of Mr. Matz — no spirits at all. But Tazzie did scare up a rabbit, and the oaks were still there, and, untamed through a hundred and fifty generations, so were the mosquitoes.

STUART KLAWANS

The Corpse in the Mirror:
The Warhol Wake

FROM GRAND STREET

ANDY WARHOL, draftsman of shoes, is dead, and the people viewing his remains are mostly wearing scuffed white sneakers. It is April 16, 1988, the first day the public can see his much-hyped relics in Sotheby's showrooms: about ten thousand objects, which have nothing in common except for having been stored for a few years in Warhol's townhouse on East Sixty-sixth Street. Published reports have portrayed Warhol as a compulsive shopper who piled never-to-be-opened boxes of flea-market junk on top of never-to-be-used antique furniture in rooms he never visited. Some of his furnishings were in fact bought for him by his associates; rumor has it that he disliked many of the pieces. Yet, through his death, these odds and ends have become The Warhol Collection, to be auctioned over the course of eleven days at Sotheby's in one of the best-publicized funerary rites of recent times. They will fetch $25.3 million, nearly twice their estimate; but that is not the concern of today's scuffed-sneaker crowd.

There are dozens of aerobics, tennis, and jogging shoes crossing the showroom floors; a few flamboyant variations, such as the pair of canvas Caribbean-print Keds worn by a wandering twelve-year-old; and a goodly number of black Reeboks, this year's office-quality sneaker. There are no basketball shoes. I do spot one pair of high-tops, laced only halfway up, on an elegant young woman; but in general Air Jordan does not come to Sotheby's.

This mild evidence of racism does not lessen one's conviction that the viewing is a people's holiday. The Saturday crowd is cheerful and curious, and Sotheby's employees are friendly in return, even though they have the unmistakable look of people called up for an all-hands operation. There is none of the solemnity one finds in a museum, and very little of the hearty scoffing that usually serves as its antidote. The visitors all seem comfortable, as if the things on display were as much their property as Warhol's. In life, he had given himself wholly to the mundane. Now, at his death, the common world has claimed him as its own, even though, among all the shoes at this wake, only one pair might have entertained him back when he was drawing ads for I. Miller: a pair of high-heeled light green pumps with gold tips on the toes, which Lana Turner might have worn in a Douglas Sirk movie, except for their being slightly baggy from wear on the streets, slightly homey in their glamour.

Warhol's relics are more than merely comfortable to the public; if you accept his way of thinking, the objects and people are transubstantial. Sotheby's has added a symbolism of its own that reinforces this idea: everything, objects and people alike, is labeled. The objects bear stickers, color-coded according to auction session, marked with the lot number, a small picture of Warhol, and the words "The Warhol Collection." The people, too, have Warhol-face stickers, only theirs are marked not with a lot number but a time of day. Sotheby's has allotted the general public an hour and a half to view the collection. Thus, entering at noon, I get a sticker with 1:30 printed in bold letters as my expiration time. It seems a bit more sinister than the legendary fifteen minutes of fame, though surely consistent with the day's funerary theme. And, of course, it is democratic, as democratic as death itself.

"Can I see 2121?" asks a man standing near me. We are at a square of display cases, which hold Warhol's watches and jewelry. The man is wearing brown penny loafers. After sneakers, penny loafers and Top-Siders are the most frequently encountered shoes at the viewing. The security guard, wearing heavy black security-guard shoes, brings out the watch. Suddenly, the man is delighted. "Hey," he cries, "it works!"

Of course it works. This watch belonged to Andy Warhol, who

earned his place in history by running mimesis smack into the wall. His supporters sometimes claimed that Warhol made mass-produced reality come alive before the viewer's eyes, that he turned the mundane into the aesthetic, as artists should. His distinction, in this account, lay in his having worked the trick so invisibly. But now, standing at the counter in Sotheby's, I decide this is exactly wrong. Warhol didn't turn a Brillo box into art; he turned art into a Brillo box. That was the achievement of his life. The achievement of his death lies in turning a cheap watch into art. Yes, this watch is part of The Warhol Collection, celebrated in magazine and newspaper articles, numbered and tagged and destined to sell for a lot more than similar watches found in any pawn shop. And yet it works — just like a real watch! The wonder of it proves death to be more traditional an artist than Warhol.

All around Sotheby's, commoners in sneakers are enjoying themselves precisely because these things — these cookie jars and stacks of Fiesta ware and old sticks of furniture — are objects from the realm of art. And yet they don't have to be treated with the delicacy due to museum pieces. They are for sale to anyone who has enough money to buy them, and the management invites your inspection. A young man in deep blue sneakers with very white laces settles into an ornate throne chair. "Comfortable?" asks his companion. She is wearing suede boots. "Yeah," he says. "Nice imperial feel." Nearby, acting without hesitation, a man in moccasins picks up a globed lantern and moves it to a chest of drawers, the better to examine a table on which the lantern had stood. A woman in blue-gray cloth slip-ons calls to her friend, "Hey, Pat! Somebody's ceremonial bowl!"

Somebody's, indeed. Sotheby's would have us believe that Warhol, by choosing the bowl, revealed something about its aesthetic qualities. But, even if he bought it himself — not always a certainty, as I've mentioned — there is an anonymity to the bowl and to everything else on display. As lots destined for auction, these things are in fact anybody's, and they look it.

More and more it seems to me that if there is a unifying element to this hodgepodge, it is not an individual's taste — much less an artist's — but rather the taste of a subculture. These are the furnishings one expects to find in the homes of many gay men of a certain age and class. The only difference is that there are so *many* of them. Instead of one piece of bloody Catholic statuary, there are a dozen. Instead of a single tin tray painted with an ad for Coca-Cola, there's a whole display case full. There are naïve paintings of the sort one finds in furnished summer cottages; a wall of tribal masks; pieces of homoerotic kitsch, such as a framed engraving of a classical nude with fig leaf. The furniture that Sotheby's calls "important" merely completes the setting. Suddenly, my thoughts fly back almost twenty years, to the first time I entered the apartment of a gay man. It was all there, the same mixture of religious melodrama, popular-culture detritus, high-art novelties, and deliberately out-of-date elegance. What if this were not The Warhol Collection but rather the contents of that apartment and the apartments of two dozen other men? Could anybody tell the difference?

Even the artworks by Warhol's peers don't identify their owner. There are drawings by Cy Twombly and Tom Wesselman dedicated to Warhol and a drawing of Warhol himself by David Hockney. But there are also drawings dedicated to other people, which seem to be neither more nor less Warhol's than the ones done especially for him. Was he that interchangeable with everyone else? He sometimes claimed to be. "I think everybody should be a machine," Warhol once said in an interview. "Someone said that Brecht wanted everybody to think alike. I want everybody to think alike. But Brecht wanted to do it through Communism, in a way. Russia is doing it under government. It's happening here all by itself. . . . Everybody looks alike and acts alike, and we're getting more and more that way."

Standing behind a stanchion, looking at Warhol's canopied bed, I note the approach of a woman who is escorted by Sotheby's officials and several bulky men who clearly are bodyguards. She, too, stands by the stanchion and nods at the bed, then leaves with her entourage. Somebody says she's the queen of Sweden. If so, she must be unlike the scuffed-sneaker crowd in material ways and probably is unlike us in her thoughts as well. But here, at the wake, she's one more gawker, staring at Warhol's heaped-up proofs of anonymity. I don't get a glimpse of the queen's shoes. But when Lily Auchincloss goes by, I notice she's wearing black pumps with half-inch heels and ornamental gold buckles.

In the spirit of generic identities, on the class level at least, I decide the queen must be wearing shoes just like those.

Near the counter where Sotheby's employees sell catalogues, a young woman with the New England prep-school look of all auction-house underlings speaks to a black security guard. "Three more hours," she says, impressed with her own weariness. The guard nods, not looking at her: "Yeah, I know." The visitors — those who have not yet expired — check estimated prices in the catalogues, which hang from the walls on strings that resemble black shoelaces.

April 23, 1988: Under an acoustical-tiled ceiling, beneath incandescent bulbs set back in chrome sleeves, one thousand folding chairs sit on a carpet the color of eight-year-old lint. It is 10:00 A.M., and the chairs — graffiti-artist gold with red seats — already are filled, except for the reserved rows at the front. In fifteen minutes, the first auction session will begin.

Movable gray partitions close off the sides of the auction pit. By the left wall, which is hung with Native American blankets, seven video and film crews stand in a row, with a gang of still photographers heading the line. By the right wall, a single photographer, no doubt Sotheby's own, has set up two tripods in front of a large print by Toulouse-Lautrec. Above us, on the third floor, horizontal banks of windows look down on the scene. Curtains are drawn across all of them except for one at the right side, which is flooded with light. These windows, I will learn, are like boxes at the opera. For now, though, they are vacant.

On my lap lies a green plastic paddle shaped like a vanity mirror. It bears the legend "SOTHEBY'S FOUNDED 1744" and, in very large white figures, the number 335. Like many of the people here, I have never before attended an auction and feel nervous about holding the paddle. Urban mythology has many tales of incautious people who, visiting an auction, scratched their noses at the wrong moment and thus bought an egg cup for three zillion dollars. Having laid my paddle across my lap, I take the further precaution of covering it with the *Times.* I would gladly get rid of it altogether, but Sotheby's will not let me.

When I arrived at 9:45, having both phoned and written the press office in advance, I discovered my credentials were nonexistent. For all Sotheby's cared, I could have been some purple-nosed guy in a hound's-tooth jacket with a police press pass slung around his neck. Would it be possible for me to get into the auction with the general public? "I don't know," the man at the press table told me. To my left, a security guard was admitting a line of people from the street. Was that the line for public admissions? "I don't know," the press officer said.

I reverted to the empirical method. Forty-five seconds later, the security guard ushered me in and pointed downstairs, where seven young prep-school graduates sat behind a long table. One of them took my name, my address, and the numbers of my credit card and driver's license. That done, she issued me a paddle, a second guard tagged me with yet another Warhol-face sticker, and I went up to the auction pit to take a seat. Members of the press, I understand, do not sit at auctions. They stand at the side, so they can get a full view of the bidding. It seems strange, then, that Sotheby's would insist on my taking a chair that might well have gone to a real bidder. But then I realize the logic of it. They will go to any length to get that paddle into your hand. I, too, am a bidder now. I take off my jacket and dump it over the *Times*.

A few people are still milling in the center aisle, looking for places to sit. They are wearing beige pumps with medium heels; gray suede calf-boots; black patent-leather pumps; black moccasins with tassels; and lots of imitation reptile. To my left is a woman with gray, tasseled slip-ons; to my right, a man with pointy-toe leather lace-ups much in need of polish. In the hope of looking respectable, I am wearing tan oxfords instead of my usual New Balance hiking boots. There are, by my count, four black people in the room: a young couple in the back, a young woman sitting at the left, and a press photographer amid the tripods. Behind us, the Sotheby's prep-schoolers have taken up their positions. At the front of the room, the price board suddenly clicks. A moment ago, it had read "Estate of Belle Linsky." Now, in preparation, it goes blank, except for the permanent headings — British pound, Swiss franc, French franc, yen, lira, and mark — and the apparent motto of the auction house, "All Conversions Approximate."

By 10:15, the stage is set. The centerpiece is a turntable draped with a tan curtain. Objects will appear and disappear on it, while behind its flimsy partitions a couple of black men take away the previous lot and position the lot to come. To the left of the turntable stand two art nouveau pieces from The Warhol Collection. A Sotheby's official, a bespectacled black man in a gray three-piece suit, has taken his place in front of this furniture. He will call out the telephone bids. To the right of the turntable stands the auctioneer's cathedra. It is massive, wooden, canopied — a true seat of power. At 10:20, the auctioneer, John L. Marion, mounts the cathedra, attended by his assistants. The show begins.

Marion, who is the chairman of Sotheby's North America, is a sleek man with straight brown hair and the genial expression of someone who is about to make a lot of money. Fill in the jowls and turn the hair white, and he could double as Edwin Meese. "I am pleased to welcome for your competition this morning and continuing for the next ten days The Andy Warhol Collection," he begins. Many of the bidders are new to auctions, he says, and he graciously predicts that he and the audience will get to know each other better. But Marion must be overestimating the number of newcomers, since there is general applause at his next announcement: that the auctions benefit the Andy Warhol Foundation for the Visual Arts, and Sotheby's therefore will not have to collect sales tax. Bear in mind: somebody at Sotheby's will eventually pay $23,000 for two cookie jars and a set of salt and pepper shakers. I assume you have to be used to auctions to throw that kind of money around and yet protest against a sales tax.

But now the turntable revolves, a silver plate appears, and bidding begins on Lot 1. In his strong baritone, Marion announces the bidding will start at $500. Twenty seconds later, the plate goes for $950.

Lot 2: $2,600, 35 seconds.
Lot 3: $2,400, 30 seconds.
Lot 4: $1,000, 45 seconds.
Lot 5: $7,000, 45 seconds.

I begin to get the idea. This is going to be as boring as bad opera. The next two hours will give me ample time to reflect on the justice of the comparison.

The minor coincidences are easiest to remark. For example: estate auctions and bad opera alike have a turntable as the central element of the set. Both require the performance of mechanical, seemingly endless oral repetition — of the score in the case of opera, of numbers at an auction. Indeed, at either event, the most impressive feature is the performer's sheer endurance. As the auction wears on, I gain great respect for John Marion, who never pauses in his patter and never takes so much as a sip of water. At the 91-minute mark, his voice breaks; at 96 minutes, he swallows in midchant. Otherwise, he talks steadily for 132 minutes, a feat as doughty as that of any Wagnerian tenor. And, as at a bad opera, the audience gets most of its thrill from seeing how his performance varies from the score. The score-readers in Sotheby's are everywhere, following the estimates in their catalogues. When something goes for much more than was foreseen, there is applause. In this sense, Saturday morning's great aria is the calling of Lot 56, a French silver and aventurine tureen and cover made by Jean Puiforcat, circa 1930–40. The estimate was $10,000–$15,000; the bidding stops at $50,000, and the crowd goes wild. Yet there are many people here, as at the opera, who are deaf to such music. They are attending out of a sense of duty but don't quite know why. Throughout the morning, one sees a steady stream of them walking out, signs of stupefaction on their faces.

But all these are surface resemblances. At the deeper level of purpose, the coincidence of opera with auction is still more telling: both are rituals of death. In opera — indeed, in all classical music — the performers subject themselves to strictly prescribed rigors so they may call up the spirits of the dead. Sometimes it works, too. At a good opera, Mozart once more dwells among the living. At a bad one, the necromancy having failed, the audience sits through three hours of meaningless yammer. Consider auctions, then, to be like operas that are always bad. They are bad because the dead are meant to stay that way. Spirit is out of the question. The gravediggers have taken care of one part of the corpse, and the auctioneer is there to dispose of the rest. In this sense, the Warhol auction really is the greatest of its kind. It celebrates the obsequies of the artist who wanted people to be like machines, who was indifferent to distinctions between living beings and merchandise. No eulogy for Warhol could be more fitting than this endless repetition of prices.

Above us, at the banks of windows, the Sotheby's employees have abandoned their boxes. Even they do not want to watch any longer. It is 12:25, and all the film crews have gone. Although new viewers have entered periodically as seats became available, the auction pit is emptying rapidly. John Marion sings on. Earlier, when the bidding sometimes turned sluggish, he had enlivened the audience with a touch of humor, jovially urging us to raise the price. Now he calls out the numbers single-mindedly. At 12:32, he lowers the gavel for the last time; 143 lots have been sold.

I direct my tan oxfords out of the room. The Sotheby's preppies have set up a table here on the second floor, where they collect my paddle. Though many shoes are passing — some on bidders, some on the crowd viewing the collection — I no longer pay attention. Dispirited and weary, I walk out to the damp, chilly street. It always rains at funerals.

May 1, 1988: The women are wearing high-heeled pumps in soft shades of satin. The men are in black patent leather, sometimes with velvet bows. It is evening, and Sotheby's is deserted except for these patrons of the American Academy in Rome. They are holding a formal-dress benefit, with Warhol's collection of contemporary art as one of the main attractions.

Though dressed in nothing better than a dark suit and a pair of shiny Florsheims, I have wangled an invitation to the earlier part of this event, when the Academy patrons wander among contemporary painting and sculpture. The Warhol auctions have wound down to their last days, so his collection, though still the centerpiece, now has company in Sotheby's. The showrooms are filled with other collections, scheduled for auction to benefit the American Academy in Rome and the AIDS unit at St. Vincent's Hospital. Whatever the provenance of the works, though, the art barely attracts the gaze of the Academy patrons. They are mostly interested in seeing each other.

Lily Auchincloss, with Kirk Varnedoe in attendance, stands near the bar, wearing shoes like the ones she shared with the queen of Sweden, though with higher heels. To her right hangs a picture Warhol had owned, a drawing by Jasper Johns of a man's shoe. A costumed trio plays Renaissance music on period instruments; their outfits are faithful enough, except for the brown walkers on one of the men. The music is pleasant, and the bar is well stocked; but The Warhol Collection has grown familiar to me, so I depart for the ground floor. And there, finally, I see the element that was missing from The Warhol Collection: pictures by Warhol himself.

The earliest is a drawing from the 1950s, done with considerable charm, of an ice cream cone sailing through the skies, festooned like a hot-air balloon. Warhol signed the drawing with his full name, using an ornate, old-fashioned script, much like Saul Steinberg's. And that's the problem with this drawing. It's entertaining, but it plainly resembles two Steinberg pieces from the same period, hung above and below. There is something mysterious about the Steinbergs, some complexity to their arrangements of line and color that hints at hidden meanings. The Warhol, though similar, has the one-time appeal of the average magazine illustration.

But the ice cream cone, whatever its shortcomings, is better than a later Warhol hung nearby: a small, jeeringly ugly silk screen of a dollar sign. By calling the cone *better,* I refer of course to its visual appeal, not its economic value. In fact, the dollar sign will cost much more. This seems puzzling at first, but it becomes logical once the artist's identity is figured into the price. Warhol's cone was imitative. With the dollar sign, though, he had come into his own. He had learned to show us the corpse in the mirror.

For a very long time, art had been the mirror of life. Then, at the turn of this century, painters stopped reflecting the world. They no longer made representations; they created images, which were meant to be understood as real in themselves, on the same level of existence as anything else. When, in the 1950s, representation began to creep back, artists still did not depict the world at large. They painted representations of things that were already images: the American flag, a comic-book panel, Marilyn Monroe's poster face.

It was Warhol's contribution to turn these images-reflecting-images into art in the older sense, a mirror of the world. All it took was the assumption that the world was dead. Why not? Images already had been granted equal status with living beings. For most people, that claim was based on the logic of art history. Warhol, though, seemed to rely on a more compelling argument. Artworks had become more valuable than people; and the century that had learned to mass-produce images was also the century of mass-produced death. Why not decide that the world was as inanimate as the art — that the figure in the mirror was a corpse? That way the art, at least, could retain its integrity. Even though we are nothing more than cheap commodities aspiring to the condition of machines, the art that reflects us can stay true to the principles of modernism — a small triumph, though nobody's left to enjoy it.

It makes no sense to argue with this point of view. Warhol was persuasive enough to make himself part of history, a much greater part than most artists; no one can dispute him out of existence. But those who still imagine themselves to be alive might recall a different vision of art and of the world. There is no evidence today that would favor this vision; but then, there was none two centuries ago, when William Blake spoke up for it. All he had was the crazy conviction that the spirit of John Milton had entered him through his left foot. We don't know why Milton chose the foot, rather than some other part of the body, and it's hard to say why he should have come in through the left one instead of the right. Nevertheless, Blake saw it happen, and that was enough to inspire in him the greatest shoe-poetry in the English language:

> And all this Vegetable World appeared on my left Foot,
> As a bright sandal formd immortal of precious stones & gold:
> I stooped down & bound it on to walk forward thro' Eternity.

We who live in the Vegetable World still can bind it to ourselves, however shriveled and decayed it might seem, not as matter paired with our own doomed matter but as a shoe, which eases the imagination's steps. I. Miller cannot sell this shoe. Andy Warhol could not draw it. But it's there, ready to be used. All we need to do is step out.

In a corner of the ground-floor showroom, I find a painting by someone who seems to want to do just that. It is a recent nude by Philip Pearlstein, whose work was never all that fashionable even during its fifteen minutes of fame. Now, Pearlstein is suffering the sort of hanging that in nineteenth-century salons used to incite secessions and manifestos. His painting is tucked next to a doorway, out of the light. Even if one should notice the picture, there is no backing-up space; one can't take in the painting as a whole. Yet, despite this disadvantage, the Pearlstein nude stands out in this company like a Bach fugue interrupting *The Monkees' Greatest Hits.* It is unquestionably a modernist painting — a textbook example of flattened space, tilted perspective, photographic composition, and all the rest of the image-making apparatus. It is also a painting about light and flesh and physical tension and the personality of a particular woman. A friend, looking at the Pearlstein with me, remarks that its estimate seems very low. I agree. "The estimate for that Warhol," I say, pointing to *210 Coca-Cola Bottles,* "is around $800,000."

"Is that with or without the deposits?" says my friend.

Upstairs, amid The Warhol Collection, Philip Pearlstein is standing in a quiet corner of the room, chatting with one of the other guests. He is a diminutive man, wearing an ancient-looking dinner jacket and a red vest. His shoes, for those who care to notice, are just like the clunkers on the security guards.

NATALIE KUSZ

Vital Signs

FROM THE THREEPENNY REVIEW

I. In Hospital

I WAS ALWAYS waking up, in those days, to the smell of gauze soaked with mucus and needing to be changed. Even when I cannot recall what parts of me were bandaged then, I remember vividly that smell, a sort of fecund, salty, warm one like something shut up and kept alive too long in a dead space. Most of the details I remember from that time are smells, and the chancest whiff from the folds of surgical greens or the faint scent of ether on cold fingers can still drag me, reflexively, back to that life, to flux so familiar as to be a constant in itself. Years after Children's Hospital, when I took my own daughter in for stitches in her forehead, and two men unfolded surgical napkins directly under my nose, I embarrassed us all by growing too weak to stand, and had to sit aside by myself until all the work was over.

It seems odd that these smells have power to bring back such horror, when my memories of that time are not, on the whole, dark ones. Certainly I suffered pain, and I knew early a debilitating fear of surgery itself, but the life I measured as months inside and months outside the walls was a good one, and bred in me understandings that I would not relinquish now.

There was a playroom in the children's wing, a wide room full of light, with colored walls and furniture, and carpets on the floor. A wooden kitchen held the corner alongside our infirmary, and my friends and I passed many hours as families, cooking pudding for our dolls before they were due in therapy. Most of the dolls had amputated arms and legs, or had lost their hair to chemotherapy, and when we put on our doctors' clothes we taught them to walk with prostheses, changing their dressings with sterile gloves.

We had school tables, and many books, and an ant farm by the window so we could care for something alive. And overseeing us all was Janine, a pink woman, young even to seven-year-old eyes, with yellow, cloudy hair that I touched when I could. She kept it long, parted in the middle, or pulled back in a ponytail like mine before the accident. My hair had been blond then, and I felt sensitive now about the coarse brown stubble under my bandages. Once, on a thinking day, I told Janine that if I had hair like hers I would braid it and loop the pigtails around my ears. She wore it like that the next day, and every day after for a month.

Within Janine's playroom, we were some of us handicapped, but none disabled, and in time we were each taught to prove this for ourselves. While I poured the flour for new play dough, Janine asked me about my kindergarten teacher: what she had looked like with an eye patch, and if she was missing my same eye. What were the hard parts, Janine said, for a teacher like that? Did I think it was sad for her to miss school sometimes, and did she talk about the hospital? What color was her hair, what sort was her eye patch, and did I remember if she was pretty? What would I be, Janine asked, when I was that age and these surgeries were past? Over the wet salt smell of green dough, I wished to be a doctor with one blue eye, who could talk like this to the sick, who could tell them they were still real. And with her feel for when to stop talking, Janine turned and left me, searching out volunteers to stir up new clay.

She asked a lot of questions, Janine did, and we answered her as we would have answered ourselves, slowly and with purpose. When called to, Janine would even reverse her words, teaching opposite lessons to clear the mist in between; this happened for Thomas and Nick in their wheelchairs, and I grew as much older from watching as they did from being taught. Both boys were eleven, and though I've forgotten their histories, I do remember their natures, the differences that drew them together.

They were roommates and best friends, and their dispositions reverberated within one another, the self-reliant and the needy. Thomas was the small one, the white one, with blue veins in his forehead and pale hair falling forward on one side. He sat always leaning on his elbows, both shoulders pressing up around his ears, and he rested his head to the side when he talked. He depended on Nick, who was tight-shouldered and long, to take charge for him, and he asked for help with his eyes half open, breathing out words through his mouth. And Nick reached the far shelves and brought Thomas books, and proved he could do for them both, never glancing for help at those who stood upright. His skin was darker than Thomas's, and his eyes much lighter, the blue from their centers washing out into the white.

When they played together, those boys, Thomas was the small center of things, the thin planet sunken into his wheelchair, pulling his friend after him. It must not have seemed to Nick that he was being pulled, because he always went immediately to Thomas's aid, never expecting anyone else to notice. Janine, of course, did. When Thomas wanted the television switched, and Nick struggled up to do it, she said, "Nick, would you like me to do that?"

"I can do it," he said.

"But so can I," Janine said, and she strode easily to the television and turned the knob to *Sesame Street*. "Sometimes," she said to Nick, "you have to let your friends be kind; it makes them feel good." She went back to sit beside Thomas, and she handed him the Erector set. How would he turn the channel, she said, if no one else was here? What could he do by himself? And as the TV went unnoticed, Thomas imagined a machine with gears and little wheels, and Janine said she thought it could work. After that, Thomas was always building, though he still asked for help, and he still got it. Nick never did ask, as long as I knew him, but in time he managed to accept what was offered, and even, in the end, to say thanks.

In this way and in others, Janine encouraged us to change. When we had new ideas, they were outstanding ones, and we could count almost always on her blessing. We planned wheelchair races, and she donated the trophy — bubble-gum ice cream all around. When she caught us blowing up surgical gloves we had found in the trash, she swiped a whole case of them, conjuring a helium bottle besides; that afternoon the playroom smelled of synthetic, powdery rubber, and we fought at the tables over colored markers, racing to decorate the brightest balloon. Janine's was the best — a cigar-smoking man with a four-spiked mohawk — and she handed it down the table to someone's father.

She always welcomed our parents in, so long as they never interfered, and they respected the rule, and acted always unsurprised. When Sheldon's mother arrived one day, she found her son — a four-year-old born with no hands — up to his elbows in orange fingerpaints. She stood for a moment watching, then offered calmly to mix up a new color.

We children enjoyed many moments like these, granted us by adults like Janine and our parents, and these instants of contentment were luxuries we savored, but on which, by necessity, we did not count. I've heard my father, and other immigrant survivors of World War II, speak of behavior peculiar to people under siege, of how they live in terms not of years but of moments, and this was certainly true of our lives. That time was fragmentary, allowing me to remember it now only as a series of flashes, with the most lyrical event likely at any moment to be interrupted. We children were each at the hospital for critical reasons, and a game we planned for one day was likely to be missing one or two players the next, because Charlie hemorrhaged in the night, Sarah was in emergency surgery, or Candice's tubes had pulled out. I myself missed many outings on the lawn because my bone grafts rejected or because my eye grew so infected that I had to be quarantined. At these times, I would watch the others out the closed window, waiting for them to come stand beyond the sterile curtain and shout to me a summary of the afternoon.

In the same way that the future seemed — because it might never arrive — generally less important than did the present, so too was the past less significant. Although each of us children could have recited his own case history by heart, it was rare that any of us required more than a faint sketch of another child's past; we found it both interesting and difficult enough to keep a current daily record of who had been examined, tested, or operated on, and whether it had hurt, and if so, whether they had cried. This last question was always of interest to us, and tears we looked on as marks not of cowards but of heroes, playmates who had endured torture and lived to testify. The older a child was, the greater our reverence when her roommate reported back after an exam; we derived some perverse comfort from the fact that even twelve-year-olds cracked under pressure.

Those of us who did choose to abide vigorously in each instant were able to offer ourselves, during the day, to one another, to uphold that child or parent who began to weaken. If her need was to laugh, we laughed together; if to talk, we listened, and once, I remember, I stood a whole morning by the chair of a fifteen-year-old friend, combing her hair with my fingers, handing her Kleenex and lemon drops, saying nothing. At night, then, we withdrew, became quietly separate, spoke unguardedly with our families. We spent these evening hours regrouping, placing the days into perspective, each of us using our own methods of self-healing. My mother would read to me from the Book of Job, about that faithful and guiltless man who said, "The thing that I so greatly feared has come upon me," and she would grieve, as I learned later, for me and for us all. Or she would sit with me and write letters to our scattered family — my father at work in Alaska, my younger brother and sister with an aunt in Oregon. Of the letters that still exist from that time, all are full of sustenance, of words like "courage" and "honor." It should have sounded ludicrous to hear a seven-year-old speaking such words, but I uttered them without embarrassment, and my parents did not laugh.

For most of us, as people of crisis, it became clear that horror can last only a little while, and then it becomes commonplace. When one cannot be sure that there are many days left, each single day becomes as important as a year, and one does not waste an hour in wishing that that hour was longer, but simply fills it, like a smaller cup, as high as it will go without spilling over. Each moment, to the very ill, seems somehow slowed down and more dense with importance, in the same way that a poem is more compressed than a page of prose, each word carrying more weight than a sentence. And though it is true I learned gentleness, and the spareness of time, this was not the case for everyone there, and in fact there were some who never embraced their mortality.

*

I first saw Darcy by a window, looking down into her lap, fingering glass beads the same leafy yellow as her skin. She was wearing blue, and her dress shifted under her chin as she looked up, asking me was I a boy, and why was my hair so short. Behind us, our mothers started talking, exchanging histories, imagining a future, and Darcy and I listened, both grown accustomed by now to all this talk of ourselves. Darcy was ten, and she was here for her second attempted kidney transplant, this time with her father as donor. The first try had failed through fault, her mother said, of the surgeons, and Washington State's best lawyer would handle the suit if anything went wrong this time. This threat was spoken loudly and often as long as I knew Darcy, and it was many years before I realized that her parents were afraid, and that they displayed their fear in anger and those thousand sideways glances at their daughter.

As a playmate, Darcy was pleasant, and she and I made ourselves jewelry from glitter and paste, and dressed up as movie stars or as rich women in France. We played out the future as children do, as if it were sure to come and as if, when it did, we would be there. It was a game we all played on the ward, even those sure to die, and it was some time before I knew that to Darcy it was not a game, that she believed it all. We were holding school, and Nick was the teacher, and Darcy was answering that when she grew up she would own a plane, and would give us free rides on the weekends.

"What if," Nick said to her, "what if you die before then?"

Darcy breathed in and out once, hard, and then she said, "I'm telling my mother you said that." Then she stood and left the playroom, and did not come back that day. Later, her father complained to Nick's, called him foolish and uncaring, and demanded that such a thing not happen again.

After that, Darcy came to play less often, and when she did, her parents looked on, even on days when Janine took us outside to look at the bay. Darcy grew fretful, and cried a good deal, and took to feeling superior, even saying that my father didn't love me or he wouldn't be in Alaska. When I forgave her, it was too late to say so, because I was gone by then and didn't know how to tell her.

Darcy's absence was a loss, not just to her but to us other children as well. Just as we had no chance to comfort her, to offer

our hands when she was weak, we could not count on her during
our worst times, for she and her family suffered in that peculiar
way that admits no fellowship. I don't remember, if I ever knew,
what became of Darcy, because I came down with chicken pox
and was discharged so as not to jeopardize her transplant. I like
to think she must have lived, it was so important to her, and as I
think this, I hope she did survive, and that one day she grew, as
we all did in some way, to be thankful.

One of my smallest teachers during this time was a leukemia
patient, just three years old, who lived down the hall. Because of
his treatments, Samuel had very little hair, and what he did have
was too blond to see. There were always, as I remember, deep
moons under his eyes, but somehow, even to us other children,
he was quite beautiful. His teeth were very tiny in his mouth,
and he chuckled rather than laughed out loud; when he cried,
he only hummed, drawing air in and out his nose, with his eyes
squeezed shut and tears forming in the cracks where there should
have been lashes. Most children's wards have a few favorite patients, and Samuel was certainly among ours. Those few afternoons when his parents left the hospital together, they spent
twenty minutes, on their return, visiting every room to find who
had taken off with their son. More often than not, he was strapped
to a lap in a wheelchair, his IV bottle dangling overhead like an
antenna, getting motocross rides from an amputee.

Samuel possessed, even for his age, and in spite of the fact
that he was so vulnerable, an implicit feeling of security, and it
was partly this sense of trust that lent him that dignity I have
found in few grown people. His mother, I remember, was usually the one to draw him away from our games when it was time
for treatments, and, although he knew what was coming, he never
ran from it; when he asked his mother, "Do I have to?" it was
not a protest but a question, and when she replied that yes, this
was necessary, he would accept her hand and leave the playroom
on his feet.

I have heard debate over whether terminally ill children know
they are going to die, and I can't, even after knowing Samuel,
answer this question. We all, to some extent, knew what death
was, simply because each of us had been friends with someone
who was gone, and we realized that at some point many of us

were likely to die; this likelihood was enough certainty for us, and made the question of time and date too insignificant to ask. I remember the last day I spent with Samuel, how we all invited him for a picnic on the lawn, though he could not eat much. He had had treatments that morning, which made him weak, made his smile very tired, but this was the same vulnerability we had always found charming, and I can't recall anything about that afternoon that seemed unusual. The rest of us could not know that Samuel would die before we woke up next morning, and certainly some things might have been different if we had; but I tend to think we would still have had the picnic, would still have rubbed dandelion petals into our skin, would still have taught Samuel to play slapjack. And, for his part, Samuel would, as he did every day, have bent down to my wrist and traced the moon-shaped scar behind my hand.

II. Attack

Our nearest neighbors through the trees were the Turners, two cabins of cousins whose sons went to my school. Both families had moved here, as we had, from California, escaping the city and everything frightening that lived there. One of the women, Ginny, had a grown son who was comatose now since he was hit on the freeway, and she had come to Alaska to get well from her own mental breakdown, and to keep herself as far away as she could from automobiles.

Brian and Jeff Turner were my best friends then, and we played with our dogs in the cousins' houses or in the wide snowy yard in between. On weekends or days off from school, my parents took us sledding and to the gravel pit with our skates. Sometimes, if the day was long enough, Brian and Jeff and I followed rabbit tracks through the woods, mapping all the new trails we could find, and my mother gave me orders about when to be home. Bears, she said, and we laughed, and said didn't she know they were asleep, and we could all climb trees anyway. We were not afraid, either, when Mom warned of dog packs. Dogs got cabin fever, too, she said, especially in the cold. They ran through the woods, whole crowds of them, looking for someone to gang up on.

That's okay, I told her. We carried pepper in our pockets in case of dogs: sprinkle it on their noses, we thought, and the whole pack would run away.

In December, the day before my birthday, when the light was dim and the days shorter than we had known before, Dad got a break at the union hall, a job at Prudhoe Bay that would save us just in time, before the stove oil ran out and groceries were gone. Mom convinced us children that he was off on a great adventure, that he would see foxes and icebergs, that we could write letters for Christmas and for New Year's, and afford new coats with feathers inside. In this last I was not much interested, because I had my favorite already — a red wool coat that reversed to fake leopard — but I would be glad if this meant we could get back from the pawn shop Dad's concertina, and his second violin, and mine, the half-size with a short bow, and the guitar and mandolin and rifles and pistol that had gone that way one by one. Whether I played each instrument or not, it had been good to have them around, smelling still of campfires and of songfests in the summer.

It was cold after Dad left, cold outside and cold in our house. Ice on the trailer windows grew thick and shaggy, and my sister and I melted handprints in it and licked off our palms. There had been no insulation when the add-on went up, so frost crawled the walls there, too, and Mom had us wear long johns and shoes unless we were in our beds. Brian and Jeff came for my birthday, helped me wish over seven candles, gave me a comb and a mirror. They were good kids, my mother said, polite and with good sense, and she told me that if I came in from school and she was not home, I should take Hobo with me and walk to their house. You're a worrywart, Mommy, I said. I'm not a baby, you know.

On January 10, only Hobo met me at the bus stop. In the glare from the school bus headlights his blue eye shone brighter than his brown, and he watched until I took the last step to the ground before tackling me in the snow. Most days, Hobo hid in the shadow of the spruce until Mom took my book bag, then he erupted from the dark to charge up behind me, run through my legs and on out the front. It was his favorite trick. I usually lost my balance and ended up sitting in the road with my feet thrown wide out front and steaming dog tongue all over my face.

Hobo ran ahead, then back, brushing snow crystals and fur against my leg. I put a hand on my skin to warm it and dragged nylon ski pants over the road behind me. Mom said to have them along in case the bus broke down, but she knew I would not wear them, could not bear the plastic sounds they made between my thighs.

No light was on in our house.

If Mom had been home, squares of yellow would have shown through the spruce and lit the fog of my breath, turning it bright as I passed through. What light there was now came from the whiteness of snow and from the occasional embers drifting up from our stovepipe. I laid my lunchbox on the top step and pulled at the padlock, slapping a palm on the door and shouting. Hobo jumped away from the noise and ran off, losing himself in darkness and in the faint keening dog sounds going up from over near the Turners' house. I called, "Hobo. Come back here, boy," and took to the path toward Brian's, tossing my ski pants to the storage tent as I passed.

At the property line, Hobo caught up with me and growled, and I fingered his ear, looking where he pointed, seeing nothing ahead there but the high curve and long sides of a quonset hut, the work shed the Turners used also as a fence for one side of their yard. In the fall, Brian and Jeff and I had walked to the back of it, climbing over boxes and tools and parts of old furniture, and we had found in the corner a lemming's nest made from chewed bits of cardboard and paper, packed under the curve of the wall so that shadows hid it from plain sight. We all bent close to hear the scratching, and while Brian held a flashlight I took two sticks and parted the rubbish until we saw the black eyes of a mother lemming and pink naked bodies of five babies. The mother dashed deeper into the pile and we scooped the nesting back, careful not to touch the sucklings for fear that their mama would eat them if they carried scent from our fingers.

The dogs were loud now beyond the quonset, fierce in their howls and sounding many more than just three. Hobo crowded against my legs, and as I walked he hunched in front of me, making me stumble into a drift that filled my boots with snow. I called him a coward and said to quit it, but I held his neck against my thigh, turning the corner into the boys' yard and stopping on the edge. Brian's house was lit in all its windows, Jeff's was dark, and in the yard between them were dogs, new ones I had not seen before, each with its own house and tether. The dogs and their crying filled the yard, and when they saw me they grew wilder, hurling themselves to the ends of their chains, pulling their lips off their teeth. Hobo cowered and ran and I called him with my mouth, but my eyes did not move from in front of me.

There were seven. I knew they were huskies and meant to pull dogsleds, because earlier that winter Brian's grandfather had put on his glasses and shown us a book full of pictures. He had turned the pages with a wet thumb, speaking of trappers and racing people and the ways they taught these dogs to run. They don't feed them much, he said, or they get slow and lose their drive. This was how men traveled before they invented snowmobiles or gasoline.

There was no way to walk around the dogs to the lighted house. The snow had drifted and been piled around the yard in heaps taller than I was, and whatever aisle was left along the sides was narrow and pitted with chain marks where the animals had wandered, dragging their tethers behind. No, I thought, Jeff's house was closest and out of biting range, and someone could, after all, be sitting home in the dark.

My legs were cold. The snow in my boots had packed itself around my ankles and begun to melt, soaking my socks and the felt liners under my heels. I turned toward Jeff's house, chafing my thighs together hard to warm them, and I called cheerfully at the dogs to shut up. Oscar said that if you met a wild animal, even a bear, you had to remember it was more scared than you were. Don't act afraid, he said, because they can smell fear. Just be loud — stomp your feet, wave your hands — and it will run away without even turning around. I yelled "Shut up" again as I climbed the steps to Jeff's front door, but even I could barely hear myself over the wailing. At the sides of my eyes, the huskies were pieces of smoke tumbling over one another in the dark.

The wood of the door was solid with cold, and even through deerskin mittens it bruised my hands like concrete. I cupped a hand to the window and looked in, but saw only black — black, and the reflection of a lamp in the other cabin behind me. I

turned and took the three steps back to the ground; seven more
and I was in the aisle between doghouses, stretching my chin far
up above the frenzy, thinking hard on other things. This was
how we walked in summertime, the boys and I, escaping from
bad guys over logs thrown across ditches: step lightly and fast,
steady on the hard parts of your soles, arms extended outward,
palms down and toward the sound. That ditch, this aisle, was a
river, a torrent full of silt that would fill your clothes and pull
you down if you missed and fell in. I was halfway across. I pointed
my chin toward the house and didn't look down.

On either side, dogs on chains hurled themselves upward,
choking themselves to reach me, until their tethers jerked their
throats back to earth. I'm not afraid of you, I whispered; this is
dumb.

I stepped toward the end of the row and my arms began to
drop slowly closer to my body. Inside the mittens, my thumbs
were cold, as cold as my thighs, and I curled them in and out
again. I was walking past the last dog and I felt brave, and I
forgave him and bent to lay my mitten on his head. He surged
forward on a chain much longer than I thought, leaping at my
face, catching my hair in his mouth, shaking it in his teeth until
the skin gave way with a jagged sound. My feet were too slow in
my boots, and as I blundered backward they tangled in the chain,
burning my legs on metal. I called out at Brian's window, expecting rescue, angry that it did not come, and I beat my arms
in front of me, and the dog was back again, pulling me down.

A hole was worn into the snow, and I fit into it, arms and legs
drawn up in front of me. The dog snatched and pulled at my
mouth, eyes, hair; his breath clouded the air around us, but I
did not feel its heat, or smell the blood sinking down between
hairs of his muzzle. I watched my mitten come off in his teeth
and sail upward, and it seemed unfair then and very sad that
one hand should freeze all alone; I lifted the second mitten off
and threw it away, then turned my face back again, overtaken
suddenly by loneliness. A loud river ran in my ears, dragging
me under.

My mother was singing. *Lu-lee, lu-lay, thou little tiny child,* the song
to the Christ child, the words she had sung, smoothing my hair,
all my life before bed. Over a noise like rushing water I called to

her and heard her answer back, Don't worry, just sleep, the ambulance is on its way. I drifted back out and couldn't know then what she prayed, that I would sleep on without waking, that I would die before morning.

She had counted her minutes carefully that afternoon, sure that she would get to town and back, hauling water and mail, with ten minutes to spare before my bus came. But she had forgotten to count one leg of the trip, had skidded up the drive fifteen minutes late, pounding a fist on the horn, calling me home. On the steps, my lunchbox had grown cold enough to burn her hands. She got the water, the groceries, and my brother and sisters inside, gave orders that no one touch the wood stove or open the door, and she left down the trail to Brian's, whistling Hobo in from the trees.

I know from her journal that Mom had been edgy all week about the crazed dog sounds next door. Now the new huskies leaped at her and Hobo rumbled warning from his chest. Through her sunglasses, the dogs were just shapes, indistinct in window light. She tried the dark cabin first, knocking hard on the windows, then turned and moved down the path between doghouses, feeling her way with her feet, kicking out at open mouths. Dark lenses frosted over from her breath, and she moved toward the house and the lights on inside.

"She's not here." Brian's mother held the door open and air clouded inward in waves. Mom stammered out thoughts of bears, wolves, dogs. Ginny grabbed on her coat. She had heard a noise out back earlier — they should check there and then the woods.

No luck behind the cabin and no signs under the trees. Wearing sunglasses and without any flashlight, Mom barely saw even the snow. She circled back and met Ginny under the window light. Mom looked that way and asked about the dogs. "They seem so hungry," she said.

Ginny said, "No. Brian's folks just got them last week, but the boys play with them all the time." All the same, she and Mom scanned their eyes over the kennels, looking through and then over their glasses. Nothing seemed different. "Are you sure she isn't home?" Ginny said. "Maybe she took a different trail."

Maybe. Running back with Ginny behind her, Mom called my name until her lungs frosted inside and every breath was a cough.

The three younger children were still the only ones at home, and Mom handed them their treasure chests, telling them to play on the bed until she found Natalie. Don't go outside, she said. I'll be back right soon.

Back at the Turners', Ginny walked one way around the quonset and Mom the other. Mom sucked air through a mitten, warming her lungs. While Ginny climbed over deeper snow, she approached the sled dogs from a new angle. In the shadow of one, a splash of red — the lining of my coat thrown open. "I've found her," she shouted, and thought as she ran, Oh, thank God. Thank, thank God.

The husky stopped its howling as Mom bent to drag me out from the hole. Ginny caught up and seemed to choke. "Is she alive?" she said.

Mom said, "I think so, but I don't know how." She saw one side of my face gone, one red cavity with nerves hanging out, scraps of dead leaves stuck on to the mess. The other eye might be gone, too; it was hard to tell. Scalp had been torn away from my skull on that side, and the gashes reached to my forehead, my lips, had left my nose ripped wide at the nostrils. She tugged my body around her chest and carried me inside.

III. Vital Signs

I had little knowledge of my mother's experience of the accident until many months afterward, and even then I heard her story only after I had told mine, after I had shown how clearly I remembered the dogs, and their chains, and my own blood on the snow — and had proven how little it bothered me to recall them. When I said I had heard her voice, and named for her the songs she had sung to me then, my mother searched my face, looking into me hard, saying, "I can't believe you remember." She had protected me all along, she said, from her point of view, not thinking that I might have kept my own, and that mine must be harder to bear. But after she knew all this, Mom felt she owed me a history, and she told it to me then, simply and often, in words that I would draw on long after she was gone.

She said that inside the Turners' cabin, she laid me on Ginny's

couch, careful not to jar the bleeding parts of me, expecting me
to wake in an instant and scream. But when I did become conscious, it was only for moments, and I was not aware then of my
wounds, or of the cabin's warmth, or even of pressure from the
fingers of Brian's grandfather, who sat up close and stroked the
frozen skin of my hands.

Ginny ordered Brian and Jeff to their room, telling them to
stay there until she called them, and then she stood at Mom's
shoulder, staring down and swaying on her legs.

Mom looked up through her glasses and said, "Is there a phone
to call an ambulance?"

Ginny was shaking. "Only in the front house, kid, and it's
locked," she said. "Kathy should be home in a minute, but I'll
try to break in." She tugged at the door twice before it opened,
and then she went out, leaving my mother to sing German lul-
labies beside my ear. *When morning comes,* the words ran, *if God
wills it, you will wake up once more.* My mother sang the words and
breathed on me, hoping I would dream again of summertime,
all those bright nights when the music played on outside, when
she drew the curtains and sang us to sleep in the trailer. Long
years after the accident, when she felt healed again and stronger,
Mom described her thoughts to me, and when she did she closed
her eyes and sat back, saying, "You can't know how it was to keep
singing, to watch air bubble up where a nose should have been,
and to pray that each of those breaths was the last one." Many
times that night she thought of Job, who also had lived in a spa-
cious, golden land, who had prospered in that place, yet had
cried in the end, "The thing that I so greatly feared has come
upon me." The words became a chant inside her, filling her head
and bringing on black time.

The wait for the ambulance was a long one, and my mother
filled the time with her voice, sitting on her heels and singing.
She fingered my hair and patted my hands and spoke low words
when I called out. Brian's grandfather wept and warmed my
fingers in his, and Mom wondered where were my mittens, and
how were her other children back home.

Ginny came back and collapsed on a chair, and Kathy, her
sister-in-law, hurried in through the door. Ginny began to choke,
rocking forward over her knees, telling Kathy the story. Her

voice stretched into a wail that rose and fell like music. "It's happening again," she said. "No matter where you go, its always there."

Kathy brought out aspirin, then turned and touched my mother's arm. She said that as soon as Ginny was quiet, she would leave her here and fetch my siblings from the trailer.

"Thank you," Mom told her. "I'll send someone for them as soon as I can." She looked at Ginny then, wishing she had something to give her, some way to make her know that she was not to blame here; but for now Mom felt that Ginny had spoken truth when she said that sorrow followed us everywhere, and there was little else she could add.

The ambulance came, and then everything was movement. I drifted awake for a moment as I was lifted to a stretcher and carried toward the door. I felt myself swaying in air, back and forth and back again. Brian's whisper carried over the other voices in the room, as if blown my way by strong wind. "Natalie's dying," he said; then his words were lost among other sounds, and I faded out again. A month later, when our first-grade class sent me a box full of valentines, Brian's was smaller than the rest, a thick, white heart folded in two. Inside it read, "I love you, Nataly. Pleas dont die." When I saw him again, his eyes seemed very big, and I don't remember that he ever spoke to me anymore.

It was dark inside the ambulance, and seemed even darker to my mother, squinting through fog on her sunglasses. She badgered the medic, begging him to give me a shot for pain. Any minute I would wake up, she said, and I would start to scream. The man kept working, taking my pulse, writing it down, and while he did, he soothed my mother in low tones, explaining to her about physical shock, about the way the mind estranges itself from the body and stands, unblinking and detached, on the outside. "If she does wake up," he said, "she'll feel nothing. She won't even feel afraid." When Mom wrote this in her journal, her voice was filled with wonder, and she asked what greater gift there could be.

At the hospital there were phone calls to be made, and Mom placed them from outside the emergency room. First she called

Dick and Esther Conger, two of the only summertime friends
who had stayed here over winter. We had met this family on the
way up the Alcan, had been attracted to their made-over school
bus with its sign, "Destination: Adventure," and to the Alaskan
license plates bolted to each bumper. Sometime during the drive
up, or during the summer when we shared the same campfires,
the children of our families had become interchangeable; Toni
and Barry were in the same age group as we were, and discipline
and praise were shared equally among us all. It was never shocking to wake up in the morning and find Toni and Barry in one
of our beds; we just assumed that the person who belonged there
was over sleeping in their bus. Now, as my mother explained the
accident to Dick, our friend began to cry, saying, "Oh, Verna.
Oh, no," and Esther's voice in the background asked, "What's
happened? Let me talk to her." Mom asked the Congers to drive
out for my brother and sisters, to watch them until my father
came.

Leaning her head to the wall, Mom telephoned a message to
the North Slope. She spoke to Dad's boss there, explaining only
that "our daughter has been hurt." Just now, she thought, she
couldn't tell the whole story again, and besides, the worst "hurt"
my father would imagine could not be this bad. The crew boss
said a big snowstorm was coming in, but they would try to fly my
father out beforehand; if not, they would get him to the radio
phone and have him call down. A nurse walked up then and
touched Mom's shoulder, saying, "Your daughter is awake, and
she's asking for you." A moment before, Mom had been crying,
pressing a fist to her teeth, but now she closed up her eyes like a
faucet and walked after the nurse, pulling up her chin and
breathing deeply in her chest. She had trembled so that she could
hardly wipe her glasses, but when she moved through the door
and saw the white lights and me lying flat on a table, she was
suddenly calm, and the skin grew warmer on her face.

Mom positioned herself in front of my one eye, hoping as she
stood there that she wasn't shaking visibly, that her face was not
obviously tense. She need not have bothered; as I lay staring
right to where my eye veered off, the room was smoky gray, and
I was conscious only of a vicious thirst that roughened the edges
of my tongue, made them stick to my teeth. I was allowed no

water, had become fretful, and when my mother spoke to me, I complained that the rag in my mouth had not been damp enough, and that these people meant to cut my favorite coat off of me. I have to think now that my mother acted courageously, keeping her face smooth, listening to me chatter about school, about the message I had brought from my teacher, that they would skip me to the second grade on Monday. Mom's answers were light, almost vague, and before she left the pre-op room, she told me to listen to the nurses, to let them do all they needed to; they were trying to help me, she said. A little later, after I was wheeled into surgery, a nurse handed her the things they had saved: my black boots and the Alice in Wonderland watch Mom had given me for Christmas.

My mother made more phone calls, to churches in town and to ones in California that we'd left behind, telling the story over again, asking these people to pray. Old friends took on her grief, asking did she need money, telling her to call again when she knew more. These people knew, as my mother did, that money was not so much the question now, but it was something they could offer, and so they did. And for months and years after this they would send cards and letters and candy and flowers and toys, making themselves as present with us as they could. For now, on this first night, they grieved with my mother, and they said to go lie down if she could, they would take over the phones. And each of these people made another call, and another, until, as my mother walked back to the waiting room, she knew she was lifted up by every friend we had ever made.

The Turners had arrived, and for a little while they all sat along the waiting room walls, stuffing fists into their pockets and closing their eyes. None of them wanted to talk about the accident, or to wonder about the progress in surgery, and when my mother said to Kathy, "I just talked to some people in California who would never *believe* the way we live here," her words seemed terribly funny, and started the whole room laughing. It wasn't so much, she said later, that they were forgetting why they were there; in fact, they remembered very well — so well that, compared to that fact, everything else was hilarious. And they could not possibly have continued for as long as they had been, she said, pressing their backs to the walls and waiting. So for hours after Mom's joke, and far into the night, the adults invented names for our kind — "the outhouse set," "the bush league" — and they contributed stories about life in Alaska that would shock most of the people Outside. They joked about Styrofoam out-house seats — the only kind that did not promote frostbite — about catalogues that no one could afford to buy from, but whose pages served a greater purpose, about the tremendous hardship of washing dishes from melted snow and then tossing the gray water out the door. From time to time, Ginny got up from her seat to walk alone in the hall, but when she came back in she was ready again to laugh.

My father arrived about midnight, dressed in a week's growth of beard and in an army surplus parka and flight pants. Mom met him in the hall and stood looking up; Dad dropped his satchel to the floor, panting, and he watched my mother's face, the eyes behind her glasses. He spoke first, said his was the last plane out in a heavy snowstorm. Then: "How did it happen," he said. "Did she fall out the door?"

My mother waited a beat and looked at him. "It wasn't a car accident, Julius," she said. She started telling the story again, and my father looked down then at the blood crusted on her sweater, and he closed his eyes and leaned into the wall. My mother told him, "You can't appreciate how I feel, because you haven't seen her face. But I wish that when you pray you'd ask for her to die soon."

Dad opened his eyes. "That must seem like the best thing to ask," he said. "But we don't make decisions like that on our own. We never have, and we can't start now."

Sometime after two A.M., my three surgeons stepped in. My mother said later that, had they not still worn their surgical greens, she would not have recognized them; during the night she had forgotten their faces.

The men sagged inside their clothes, three sets of shoulders slumped forward under cloth. I was still alive, they said, but only barely, and probably not for long. I had sustained over one hundred lacerations from the shoulders up, and had lost my left cheekbone along with my eye. They'd saved what tissue they could,

filling the bulk of the cavity with packings, and what bone fragments they had found were now wired together on the chance
that some of them might live.

My father groped for a positive word. "At least she doesn't
have brain damage. I heard she was lucid before surgery."

Dr. Butler brushed the surgical cap from his head and held it,
twisting it in his hands. His eyes were red as he looked up, explaining as kindly as it seemed he could. A dog's mouth, he said,
was filthy, filthier than sewage, and all of that impurity had passed
into my body. They had spent four hours just cleaning out the
wounds, pulling out dirt and old berry leaves and dog feces.
Even with heavy antibiotics, I would likely have massive infections, and they would probably spread into my brain. His voice
turned hoarse and he looked across at Dr. Earp, asking the man
to continue.

Dr. Earp rubbed hard at the back of his head and spoke softly,
working his neck. For now, Dr. Earp said, they had been able to
reconstruct the eyelids; that would make the biggest visible difference.

On my parents' first hourly visit to Intensive Care, Mom stopped
at the door and put her hand to my father's chest. "No matter
how she looks," she said, "don't react. She'll be able to tell what
you're thinking."

The nurse at the desk sat under a shaded lamp, the only real
light in the room. She stood and whispered that mine was the
first bed to the left. "She wakes up for a minute or so at a time,"
she said. "She's been asking for you."

"First one on the left," my father said after her, a little too
loud for that place, and from somewhere inside a great rushing
river I heard him and called out. At my bed, Mom watched him
as he stood looking down, and when the lines in his face became
deeper, she turned from him, pinching his sleeve with her fingers. She walked closer to me and held the bedrail.

IV. The Fear

It had to happen eventually, that I found a mirror and looked
in. For the first days after my accident, I had stayed mostly in

bed, leaning my bandages back on the pillow and peeling frostbite blisters from my hands. The new skin was pink, and much
thinner than the old, as sensitive to touch as the nail beds I un-
covered by chewing down to them. I had taken to running two
fingers over stitches standing up like razor stubble on my face,
then over the cotton that covered the right side and the rest of
my head. The whole surgical team came in daily to lift me into a
chair and unwind the gauze, releasing into the room a smell like
old caves full of bones. And all this time I had never seen myself,
never asked what was under there, in the place where my eye
belonged.

I had asked my mother once if I would again see out of that
eye. It was an hour after my dressings had been changed, and
the smell of hot ooze still hovered in my room. Mom stood up
and adjusted my bedrail. "Do you want your feet a little higher?"
she said. "I can crank them up if you like."

I said, "Mommy, my eye. Will I be able to see from it?"

"Hang on," she said. "I need to use the little girls' room." She
started to the door and I screamed after her, "Mommy, you're
not answering me." But she was gone, and after that I did not
ask.

Later, when the light was out, I lay back and looked far right,
then left, concentrating hard, trying to feel the bandaged eye
move. I thought I could feel it, rolling up and then down, ceiling
to floor, matching its moves with my other eye. Even after I was
grown, I could swear that I felt it blink when I pressed my two
lids together.

Men from down the hall visited me during the day, rolling in on
wheelchairs or walking beside their IV racks. They all wore two
sets of pajamas, one wrong way forward so their backsides were
covered. The hospital floor was old, its tiles starting to bubble,
and the wheels on my friends' IV racks made rumbling sounds
as they passed over. If a nurse passed by the door and looked
in, the men waved her away, saying, "It's all right, dear. I'm visiting my granddaughter." For a kiss they gave me a sucker and
a story about bears, or they carried me to a wheelchair and took
me around to visit. In this way, I passed from room to room,
brushing at the green curtains between beds, pouring water into

plastic glasses, gathering hugs and learning to shake hands in the "cool" way. I signed plaster casts in big red letters, and I visited the baby room, pressing my chin to the glass.

On a day when I felt at my smallest and was in my bed still sleeping, one of my favorite men friends checked out, leaving on my nightstand a gift and a note that said he would miss me. The gift was a music box in pink satin, with a ballerina inside who pirouetted on her toes when I wound the key. And behind her inside the lid, a triangular looking glass not much bigger than she was.

My mother came in behind me as I was staring into the mirror, holding it first from one angle, then from another, and she stood by the bed for a moment, saying nothing. When I turned, she was looking at me with her shoulders forward, and she seemed to be waiting.

"My eye is gone, isn't it?" I said.

She kept looking at me. She said, "Yes it is."

I turned again and lifted the box to my face. "I thought so," I said. "Those dogs were pretty mean."

I didn't understand, or was too small to know, what my mother thought she was protecting me from. It must be something very bad, I thought, for her to avoid every question I asked her. "Mommy," I said once, "I don't *feel* like I'm going to die."

She looked up from her book and the light shone off her glasses. She said, "Oh, no. You're certainly not going to do anything like that."

"Then will I be blind?"

"Well," she said. "You can see now, can't you?" And when I pressed her with more questions, she looked toward the door and said, "Shh. Here comes your lunch tray."

It all made me wonder if my wounds were much worse than everyone said — and of course they were, but there were long years of surgery still ahead, and no one wanted me to feel afraid. I was angry, too — as angry as a seven-year-old can be — that Mom patted my cheek with her palm and said she'd be taking my malemute to the pound before I came home. I stared at her then with my head up and sputtered out a peevish tirade, telling her I didn't hate all dogs, or even most dogs, but just the ones who bit me. It didn't occur to me until my own daughter was seven, the same age I was when I was hurt, that Mom might have been sending my dog away for her own sake.

V. Small Purchase

I have bought a one-eyed fish. As he drifts around the tank near my desk, his skin ripples silver like well-pressed silk, and he moves under the light and hovers with his one bronze eye turned toward me, waiting to be fed. His body is smooth and flat, like a silver dollar but twice the size, and his fins are mottled gold. He is a relative of the piranha, a meat eater with a bold round mouth, but even when the smaller fish challenge him, swishing their tails at his eye, he leaves them alone and swims off. He has not eaten one of them.

I call him Max, because my sister said I should. She did not remind me, when I brought him home, that I had wanted no pets, nothing with a life span shorter than my own, nothing that would die or have to be butchered as soon as I had given it a name. She just looked up with her face very serious as if she knew well how one could become attached to a fish, and she said to me, Max. Yes, that should be his name.

I had told us both, when I bought the aquarium, that fish were low-maintenance animals, without personalities and incapable of friendliness, and if one of them died you just flushed it away and got another. And besides, I said, I needed a fish tank. I had begun to feel stale, inert. I needed the sounds of moving water in my house, and I needed, too, something alive and interesting to stare at when I stopped typing to think of a new sentence.

Last summer, when I was tired and the writing was going badly, I got superstitious about the sea and thought that the lurch and pull of waves would freshen my ears and bring on clean thoughts. So I packed some books and a portable typewriter, drove to Homer on the coast, and rented a cabin near the beach. Something about the place, or its fishy air, or my aloneness in the middle of it worked somehow, and I breathed bigger there in my chest and wrote more clearly on the page. I had forgotten about tides and about the kelp and dried crabs that came in with them, and every morning I shivered into a sweater, put combs in my hair, and walked out to wade and to fill my pockets with what I found. I liked it best when the wind was blowing and the sky was gray, and the sounds of seagulls and my own breathing were carried out with the water.

Kelp pods washed up around my feet, and I stomped on them with tennis shoes to find what was inside. I collected driftwood, and urchins, and tiny pink clam shells dropped by gulls, thin enough to see through and smaller than a thumbnail. When the tide had gone far out, I climbed the bluff back to my cabin and sat writing in front of the window, eating cheese on bread and drinking orange spritzers or tea. The walls and windows there had space in between, and they let in shreds of wind and the arguing of birds and the metal smell of seaweed drying out on the beach. When the tide started back in, I took pen and notebook and sat on a great barnacled rock, letting water creep up and surround me, then jumping to shore just in time. An hour later, the rock would be covered, three feet or more under the gray, and I would know where it lay only because of the froth and swirl of whirlpools just above it.

When I came home I threw my bags on the bed and unfastened them, and a thousand aromas opened up then into my face, drifting out from the folds of my clothes, the seams in my shoes, the pages of my notebook. I had carried them back with me, the smells of wet sand and fish fins, of eagle feathers floating in surf, of candle wax burned at midnight and filled with the empty bodies of moths. I had grieved on the drive home for that place I was leaving, and for the cold wind of that beach, and I had decided that somehow water should move in my house, should rush and bubble in my ears, should bring in the sound of the sea, and the wind and dark currents that move it.

So I bought an aquarium, and fish to go in it, and a water pump strong enough to tumble the surface as it worked. I bought plants for the tank, and waved their smell into the room, and when I thought I was finished I made one more trip to a pet store, just to see what they had.

The shop was a small one, in an old wooden building with low ceilings, and the fish room in back was dark and smelled submarine — humid and slippery and full of live things. All light in the place came from the fish tanks themselves, and the plants inside them absorbed the glow and turned it green, casting it outward to move in shadowed patterns on my skin. When I closed my eyes, the sound was of rivers running out to the coast to be carried away mixed with salt. And the fish inside waved their fins and wandered between the rocks, opening and closing their mouths.

I glanced, but didn't look hard at the larger fish, because I had found already that they were always very expensive. I browsed instead through tetras and guppies, gouramis and cichlids, trying to be satisfied with the small ones, because after all it was just the water and its motion that I really wanted. So when I saw the wide silver fish and a sign that said "$10," I assumed it was a mistake but decided to ask about it while I ordered some neons dipped out. With my neck bent forward, I watched as fifty neons swam fast away from the net that would always catch them anyway. Was that big fish back there really only ten? I said.

The clerk said, "You mean the Matinnis with one eye. He's such a mellow guy."

I swung my head to look at her. One eye?

The woman stared at my face for a moment and opened her mouth. Her cheeks grew pinker, but when she answered me, her voice stayed even. She said, "Yes, his former owners thought he was a piranha and put him in the tank with some. They ate out one eye before anyone could get him back up."

"They go for the eyes so their lunch will quit looking at them," I said. I told the woman I would take the Matinnis. I thought we were a match, I said.

And I was right. As absurd as I felt about my affinity with a one-eyed fish, I found myself watching him for the ways he was like me, and I did find many. Max had already learned, by the time I got him, to hold his body in the water so that whatever he was interested in lay always on the same side of him as his eye. In the same way that I situate myself in movie theaters so that my best friend sits on my right side, Max turns his eye toward the wall of his tank, watching for my arm to move toward the food box. When I drop a worm cube down to him, he shifts his eye up to look at it and then swims at it from the side so he never loses it from vision. If the smaller fish fight, or behave defiantly around him, he turns his dead eye against them and flicks himself away to a far corner of the tank.

I don't know if it is normal to befriend a fish. I think probably not. I do know that as I sit by Max's tank and write, I stop sometimes and look up, and I think then that he looks terribly dashing, swimming around with his bad eye outward, unafraid that something might attack him from his blind side. I buy him special shrimp pellets, and I feed them to him one at a time, careful always to drop them past his good eye. My friends like to feed him, too, and I teach them how, warning them to drop his food where he can see it. Now one of my friends wants to introduce me to his neighbor's one-eyed dog, and another wishes she still had her one-eyed zebra finch so she could give it to me.

That's just what I need, I think — a houseful of blind-sided pets. We could sit around together and play wink-um, wondering was that a wink or just a lid shut down over a dry eyeball. We could fight about who got to sit on whose good side, or we could make jokes about how it takes two of us to look both ways before crossing the street. I laugh, but still I intend to meet the one-eyed dog, to see if he reminds me of Max — or of me. I wonder if he holds himself differently from other dogs, if when he hears a voice he turns his whole body to look.

And I wonder about myself, about what has changed in the world. At first, I wanted fish only for the water they lived in, for the movement it would bring to my house, the dust it would sweep from my brain. I thought of fish as "safe" pets, too boring to demand much attention, soulless by nature and indistinguishable from their peers. Maybe this is true for most of them. But I know that when the smaller fish chase after Max, or push him away from the food, I find myself fiercely angry. I take a vicious pleasure in dropping down shrimp pellets too big and too hard for the small ones to eat, and I find pleasure, too, in the way Max gobbles the food, working it to bits in his mouth. When he is finished, he turns a dead eye to the others and swims away, seeking things more interesting to look at.

URSULA K. LE GUIN

The Fisherwoman's Daughter

FROM THE NEW YORK TIMES BOOK REVIEW

" 'SO OF COURSE,' wrote Betty Flanders, pressing her heels rather deeper in the sand, 'there was nothing for it but to leave.' "

That is the first sentence of Virginia Woolf's *Jacob's Room*. It is a woman writing. Sitting on the sand by the sea, writing. It's only Betty Flanders, and she's only writing a letter. But first sentences are doors to worlds. This world of Jacob's room, so strangely empty at the end of the book when the mother stands in it holding out a pair of her son's old shoes and saying, "What am I to do with these?" — this is a world in which the first thing one sees is a woman, a mother of children, writing.

On the shore, by the sea, outdoors, is that where women write? Not at a desk, in a writing room? Where does a woman write, what does she look like writing, what is my image, your image, of a woman writing? I asked my friends: "A woman writing: What do you see?" There would be a pause, then the eyes would light up, seeing. Some sent me to paintings, Fragonard, Cassatt, but mostly these turned out to be paintings of a woman reading or with a letter, not actually writing or reading the letter but looking up from it with unfocused eyes: Will he never never return? Did I remember to turn off the pot roast? . . . Another friend responded crisply, "A woman writing is taking dictation." And another said, "She's sitting at the kitchen table, and the kids are yelling."

And that last is the image I shall pursue. But first let me tell you my own first answer to my question: Jo March. From the immediacy, the authority, with which Frank Merrill's familiar illustrations of *Little Women* came to my mind as soon as I asked myself what a woman writing looks like, I know that Jo March must have had real influence upon me when I was a young scribbler. I am sure she has influenced many girls, for she is not, like most "real" authors, either dead or inaccessibly famous; nor, like so many artists in books, is she set apart by sensitivity or suffering or general superlativity; nor is she, like most authors in novels, male. She is close as a sister and common as grass. As a model, what does she tell scribbling girls? I think it worthwhile to follow the biography of Jo March the Writer until we come to that person of whom, as a child and until quite recently, I knew almost nothing: Louisa May Alcott.

We first meet Jo as a writer when sister Amy vengefully burns her manuscript, "the loving work of several years. It seemed a small loss to others, but to Jo it was a dreadful calamity." How could a book, several years' work, be "a small loss" to anyone? That horrified me. How could they ask Jo to forgive Amy? At least she nearly drowns her in a frozen lake before forgiving her. At any rate, some chapters later Jo is

> very busy in the garret . . . seated on the old sofa, writing busily, with her papers spread out on a trunk before her. . . . Jo's desk up here was an old tin kitchen . . .

— the *OED* says, "New England: a roasting pan." So Jo's room of her own at this stage is a garret furnished with a sofa, a roasting pan, and a rat. To any twelve-year-old, heaven.

> Jo scribbled away till the last page was filled, when she signed her name with a flourish. . . . Lying back on the sofa she read the manuscript carefully through, making dashes here and there, and putting in many exclamation points, which looked like little balloons; then she tied it up with a smart red ribbon and sat a minute looking at it with a sober, wistful expression, which plainly showed how earnest her work had been.

I am interested here by the counterplay of a deflating irony — the scribbling, the dashes, the balloons, the ribbon — and that wistful earnestness.

Jo sends her story to a paper, it is printed, and she reads it aloud to her sisters, who cry at the right places. Beth asks, "Who wrote it?"

The reader suddenly sat up, cast away the paper, displaying a flushed countenance, and with a funny mixture of solemnity and excitement, replied, in a loud voice, "Your sister."

The March family makes a great fuss, "for these foolish, affectionate people made a jubilee of every little household joy" — and there again is deflation, a writer's first publication reduced to a "little household joy." Does it not debase art? And yet does it not also, by refusing the heroic tone, refuse to inflate art into something beyond the reach of any "mere girl"?

So Jo goes on writing; here she is some years later, and I quote at length, for this is the central image.

> Every few weeks she would shut herself up in her room, put on her scribbling suit, and "fall into a vortex," as she expressed it, writing away at her novel with all her heart and soul, for till that was finished she could find no peace. Her "scribbling suit" consisted of a black woollen pinafore on which she could wipe her pen at will, and a cap of the same material, adorned with a cheerful red bow. . . . This cap was a beacon to the inquiring eyes of her family, who during these periods kept their distance, merely popping in their heads semi-occasionally to ask, with interest, "Does genius burn, Jo?" They did not always venture even to ask this question, but took an observation of the cap, and judged accordingly. If this expressive article of dress was drawn low upon the forehead, it was a sign that hard work was going on; in exciting moments it was pushed rakishly askew; and when despair seized the author it was plucked wholly off and cast upon the floor. At such times the intruder silently withdrew; and not until the red bow was seen gayly erect upon the gifted brow, did anyone dare address Jo.
>
> She did not think herself a genius by any means; but when the writing fit came on, she gave herself up to it with entire abandon, and led a blissful life, unconscious of want, care, or bad weather, while she sat safe and happy in an imaginary world, full of friends almost as real and dear to her as any in the flesh. Sleep forsook her eyes, meals stood untasted, day and night were all too short to enjoy the happiness which blessed her only at such times, and made these hours worth living, even if they bore no other fruit. The divine afflatus usually lasted a week or two, and then she emerged from her vortex, hungry, sleepy, cross, or despondent.

This is a good description of the condition in which the work of art is done. This is the real thing — domesticated. The cap and bow, the facetious turns and the disclaimers, deflate without degrading, and allow Alcott to make a rather extraordinary statement: that Jo is doing something very important and doing it entirely seriously and that there is nothing unusual about a young woman's doing it. This passion of work and this happiness which blessed her in doing it are fitted without fuss into a girl's commonplace life at home. It may not seem much; but I don't know where else I or many other girls like me, in my generation or my mother's or my daughters', were to find this model, this validation.

Jo writes romantic thrillers and they sell; her father shakes his head and says, "Aim at the highest and never mind the money," but Amy remarks, "The money is the best part of it." Working in Boston as a governess-seamstress, Jo sees that "money conferred power: money and power, therefore, she resolved to have; not to be used for herself alone," our author's author hastily adds, "but for those whom she loved more than self. . . . She took to writing sensation stories." Her first visit to the editorial office of the *Weekly Volcano* is handled lightly, but the three men treat her as a woman who has come to sell herself — true Lévi-Straussians, to whom what a woman does is entirely subsumed in woman as commodity. Refusing shame, Jo writes on, and makes money by her writing; admitting shame, she does not "tell them at home."

> Jo soon found that her innocent experience had given her but few glimpses of the tragic world which underlies society; so, regarding it in a business light, she set about supplying her deficiences with characteristic energy. . . . She searched newspapers for accidents, incidents, and crimes; she excited the suspicions of public librarians by asking for works on poisons; she studied faces in the street, and characters good, bad, and indifferent all about her. . . . Much describing of other people's passions and feelings set her to studying and speculating about her own — a morbid amusement, in which healthy young minds do not voluntarily indulge —

but which one might think appropriate, even needful, to the young novelist? However, "wrongdoing always brings its own punishment, and when Jo most needed hers, she got it."

Her punishment is administered by the Angel in the House, in the form of Professor Bhaer. Knowing that she is soiling her pure soul, he attacks the papers she writes for: "I do not like to think that good young girls should see such things." Jo weakly defends them, but when he leaves she rereads her stories, three months' work, and burns them. Amy doesn't have to do it for her anymore; she can destroy herself. Then she sits and wonders: "I almost wish I hadn't any conscience, it's so inconvenient!" A cry from the heart of Bronson Alcott's daughter. She tries a pious tale and a children's story, which don't sell, and gives up: she "corked up her inkstand."

Beth dies, and trying to replace her, Jo tries "to live for others" — finally driving her mother to say, "Why don't you write? That always used to make you happy." So she does, and she writes both well and successfully — until Professor Bhaer returns and marries her, evidently the only way to make her stop writing. She has his two boys to bring up, and then her two boys, and then all those Little Men in the next volume; at the end of *Little Women,* in the chapter called "Harvest Time," she says, "I haven't given up the hope that I may write a good book yet, but I can wait."

The harvest seems indefinitely deferred. But, in Rachel Blau Du Plessis's phrase, Jo writes beyond the ending. In the third volume, *Jo's Boys,* she has gone back in middle age to writing, and is rich and famous. There is realism, toughness, and comedy in the descriptions of her managing the household, mothering the teenagers, writing her chapters, and trying to avoid the celebrity hunters. In fact this, like the whole story of Jo the Writer, is quite close to Louisa Alcott's own story, with one large difference. Jo marries and has children. Lu did not.

And yet she undertook the responsibility for a family, some of whom were as improvident and self-centered as any baby. There is a heartbreaking note in her journal for April 1869, when she was suffering a "bad spell" of mercury poisoning (the calomel given her to cure fever when she was a nurse in the Civil War made her sick the rest of her life):

> Very poorly. Feel quite used up. Don't care much for myself, as rest is heavenly, even with pain; but the family seems so panic-stricken and helpless when I break down, that I try to keep the mill going. Two short tales for L., $50; two for Ford, $20; and did my editorial work, though two months are unpaid for. Roberts wants a new book, but am afraid to get into a vortex lest I fall ill.

Alcott used the same word Jo used for her passions of writing; here are a couple of journal passages comparable to the "vortex" passage in *Little Women*.

> August 1860 — "Moods" [a novel]. Genius burned so fiercely that for four weeks I wrote all day and planned nearly all night, being quite possessed by my work. I was perfectly happy, and seemed to have no wants.

> February 1861 — Another turn at "Moods," which I remodelled. From the 2d to the 25th I sat writing, with a run at dusk; could not sleep, and for three days was so full of it I could not stop to get up. Mother made me a green silk cap with a red bow, to match the old green and red party wrap, which I wore as a "glory cloak." Thus arrayed sat in a grove of manuscripts, "living for immortality" as May said. Mother wandered in and out with cordial cups of tea, worried because I couldn't eat. Father thought it fine, and brought his reddest apples and hardest cider for my Pegasus to feed upon. . . . It was very pleasant and queer while it lasted. . . .

And it is pleasant to see how the family whose debts she slaved to pay off, and which she strove so to protect and keep in comfort, tried to protect and help her in return.

Like so many women of her century, then, Lu Alcott had a family, though she did not marry. "Liberty is a better husband than love to many of us," she wrote, but in fact she had very little liberty, in the sense of freedom from immediate, personal responsibilities. She even had a baby — her sister May's. Dying from complications of childbirth, May asked the beloved older sister, then forty-eight, to bring up little Lu, which she did until her death eight years later.

All this is complex, more complex, I think, than one tends to imagine, for the Victorian script calls for a clear choice — either books or babies for a woman, not both. And Jo *seems* to make that choice. I was annoyed at myself when I realized that I had forgotten Jo's survival as a writer — that my memory, except for one nagging scrap that led me to look up *Jo's Boys* at last, had followed the script. That, of course, is the power of the script: you play the part without knowing it.

Here is a classic — a scriptural — description of a writing woman, the mother of children, one of whom is just now in the process of falling down the stairs.

Mrs Jellyby was a pretty, very diminutive, plump woman, of from forty to fifty, with handsome eyes, though they had a curious habit of seeming to look a long way off. . . . [She] had very good hair, but was too much occupied with her African duties to brush it. . . . We could not help noticing that her dress didn't nearly meet up the back, and that the open space was railed across with a latticework of stay-laces — like a summer-house.

The room, which was strewn with papers and nearly filled by a great writing-table covered with similar litter, was, I must say, not only very untidy, but very dirty. We were obliged to take notice of that with our sense of sight, even while, with our sense of hearing, we followed the poor child who had tumbled downstairs: I think into the back kitchen, where somebody seemed to stifle him. But what principally struck us was a jaded and unhealthy-looking, though by no means plain girl, at the writing-table, who sat biting the feather of her pen, and staring at us. I suppose nobody ever was in such a state of ink.

I will, with difficulty, restrain myself from reading you the rest of *Bleak House*. I love Dickens and will defend his Mrs. Jellyby and her correspondence with Borrioboola-Gha as an eternal send-up of those who meddle with foreign morals while remaining oblivious of the misery under their nose. But I observe also that he uses a woman to make this point, probably because it was, and is, safe: few readers would question the assumption that a woman should put family before public responsibility, or that if she does work outside the "private sphere" she will be neglectful of her house, indifferent to the necks of her children, and incompetent to fasten her clothing. Mrs. Jellyby's daughter is saved from her enforced "state of ink" by marriage, but Mrs. Jellyby will get no help from her husband, a man so inert that their marriage is described as the union of mind and matter. Mrs. Jellyby is a joy to me, she is drawn with so much humor and good nature; and yet she troubles me because behind her lurks the double standard. Nowhere among Dickens's many responsible, intelligent women is there one who does real artistic or intellectual work, to balance Mrs. Jellyby and reassure us that it isn't what she does but how she does it that is deplorable. And yet the passage just quoted is supposed to have been written by a woman — the character Esther Summerson. Esther herself is a problem. How does she write half Dickens's novel for him while managing Bleak House and getting smallpox and everything else? We never catch her at it. As a woman writing, Esther is invisible. She is not in the script.

There may be a sympathetic portrait of a woman writer with children in a novel written by a man. I have read versions of this paper in Rhode Island, Ohio, Georgia, Louisiana, Oregon, and California, and asked each audience please to tell me if they knew of any such. I wait in hope. Indeed, the only sympathetic picture of a woman novelist in a man's novel that I know is the protagonist of *Diana of the Crossways*. Meredith shows her writing novels for her living, doing it brilliantly, and finding her freedom in her professionalism. But, self-alienated by a disastrous infatuation, she begins to force her talent and can't work — the script apparently being that love is incidental for a man, everything for a woman. At the end, well off and happily married, she is expecting a baby, but not, it appears, a book. All the same, Diana still stands, nearly a century later, quite alone at her crossways.

Invisibility as a writer is a condition that affects not only characters but authors, and even the children of authors. Take Elizabeth Barrett Browning, whom we have consistently put to bed with a spaniel, ignoring the fact that when she wrote *Aurora Leigh* she was the healthy mother of a healthy four-year-old — ignoring, in fact, the fact that she wrote *Aurora Leigh,* a book about being a woman writer, and how difficult one's own true love can make it for one.

Here is a woman who had several children and was a successful novelist, writing a letter to her husband about a hundred and fifty years ago, or maybe last night:

> If I *am* to write, I must have a room to myself, which shall be *my* room. All last winter I felt the need of some place where I could go and be quiet. I could not [write in the dining room] for there was all the setting of tables and clearing up of tables and dressing and washing of children, and everything else going on, and . . . I never felt comfortable there, though I tried hard. Then if I came into the parlor where you were, I felt as if I were interrupting you, and you know you sometimes thought so too.

What do you mean? Not at all! Silly notion! Just like a woman!

Fourteen years and several more children later, that woman wrote *Uncle Tom's Cabin* — most of it at the kitchen table.

A room of one's own — yes. One may ask why Mr. Harriet
Beecher Stowe got a room to himself to write in, while the woman
who wrote the most morally effective American novel of the
nineteenth century got the kitchen table. But then one may also
ask why she accepted the kitchen table. Any self-respecting man
would have sat there for five minutes and then stalked out
shouting, "Nobody can work in this madhouse, call me when
dinner's ready!" But Harriet, a self-respecting woman, went on
getting dinner with the kids all underfoot *and* writing her novels.
The first question, to be asked with awe, is surely, How? But
then, Why? *Why* are women such patsies?

The quick-feminist-fix answer is that they are victims of and/
or accomplices with the patriarchy, which is true but doesn't really
get us anywhere new. Let us go to another woman novelist for
help. I stole the Stowe quotation (and others) from Tillie Olsen's
Silences, a book to which this paper stands in the relation of a
loving but undutiful daughter — Hey, Ma, that's a neat quotation, can I wear it? This next one I found for myself, in the
Autobiography of Margaret Oliphant, a fascinating book from the
generation just after Stowe. Oliphant was a successful writer very
young, married, had three kids, went on writing, was left a widow
with heavy debts and the three kids plus her brother's three kids
to bring up, did so, went on writing . . . When her second book
came out, she was still, like Jo March, a girl at home.

> I had a great pleasure in writing, but the success and the three edi-
> tions had no particular effect upon my mind. . . . I had nobody to
> praise me except my mother and [brother] Frank, and their ap-
> plause — well, it was delightful, it was everything in the world — it
> was life — but it did not count. They were part of me, and I of them,
> and we were all in it.

I find that extraordinary. I cannot imagine any male author
saying anything like that at all. There is a key here — something
real that has been neglected, been hidden, been denied.

> . . . The writing ran through everything. But then it was also sub-
> ordinate to everything, to be pushed aside for any little necessity. I
> had no table even to myself, much less a room to work in, but sat at
> the corner of the family table with my writing-book, with everything
> going on as if I had been making a shirt instead of writing a book.

. . . My mother sat always at needlework of some kind, and talked
to whoever might be present, and I took my share in the conversation, going on all the same with my story, the little groups of imaginary persons, these other talks evolving themselves quite undisturbed.

How's that for an image, the group of imaginary people talking in the imaginary room in the real room among the real people talking, and all of it going on perfectly quiet and unconfused
. . . But it's shocking. She can't be a real writer. Real writers
writhe on solitary sofas in cork-lined rooms, agonizing after *le
mot juste* — don't they?

My study, all the study I have ever attained to, is the little second
drawing-room where all the life of the house goes on . . .

— you recall that she was bringing up six children? —

. . . And I don't think I have ever had two hours undisturbed (except at night when everybody is in bed) during my whole literary life.
Miss Austen, I believe, wrote in the same way, and very much for the
same reason; but at her period the natural flow of life took another
form. The family were half ashamed to have it known that she was
not just a young lady like the others, doing her embroidery. Mine
were quite pleased to magnify me and to be proud of my work, but
always with a hidden sense that it was an admirable joke . . .

— perhaps artists cast off their families and go to the South Sea
Islands because they want to be perceived as heroes and their
families think they are funny? —

. . . a hidden sense that it was an admirable joke, and no idea that
any special facilities or retirement was necessary. My mother would
have felt her pride much checked, almost humiliated, if she had conceived that I stood in need of any artificial aids of that description.
That would at once have made the work unnatural to her eyes, and
also to mine.

Oliphant was a proud Scotswoman, proud of her work and
her strength; yet she wrote nonfiction potboilers rather than fight
her male editors and publishers for better pay for her novels.
So, as she says bitterly, "Trollope's worst book was better paid
than my best." Her best is said to be *Miss Marjoribanks,* but I have
never yet been able to get a copy of it; it was disappeared, along

with all her other books. Thanks to publishers such as Virago we can now get Oliphant's *Hester,* a stunning novel, and *Kirsteen* and a few others, but they are still taught, so far as I know, only in women's studies courses; they are not part of the Canon of English Literature, though Trollope's potboilers are. No book by a woman who had children has ever been included in that august list.

I think Oliphant gives us a glimpse of why a novelist might not merely endure writing in the kitchen or the parlor amidst the children and the housework, but might endure it willingly. She seems to feel that she profited, that her writing profited, from the difficult, obscure, chancy connection between the artwork and the emotional/manual/managerial complex of skills and tasks called housework, and that to sever that connection would put the writing itself at risk, would make it, in her word, unnatural.

The received wisdom, of course, is just the opposite: that any attempt to combine artwork with housework and family responsibility is impossible, unnatural. And the punishment for unnatural acts, among the critics and the Canoneers, is death.

What is the ethical basis of this judgment and sentence upon the housewife-artist? It is a very noble and austere one, with religion at its foundation: it is the idea that the artist must sacrifice himself to his art. (I use the pronoun advisedly.) His responsibility is to his work alone. It is a motivating idea of the Romantics; it guides the careers of poets from Rimbaud to Dylan Thomas to Richard Hugo; it has given us hundreds of hero figures, typical of whom is James Joyce himself and his Stephen Dedalus. Stephen sacrifices all "lesser" obligations and affections to a "higher" cause, embracing the moral irresponsibility of the soldier or the saint. This heroic stance, the Gauguin Pose, has been taken as the norm — as natural to the artist — and artists, both men and women, who do not assume it have tended to feel a little shabby and second rate.

Not, however, Virginia Woolf. She observed factually that the artist needs a small income and a room to work in, but did not speak of heroism. Indeed, she said, "I doubt that a writer can be a hero. I doubt that a hero can be a writer." And when I see a writer assume the full heroic posture, I incline to agree. Here, for example, is Joseph Conrad:

For twenty months I wrestled with the Lord for my creation . . . mind and will and conscience engaged to the full, hour after hour, day after day . . . a lonely struggle in a great isolation from the world. I suppose I slept and ate the food put before me and talked connectedly on suitable occasions, but I was never aware of the even flow of daily life, made easy and noiseless for me by a silent, watchful, tireless affection.

A woman who boasted that her conscience had been engaged to the full in such a wrestling match would be called to account by both women and men; and women are now calling men to account. What "put food" before him? What made daily life so noiseless? What in fact was this "tireless affection," which sounds to me like an old Ford in a junkyard but is apparently intended as a delicate gesture toward a woman whose conscience was engaged to the full, hour after hour, day after day, for twenty months, in seeing to it that Joseph Conrad could wrestle with the Lord in a very relatively great isolation, well housed, clothed bathed, and fed?

Conrad's "struggle" and Jo March / Lu Alcott's "vortex" are descriptions of the same kind of all-out artistic work; and in both cases the artist is looked after by the family. But I feel an important difference in their perceptions. Where Alcott receives a gift, Conrad asserts a right; where she is taken into the vortex, the creative whirlwind, becoming part of it, he wrestles, struggles, seeking mastery. She is a participant; he is a hero. And her family remain individuals, with cups of tea and timid inquiries, while his is depersonalized to "an affection."

Looking for a woman writer who might have imitated this heroic infantilism, I thought of Gertrude Stein, under the impression that she had used Alice Toklas as a "wife" in this utilitarian sense; but that, as I should have guessed, is an anti-lesbian canard. Stein certainly took hero-artist poses and indulged an enormous ego, but she played fair; and the difference between her domestic partnership and that of Joyce or Conrad is illuminating. And indeed, lesbianism has given many artists the network of support they need — for there *is* a heroic aspect to the practice of art; it is lonely, risky, merciless work, and every artist needs some kind of moral support or sense of solidarity and validation.

The artist with the least access to social or aesthetic solidarity or approbation has been the artist-housewife. A person who undertakes responsibility both to her art and to her dependent children, with no "tireless affection" or even tired affection to call on, has undertaken a full-time double job that can be simply, practically, destroyingly impossible. But that isn't how the problem is posed — as a recognition of immense practical difficulty. If it were, practical solutions would be proposed, beginning with childcare. Instead the issue is stated, even now, as a moral one, a matter of ought and ought not. The poet Alicia Ostriker puts it neatly: "That women should have babies rather than books is the considered opinion of Western civilization. That women should have books rather than babies is a variation on that theme."

Freud's contribution to this doctrine was to invest it with such a weight of theory and mythology as to make it appear a primordial, unquestionable fact. It was, of course, Freud who, after telling his fiancée what it is a woman wants, said that what we shall never know is what a woman wants. Lacan is perfectly consistent in following him, if I as a person without discourse may venture to say so. A culture or a psychology predicated upon man as human and woman as other cannot accept a woman as artist. An artist is an autonomous, choice-making self: to be such a self a woman must unwoman herself. Barren, she must imitate the man — imperfectly, it goes without saying.*

Hence the approbation accorded Austen, the Brontës, Dickinson, and Plath, who though she made the mistake of having two children compensated for it by killing herself. The misogynist Canon of Literature can include these women because they can be perceived as incomplete women, as female men.

---

*A particularly exhilarating discussion of this issue is the essay "Writing and Motherhood" by Susan Rubin Suleiman, in *The (M)other Tongue: Essays in Feminist Psychoanalytic Interpretation,* edited by Garner, Kahane, and Springnether (Ithaca: Cornell University Press, 1985). Suleiman gives a short history of the nineteenth-century books-or-babies theory and its refinement in the twentieth century by such psychologists as Helene Deutsch, remarking that "it took psychoanalysis to transform moral obligation into a psychological 'law,' equating the creative impulse with the procreative one and decreeing that she who has a child feels no need to write books." Suleiman presents a critique of the feminist reversal of this theory (she who has a book feels no need to have children) and analyzes current French feminist thinking on the relationship between writing and femininity/motherhood.

Still, I have to grit my teeth to criticize the either-books-or-babies doctrine, because it has given real, true comfort to women who could not or chose not to marry and have children, and saw themselves as "having" books instead. But though the comfort may be real, I think the doctrine false. And I hear that falseness when a Dorothy Richardson tells us that other women can have children but nobody else can write *her* books. As if "other women" could have had *her* children — as if books came from the uterus! That's just the flip side of the theory that books come from the scrotum. This final reduction of the notion of sublimation is endorsed by our chief macho dodo writer, who has announced that "the one thing a writer needs to have is balls." But he doesn't carry the theory of penile authorship to the extent of saying that if you "get" a kid you can't "get" a book and so fathers can't write. The analogy collapsed into identity, the you-can't-create-if-you-procreate myth, is applied to women only.

I've found I have to stop now and say clearly what I'm not saying. I'm not saying a writer ought to have children, I'm not saying a parent ought to be a writer, I'm not saying any woman *ought* to write books *or* have kids. Being a mother is one of the things a woman can do — like being a writer. It's a privilege. It's not an obligation, or a destiny. I'm talking about mothers who write because it is almost a taboo topic — because women have been told that they *ought not* to try to be both a mother and a writer because both the kids and the books will *pay* — because it can't be done — because it is unnatural.

This refusal to allow both creation and procreation to women is cruelly wasteful: not only has it impoverished our literature by banning the housewives, but it has caused unbearable personal pain and self-mutilation: Woolf obeying the wise doctors who said she must not bear a child; Plath who put glasses of milk by her kids' beds and then put her head in the oven.

A sacrifice, not of somebody else but of oneself, is demanded of women artists (while the Gauguin Pose demands of men artists only that they sacrifice others). I am proposing that this ban on a woman artist's full sexuality is harmful not only to the woman but to the art.

There is less censure now, and more support, for a woman who wants both to bring up a family and to work as an artist. But it's a small degree of improvement. The difficulty of trying

to be responsible, hour after hour, day after day for maybe twenty
years, for the well-being of children and the excellence of books,
is immense: it involves an endless expense of energy and an impossible weighing of competing priorities. And we don't know
much about the process, because writers who are mothers haven't
talked much about their motherhood — for fear of boasting? for
fear of being trapped in the Mom trap, discounted? — nor have
they talked much about their writing as in any way connected
with their parenting, since the heroic myth demands that the
two jobs be considered utterly opposed and mutually destructive.

But we heard a hint of something else from Oliphant; and
here (thanks, Tillie) is the painter Käthe Kollwitz:

> I am gradually approaching the period in my life when work comes
> first. When both the boys were away for Easter, I hardly did anything
> but work. Worked, slept, ate, and went for short walks. But above all
> I worked.
>   And yet I wonder whether the "blessing" isn't missing from such
> work. No longer diverted by other emotions, I work the way a cow
> grazes.

That is marvelous — "I work the way a cow grazes." That is the
best description of the "professional" at work I know.

> Perhaps in reality I accomplish a little more. The hands work and
> work, and the head imagines it's producing God knows what, and yet,
> formerly, when my working time was so wretchedly limited, I was
> more productive, because I was more sensual; I lived as a human
> being must live, passionately interested in everything. . . . Potency,
> potency is diminishing.

This *potency* felt by a woman is a potency from which the Hero-
Artist has (and I choose my words carefully) cut himself off, in
an egoism that is ultimately sterile. But it is a potency that has
been denied by women as well as men, and not just women eager
to collude with misogyny.

Back in the seventies Nina Auerbach wrote that Jane Austen
was able to write because she had created around her "a child-
free space." Germ-free I knew, odor-free I knew, but child-free?
And Austen? who wrote in the parlor, and was a central figure
to a lot of nieces and nephews? But I tried to accept what Auer-

bach said, because although my experience didn't fit it, I was, like many women, used to feeling that my experience was faulty, not right — that it was *wrong*. So I was probably wrong to keep on writing in what was then a fully child-filled space. However, feminist thinking evolved rapidly to a far more complex and realistic position, and I, stumbling along behind, have been enabled by it to think a little for myself.

The greatest enabler for me was always, is always, Virginia Woolf. And I quote now from the first draft of her paper "Professions for Women," where she gives her great image of a woman writing.

> I figure her really in an attitude of contemplation, like a fisherwoman, sitting on the bank of a lake with her fishing rod held over its water. Yes that is how I see her. She was not thinking; she was not reasoning; she was not constructing a plot; she was letting her imagination down into the depths of her consciousness while she sat above holding on by a thin but quite necessary thread of reason.

Now I interrupt to ask you to add one small element to this scene. Let us imagine that a bit farther up the bank of the lake sits a child, the fisherwoman's daughter. She's about five, and she's making people out of sticks and mud and telling stories with them. She's been told to be very quiet please while Mama fishes, and she really is very quiet except when she forgets and sings or asks questions; and she watches in fascinated silence when the following dramatic events take place. There sits our woman writing, our fisherwoman, when

> suddenly there is a violent jerk; she feels the line race through her fingers.
> The imagination has rushed away; it has taken to the depths; it has sunk heaven knows where — into the dark pool of extraordinary experience. The reason has to cry "Stop!" the novelist has to pull on the line and haul the imagination to the surface. The imagination comes to the top in a state of fury.
> Good heavens she cries — how dare you interfere with me — how dare you pull me out with your wretched little fishing line? And I — that is, the reason — have to reply, "My dear you were going altogether too far. Men would be shocked." Calm yourself I say, as she sits panting on the bank — panting with rage and disappointment. We have only got to wait fifty years or so. In fifty years I shall be able

to use all this very queer knowledge that you are ready to bring me. But not now. You see I go on, trying to calm her, I cannot make use of what you tell me — about womens bodies for instance — their passions — and so on, because the conventions are still very strong. If I were to overcome the conventions I should need the courage of a hero, and I am not a hero.

I doubt that a writer can be a hero. I doubt that a hero can be a writer.

. . . Very well, says the imagination, dressing herself up again in her petticoat and skirts, we will wait. We will wait another fifty years. But it seems to me a pity.

It seems to me a pity. It seems to me a pity that more than fifty years have passed and the conventions, though utterly different, still exist to protect men from being shocked, still admit only male experience of women's bodies, passions, and existence. It seems to me a pity that so many women, including myself, have accepted this denial of their own experience and narrowed their perception to fit it, writing as if their sexuality were limited to copulation, as if they knew nothing about pregnancy, birth, nursing, mothering, puberty, menstruation, menopause, except what men are willing to hear, nothing except what men are willing to hear about housework, childwork, lifework, war, peace, living, and dying as experienced in the female body and mind and imagination. "Writing the body," as Woolf asked and Hélène Cixous asks, is only the beginning. We have to rewrite the world.

White writing, Cixous calls it, writing in milk, in mother's milk. I like that image, because even among feminists, the woman writer has been more often considered in her sexuality as a lover than in her sexuality as pregnant-bearing-nursing-childcaring. Mother still tends to get disappeared. And in losing the artist-mother we lose where there's a lot to gain. Alicia Ostriker thinks so. "The advantage of motherhood for a woman artist," she says — have you ever heard anybody say that before? the *advantage* of motherhood for an artist? —

> The advantage of motherhood for a woman artist is that it puts her in immediate and inescapable contact with the sources of life, death, beauty, growth, corruption. . . . If the woman artist has been trained to believe that the activities of motherhood are trivial, tangential to

the main issue of life, irrelevant to the great themes of literature, she should untrain herself. The training is misogynist, it protects and perpetuates systems of thought and feeling which prefer violence and death to love and birth, and it is a lie.

. . . "We think back through our mothers, if we are women," declares Woolf, but through whom can those who are themselves mothers . . . do their thinking? . . . We all need data, we need information, . . . the sort provided by poets, novelists, artists, from within. As our knowledge begins to accumulate, we can imagine what it would signify to all women, and men, to live in a culture where childbirth and mothering occupied the kind of position that sex and romantic love have occupied in literature and art for the last five hundred years, or . . . that warfare has occupied since literature began.

My book *Always Coming Home* was a rash attempt to imagine such a world, where the Hero and the Warrior are a stage adolescents go through on their way to becoming responsible human beings, where the parent-child relationship is not forever viewed through the child's eyes but includes the reality of the mother's experience. The imagining was difficult, and rewarding.

Here is a passage from a novel where what Woolf, Cixous, and Ostriker ask for is happening, however casually and unpretentiously. In Margaret Drabble's *The Millstone*, Rosamund, a young scholar and free-lance writer, has a baby about eight months old, Octavia. They share a flat with a friend, Lydia, who's writing a novel. Rosamund is working away on a book review:

> I had just written and counted my first hundred words when I remembered Octavia; I could hear her making small happy noises. . . .
>
> I was rather dismayed when I realized she was in Lydia's room and that I must have left the door open, for Lydia's room was always full of nasty objects like aspirins, safety razors and bottles of ink; I rushed along to rescue her and the sight that met my eyes when I opened the door was enough to make anyone quake. She had her back to the door and was sitting in the middle of the floor surrounded by a sea of torn, strewed, chewed paper. I stood there transfixed, watching the neat small back of her head and her thin stalk-like neck and flowery curls: suddenly she gave a great screech of delight and ripped another sheet of paper. "Octavia," I said in horror, and she started guiltily, and looked round at me with a charming deprecating smile: her mouth, I could see, was wedged full of wads of Lydia's new novel.

I picked her up and fished the bits out and laid them carefully on the bedside table with what was left of the typescript; pages 70 to 123 seemed to have survived. The rest was in varying stages of dissolution: some pages were entire but badly crumpled, some were in large pieces, some in small pieces, and some, as I have said, were chewed up. The damage was not, in fact, as great as it appeared at first sight to be, for babies, though persistent, are not thorough: but at first sight it was frightful. . . . In a way it was clearly the most awful thing for which I had ever been responsible, but as I watched Octavia crawl around the sitting room looking for more work to do, I almost wanted to laugh. It seemed so absurd, to have this small living extension of myself, so dangerous, so vulnerable, for whose injuries and crimes I alone had to suffer. . . . It really was a terrible thing . . . and yet in comparison with Octavia being so sweet and so alive it did not seem so very terrible.

Confronted with the wreckage, Lydia is startled, but not deeply distressed:

. . . and that was it, except for the fact that Lydia really did have to rewrite two whole chapters as well as doing a lot of boring sellotaping, and when it came out it got bad reviews anyway. This did succeed in making Lydia angry.

I have seen Drabble's work dismissed with the usual list of patronizing adjectives reserved for women who write as women, not imitation men. Let us not let her be disappeared. Her work is deeper than its bright surface. What is she talking about in this funny passage? Why does the girl-baby eat not her mother's manuscript but another woman's manuscript? Couldn't she at least have eaten a manuscript by a man? — no, no, that's not the point. The point, or part of it, is that babies eat manuscripts. They really do. The poem not written because the baby cried, the novel put aside because of a pregnancy, and so on. Babies eat books. But they spit out wads of them that can be taped back together; and they are babies only for a couple of years, while writers live for decades; and it is terrible, but not very terrible. The manuscript that got eaten *was* terrible; if you know Lydia you know the reviewers were right. And that's part of the point too — that the supreme value of art depends on other equally supreme values. But that subverts the hierarchy of values; "men would be shocked. . . ."

In Drabble's comedy of morals the absence of the Hero-Artist is a strong ethical statement. Nobody lives in a great isolation, nobody sacrifices human claims, nobody even scolds the baby. Nobody is going to put their head, or anybody else's head, into an oven: not the mother, not the writer, not the daughter — these three and one who, being women, do not separate creation and destruction into *I create* / *You are destroyed,* or vice versa. Who are responsible, take responsibility, for both the baby and the book.*

But I want now to turn from fiction to biography and from general to personal; I want to talk a bit about my mother, the writer.

Her maiden name was Theodora Kracaw; her first married name was Brown; her second married name, Kroeber, was the one she used on her books; her third married name was Quinn. This sort of many-namedness doesn't happen to men; it's inconvenient, and yet its very cumbersomeness reveals, perhaps, the being of a woman writer as not one simple thing — the author — but a multiple, complex process of being, with various responsibilities, one of which is to her writing.

Theodora put her personal responsibilities first — chronologically. She brought up and married off her four children before she started to write. She took up the pen, as they used to say — she had the most amazing left-handed scrawl — in her mid-fifties. I asked her once, years later, "Did you want to write, and

---

*My understanding of this issue has been much aided by Carol Gilligan's *In a Different Voice* (Cambridge: Harvard University Press, 1982), as well as by Jean Baker Miller's modestly revolutionary *Toward a New Psychology of Women* (Boston: Beacon Press, 1976). Gilligan's thesis, stated very roughly, is that our society brings up males to think and speak in terms of their rights, females in terms of their responsibilities, and that conventional psychologies have implicitly evaluated the "male" image of a hierarchy of rights as "superior" (hierarchically, of course) to the "female" image of a network of mutual responsibilities. Hence a man finds it (relatively) easy to assert his "right" to be free of relationships and dependents, à la Gauguin, while women are not granted and do not grant one another any such right, preferring to live as part of an intense and complex network in which freedom is arrived at, if at all, mutually. Coming at the matter from this angle, one can see why there are no or very few "Great Artists" among women, when the "Great Artist" is defined as inherently superior to and not responsible toward others.

put it off intentionally, till you'd got rid of us?" And she laughed
and said, "Oh, no, I just wasn't *ready*." Not an evasion or a dis-
honest answer, but not, I think, the whole answer.

She was born in 1897 in a wild Colorado mining town, and
her mother boasted of having been *born* with the vote — in Wyoming, which ratified woman suffrage along with statehood —
and rode a stallion men couldn't ride; but still, the Angel in the
House was very active in those days, the one whose message is
that a woman's needs come after everybody else's. And my mother
really came pretty close to incarnating that Angel, whom Woolf
called "the woman men wish women to be." Men fell in love with
her — all men. Doctors, garage mechanics, professors, roach ex-
terminators. Butchers saved sweetbreads for her. She was also,
to her daughter, a demanding, approving, nurturing, good-natured, loving, lively mother — a first-rate mother. And then,
getting on to sixty, she became a first-rate writer.

She started out, as women so often do, by writing some books
for children — not competing with men, you know, staying in
the "domestic sphere." One of these, *A Green Christmas,* is a lovely
book that ought to be in every six-year-old's stocking. Then she
wrote a charming and romantic autobiographical novel — still
on safe, "womanly" ground. Next she ventured into Native
American territory with *The Inland Whale;* and then she was asked
to write the story of an Indian called Ishi, the only survivor of a
people massacred by the North American pioneers, a serious
and risky subject requiring a great deal of research, moral sensitivity, and organizational and narrative skill.

So she wrote it, the first best seller, I believe, that University
of California Press ever published. *Ishi* is still in print in many
languages, still used, I think, in California schools, still de-
servedly beloved. It is a book entirely worthy of its subject, a
book of very great honesty and power.

So, if she could write that in her sixties, what might she have
written in her thirties? Maybe she really "wasn't ready." But maybe
she listened to the wrong angel, and we might have had many
more books from her. Would my brothers and I have suffered,
have been cheated of anything, if she had been writing them? I
think my aunt Betsy and the household help we had back then
would have kept things going just fine. As for my father, I don't

see how her writing could have hurt him or how her success could have threatened him. But I don't know. All I do know is that once she started writing (and it was while my father was alive, and they collaborated on a couple of things), she never stopped; she had found the work she loved.

Once, not long after my father's death, when *Ishi* was bringing her the validation of praise and success she very much needed, and while I was still getting every story I sent out rejected with monotonous regularity, she burst into tears over my latest rejection slip and tried to console me, saying that she wanted rewards and success for me, not for herself. And that was lovely, and I treasured her saying it then as I do now. That she didn't really mean it and I didn't really believe it made no difference. Of course, she didn't want to sacrifice her achievement, her work, to me — why on earth should she? She shared what she could of it with me by sharing the pleasures and anguishes of writing, the intellectual excitement, the shop talk — and that's all. No angelic altruism. When I began to publish, we shared that. And she wrote on; in her eighties she told me, without bitterness, "I wish I had started sooner. Now there isn't time." She was at work on a third novel when she died.

As for myself: I have flagrantly disobeyed the either-books-or-babies rule, having had three kids and written about twenty books, and thank God it wasn't the other way around. By the luck of race, class, money, and health, I could manage the double-tightrope trick — and especially by the support of my partner. He is not my wife; but he brought to marriage an assumption of mutual aid as its daily basis, and on that basis you can get a lot of work done. Our division of labor was fairly conventional; I was in charge of house, cooking, the kids, and novels, because I wanted to be, and he was in charge of being a professor, the car, the bills, and the garden, because he wanted to be. When the kids were babies I wrote at night; when they started school I wrote while they were at school; these days I write as a cow grazes. If I needed help he gave it without making it into a big favor, and — this is the central fact — he did not ever begrudge me the time I spent writing, or the blessing of my work.

That is the killer: the killing grudge, the envy, the jealousy, the spite that so often a man is allowed to hold, trained to hold, against anything a woman does that's not done in his service, for him, to feed his body, his comfort, his kids. A woman who tries to work against that grudge finds the blessing turned into a curse; she must rebel and go it alone, or fall silent in despair. Any artist must expect to work amid the total, rational indifference of everybody else to their work, for years, perhaps for life: but no artist can work well against daily, personal, vengeful resistance. And that's exactly what many women artists get from the people they love and live with.

I was spared all that. I was free — born free, lived free. And for years that personal freedom allowed me to ignore the degree to which my writing was controlled and constrained by judgments and assumptions which I thought were my own, but which were the internalized ideology of a male supremacist society. Even when subverting the conventions, I disguised my subversions from myself. It took me years to realize that I chose to work in such despised, marginal genres as science fiction, fantasy, young adult, precisely because they were excluded from critical, academic, canonical supervision, leaving the artist free; it took ten more years before I had the wits and guts to see and say that the exclusion of the genres from "literature" is unjustified, unjustifiable, and a matter not of quality but of politics. So too in my choice of subjects: until the mid-seventies I wrote my fiction about heroic adventures, high-tech futures, men in the halls of power, men — men were the central characters, the women were peripheral, secondary. Why don't you write about women? my mother asked me. I don't know how, I said. A stupid answer, but an honest one. I did not know how to write about women — very few of us did — because I thought that what men had written about women was the truth, was the true way to write about women. And I couldn't.

My mother could not give me what I needed. When feminism began to reawaken, she hated it, called it "those women's libbers"; but it was she who had steered me years and years before to what I would and did need, to Virginia Woolf. "We think back through our mothers," and we have many mothers, those of the body and those of the soul. What I needed was what feminism, feminist literary theory and criticism and practice, had to give me. And I can hold it in my hands — not only *Three Guineas*, my treasure in the days of poverty, but now all the wealth of *The Norton Anthology of Literature by Women* and the reprint houses and the women's presses. Our mothers have been returned to us. This time, let's hang on to them.

And it is feminism that has empowered me to criticize not only my society and myself but — for a moment now — feminism itself. The books-or-babies myth is not only a misogynist hang-up; it can be a feminist one. Some of the women I respect most, writing for publications that I depend on for my sense of women's solidarity and hope, continue to declare that it is "virtually impossible for a heterosexual woman to be a feminist," as if heterosexuality were heterosexism; and that social marginality, such as that of lesbian, childless, Black, or Native American women, "appears to be necessary" to form the feminist. Applying these judgments to myself, and believing that as a woman writing at this point I have to be a feminist to be worth beans, I find myself, once again, excluded — disappeared.

The rationale of the exclusionists, as I understand it, is that the material privilege and social approbation our society grants the heterosexual wife, and particularly the mother, prevent her solidarity with less privileged women and insulate her from the kind of anger and the kind of ideas that lead to feminist action. There is truth in this; maybe it's true for a lot of women; I can oppose it only with my experience, which is that feminism has been a life-saving *necessity* to women trapped in the wife/mother "role." What do the privilege and approbation accorded the housewife-mother by our society in fact consist of? Being the object of infinite advertising? Being charged by psychologists with total answerability for children's mental well-being, and by the government with total answerability for children's welfare, while being regularly equated with apple pie by sentimental warmongers? As a social "role," motherhood, for any woman I know, simply means that she does everything everybody else does plus bringing up the kids.

To push mothers back into "private life," a mythological space invented by the patriarchy, on the theory that their acceptance of the "role" of mother invalidates them for public, political, artistic responsibility, is to play Old Nobodaddy's game, by his rules, on his side.

In *Writing Beyond the Ending,* Du Plessis shows how women novelists write about the woman artist: they make her an ethical force, an activist trying "to change the life in which she is also immersed." To have and bring up kids is to be about as immersed in life as one can be, but it does not always follow that one drowns. A lot of us can swim.

Again, whenever I give a version of this paper, somebody will pick up on this point and tell me that I'm supporting the Superwoman syndrome, saying that a woman *should* have kids write books be politically active and make perfect sushi. I am not saying that. We're all asked to be Superwoman; I'm not asking it, our society does that. All I can tell you is that I believe it's a lot easier to write books while bringing up kids than to bring up kids while working nine to five plus housekeeping. But that is what our society, while sentimentalizing over Mom and the Family, demands of most women — unless it refuses them any work at all and dumps them onto welfare and says, Bring up your kids on food stamps, Mom, we might want them for the army. Talk about superwomen; those are the superwomen. Those are the mothers up against the wall. Those are the marginal women, without either privacy or publicity; and it's because of them more than anyone else that the woman artist has a responsibility to "try to change the life in which she is also immersed."

And now I come back round to the bank of that lake where the fisherwoman sits, our woman writer, who had to bring her imagination up short because it was getting too deeply immersed . . . The imagination dries herself off, still swearing under her breath, and buttons up her blouse, and comes to sit beside the little girl, the fisherwoman's daughter. "Do you like books?" she says, and the child says, "Oh, yes. When I was a baby I used to eat them, but now I can read. I can read all of Beatrix Potter by myself, and when I grow up I'm going to write books, like Mama."

"Are you going to wait till your children grow up, like Jo March and Theodora?"

"Oh, I don't think so," says the child. "I'll just go ahead and do it."

"Then will you do as Harriet and Margaret and so many Harriets and Margarets have done and are still doing, and hassle through the prime of your life trying to do two full-time jobs

that are incompatible with each other in practice, however en-
riching their interplay may be both to the life and the art?"

"I don't know," says the little girl. "Do I have to?"

"Yes," says the imagination, "if you aren't rich and you want
kids."

"I might want one or two," says reason's child. "But why do
women have two jobs where men only have one? It isn't reasonable, is it?"

"Don't ask me!" snaps the imagination. "I could think up a
dozen better arrangements before breakfast! But who listens to
me?"

The child sighs and watches her mother fishing. The fisherwoman, having forgotten that her line is no longer baited with
the imagination, isn't catching anything, but she's enjoying the
peaceful hour; and when the child speaks again she speaks softly.
"Tell me, Auntie. What is the one thing a writer has to have?"

"I'll tell you," says the imagination. "The one thing a writer
has to have is not balls. Nor is it a child-free space. Nor is it even,
speaking strictly on the evidence, a room of her own, though
that is an amazing help, as is the good will and cooperation of
the opposite sex, or at least the local, in-house representative of
it. But she doesn't have to have that. The one thing a writer has
to have is a pencil and some paper. That's enough, so long as
she knows that she and she alone is in charge of that pencil, and
responsible, she and she alone, for what it writes on the paper.
In other words, that she's free. Not wholly free. Never wholly
free. Maybe very partially. Maybe only in this one act, this sitting
for a snatched moment being a woman writing, fishing the mind's
lake. But in this, responsible; in this, autonomous; in this, free."

"Auntie," says the little girl, "can I go fishing with you now?"

JAY McINERNEY

Raymond Carver, Mentor

FROM THE NEW YORK TIMES BOOK REVIEW

A YEAR AFTER his death, the recurring image I associate with Raymond Carver is one of people leaning toward him, working very hard at the act of listening. He mumbled. T. S. Eliot once described Ezra Pound, qua mentor, as "a man trying to convey to a very deaf person the fact that the house is on fire." Raymond Carver had precisely the opposite manner. The smoke could be filling the room, flames streaking across the carpet, before Carver would ask, "Is it, uh, getting a little hot in here, maybe?" And you would be sitting in your chair, bent achingly forward at the waist, saying, "Beg pardon, Ray?" Never insisting, rarely asserting, he was an unlikely teacher.

I once sat in and listened while Carver was interviewed for two and a half hours. The writer conducting the interview moved the tape recorder closer and closer and finally asked if Carver would put it in his lap. A few days later the interviewer called up, near despair: Ray's voice on the tapes was nearly inaudible. The word "soft-spoken" hardly begins to do justice to his speech; this condition was aggravated whenever he was pressed into the regions of generality or prescription.

As I say, he mumbled, and if it once seemed merely a physical tic, akin to cracking knuckles or the drumming of a foot, I now think it was a function of a deep humility and a respect for the language bordering on awe, a reflection of his sense that words should be handled very, very gingerly. As if it might be almost impossible to say what you wanted to say. As if it might be dangerous, even. Listening to him talking about writing in the classroom or in the living room of the big Victorian house he shared

with Tess Gallagher in Syracuse, you sensed a writer who loved
the words of the masters who had handed the language down to
him, and who was concerned that he might not be worthy to pick
up the instrument. You feel this respect for the language — humility bordering on dread — in every sentence of his work.

Encountering Carver's fiction early in the 1970s was a trans-
forming experience for many writers of my generation, an experience perhaps comparable to discovering Hemingway's
sentences in the twenties. In fact, Carver's language was unmistakably like Hemingway's — the simplicity and clarity, the repe-
titions, the nearly conversational rhythms, the precision of physical description. But Carver completely dispensed with the
romantic egoism that made the Hemingway idiom such an awk-
ward model for other writers in the late twentieth century. The
cafés and *pensions* and battlefields of Europe were replaced by
trailer parks and apartment complexes, the glamorous occupa-
tions by dead-end jobs. The trout in Carver's streams were apt
to be pollution-deformed mutants. The good *vin du pays* was replaced by cheap gin, the romance of drinking by the dull grind
of full-time alcoholism. Some commentators found his work depressing for these reasons. For many young writers it was terribly liberating.

One aspect of what Carver seemed to say to us — even to
someone who had never been inside a lumber mill or a trailer
park — was that literature could be fashioned out of strict observation of real life, wherever and however it was lived, even if it
was lived with a bottle of Heinz ketchup on the table and the
television set droning. This was news at a time when academic
metafiction was the regnant mode. His example reinvigorated
realism as well as the short story form.

Though he was a teacher for much of his life, Carver never
consciously gathered a band of disciples around himself. But when
I was knocking around between graduate schools and the New
York publishing world in the late seventies and early eighties, no
other writer was as much discussed and mimicked by the writers
one met at readings and writers' conferences. Probably not since
Donald Barthelme began publishing in the 1960s had a story
writer generated such a buzz in the literary world.

Having fallen under Carver's spell on reading his first collection, *Will You Please Be Quiet, Please?*, a book I would have bought on the basis of the title alone, I was lucky enough to meet him a few years later and eventually to become his student at Syracuse University in the early eighties. Despite the existence of several thousand creative writing programs around the country, there is probably no good answer to the question of whether writing can be taught. Saying that Faulkner and Fitzgerald never got M.F.A.s is beside the point. Novelists and short story writers like to eat as much as anyone else, and tend to sniff out subsidies while they pursue their creative work. For writers in the twenties, the exchange rate was favorable in Paris, and in the thirties there was the WPA, and a gold rush of sorts in Hollywood. The universities have become the creative writers' WPA in recent years.

Carver was himself a product of the new system, having studied writing at the University of Iowa Writers' Workshop and at Stanford, and later earned a living teaching. It was something he did out of necessity, a role he was uncomfortable with. He did it to make a living, because it was easier than the other jobs he'd had — working at a sawmill and a hospital, working as a service station attendant, a janitor, a delivery boy, a textbook editor. Though grateful for genteel employment, he didn't really see why people who had a gift for writing should necessarily be able to teach. And he was very shy. The idea of facing a class made him nervous every time. On the days he had to teach he would get agitated, as if he himself were a student on the day of the final exam.

Like many writers in residence at universities, Ray was required to teach English courses in addition to creative writing courses. One was called Form and Theory of the Short Story, a title Ray inherited from the graduate English catalogue. His method in these classes was to assign a book of stories he liked each week, including contemporary and nineteenth-century authors as well as works in translation. We would read the books and discuss them for two hours. Flannery O'Connor, Chekhov, Ann Beattie, Maupassant, Frank O'Connor, John Cheever, Mary Robison, Turgenev, and more Chekhov. (He loved all the nineteenth-century Russians.) Class would begin with Ray saying something like, "Well, guys, how'd you like Eudora Welty?" He preferred listening to lecturing, but he would read his favorite

passages, talk about what he loved in the book he had chosen.
He dealt in specifics, stayed close to the text, and eventually there
would come a moment when the nervousness would lift off of
him as he spoke about writing that moved him.

One semester, a very earnest Ph.D. candidate found his way
into this class, composed mainly of writers. At that time, the English department, like many around the country, had become a
battleground between theorists and humanists, and post-struc-
turalism lay heavy upon the campus. After a few weeks of Carver's free-ranging and impressionistic approach to literature, the
young theorist registered a strong protest: "This class is called
Form and Theory of the Short Story but all we do is sit around
and talk about the books. Where's the form and the theory?"

Ray looked distressed. He nodded and pulled extra hard on
his cigarette. "Well, that's a good question," he said. After a long
pause, he said, "I guess I'd say that the point here is that we read
good books and discuss them. . . . And then you *form* your own
theory." Then he smiled.

As a teacher of creative writing, too, Carver had a light touch.
He did not consider it his job to discourage anyone. He said that
there was enough discouragement out there for anyone trying
against all odds to be a writer, and he clearly spoke from experience. Criticism, like fiction, was an act of empathy for Ray,
putting yourself in the other guy's shoes. He couldn't understand writers who wrote negative reviews and once chided me
for doing so. He believed fiction and poetry were fraternal enterprises. Among the very few people that Ray vocally disliked
were a poet who had refused to lend him $50 when his car broke
down in Salt Lake City, two critics who had attacked his own
work, and writers who had attacked any of his friends.

For a shy man, his gregarious generosity of spirit was remarkable. He kept up a correspondence with dozens of other writers,
students, and fans. He wrote letters of recommendation and en-
couragement, helped people get jobs and grants, editors and
agents, accompanied friends in need to their first AA meetings.

One day when I berated him for going easy on a student I
thought was turning out poor work, he told me a story: he had
recently been a judge in a prestigious fiction contest. The unan-
imous winner, whose work has since drawn much praise, turned

out to be a former student of his, probably the worst, least promising student he'd had in twenty years. "What if I had discouraged her?" he said.

His harshest critical formula was: "I think it's good you got that story behind you." Meaning, I guess, that one has to drive through some ugly country on the way to Parnassus. If Carver had had his way, classes and workshops would have been conducted entirely by students, but his approval was too highly valued for him to remain mute.

Once he sat through the reading of a long, strange story in his graduate writing workshop: as I recall, the story fleshed out two disparate characters, brought them together, followed their courtship and eventual marriage. After a series of false starts they decided to open a restaurant together, the preparations for which were described in great detail. On the day it opened a band of submachine-gun-toting terrorists burst in and killed everyone in the restaurant. End of story. After nearly everyone in the smoky seminar room had expressed dissatisfaction with this plot, we all turned to Ray. He was clearly at a loss. Finally he said softly, "Well, sometimes a story needs a submachine gun." This answer seemed to satisfy the author no less than those who felt the story in question had been efficiently put out of its misery.

My first semester, Ray somehow forgot to enter my grade for workshop. I pointed this out to him, and we went together to the English office to rectify the situation. "You did some real good work," he said, informing me that I would get an A. I was very pleased with myself, but perhaps a little less so when Ray opened the grade book and wrote an A next to my name underneath a solid column of identical grades. Everybody did good work, apparently. In workshop he approached every story with respect — treating each as if it were a living entity, a little sick, possibly, or lame, but something that could be nursed and trained to health.

Though Ray was always encouraging, he could be rigorous if he knew criticism was welcome. Fortunate students had their stories subjected to the same process he employed on his own numerous drafts. Manuscripts came back thoroughly ventilated with Carver deletions, substitutions, question marks, and chicken-scratch queries. I took one story back to him seven times; he must have spent fifteen or twenty hours on it. He was a meticulous, obsessive line editor. One on one, in his office, he almost became a tough guy, his voice gradually swelling with conviction.

Once we spent some ten or fifteen minutes debating my use of the word "earth." Carver felt it had to be "ground," and he felt it was worth the trouble of talking it through. That one exchange was invaluable; I think of it constantly when I'm working. Carver himself used the same example later in an essay he wrote that year, in discussing the influence of his mentor, John Gardner. "Ground is ground, he'd say, it means *ground*, dirt, that kind of stuff. But if you say 'earth,' that's something else, that word has other ramifications."

John Gardner, the novelist, was Ray's first writing teacher. They met at Chico State College in California in the 1960s. Ray said that all of his writing life he had felt Gardner looking over his shoulder when he wrote, approving or disapproving of certain words, phrases, and strategies. Calling fouls. He said a good writing teacher is something like a literary conscience, a friendly critical voice in your ear. I know what he meant. (I have one; it mumbles.)

After almost twenty years Carver had a reunion with his old teacher, who was living and teaching less than a hundred miles from Syracuse, in Binghamton, New York, and Gardner's approval of his work had meant a great deal to him. In the spring of 1982, I happened to stop by Ray's house a few minutes after he heard that Gardner had died in a motorcycle crash. Distraught, he couldn't sit still. We walked around the house and the back yard as he talked about Gardner.

"Back then I didn't even know what a writer looked like," Ray said. "John looked like a writer. He had that hair, and he used to wear this thing that was like a cape. I tried to copy the way he walked. He used to let me work in his office because I didn't have a quiet place to work. I'd go go through his files and steal the titles of his stories, use them on my stories."

So he must have understood when we all shamelessly cribbed from him, we students at Syracuse, and Iowa and Stanford and all the other writing workshops in the country where almost everyone seemed to be writing and publishing stories with Raymond Carver titles like "Do You Mind If I Smoke?" or "How About This, Honey?" He certainly didn't want clones. But he knew that imitation was part of finding your own voice.

I encountered Carver near the beginning of what he liked to call his "second life," after he had quit drinking. I heard stories about the bad old Ray, stories he liked to tell on himself. When I met him I thought of writers as luminous madmen who drank too much and drove too fast and scattered brilliant pages along their doomed trajectories. Maybe at one time he did, too. In his essay "Fires," he says, "I understood writers to be people who didn't spend their Saturdays at the laundromat." Would Hemingway be caught dead doing laundry? No, but William Carlos Williams would. Ditto Carver's beloved Chekhov. In the classroom and on the page, Carver somehow delivered the tonic news that there was laundry in the kingdom of letters.

Not that, by this time, Ray was spending much time at the laundromat, life having been good to him toward the end in a way for which he seemed constantly to be grateful. But hearing the typewriter of one of the masters of American prose clacking just up the street, while a neighbor raked leaves and some kids threw a Frisbee as the dogs went on with their doggy life — this was a lesson in itself for me. Whatever dark mysteries lurk at the heart of the writing process, he insisted on a single trade secret: that you had to survive, find some quiet, and work hard every day. And seeing him for coffee, or watching a ball game or a dumb movie with him, put into perspective certain dangerous myths about the writing life that he preferred not to lecture on — although he sometimes would, if he thought it might help. When we first became acquainted, in New York, he felt obliged to advise me, in a series of wonderful letters, and a year later I moved upstate to become his student.

Reading the dialogues of Plato, one eventually realizes that Socrates' self-deprecation is something of a ploy. Ray's humility, however, was profound and unself-conscious and one of the most astonishing things about him. When he asked a student, "What do you think?" he clearly wanted to know. This seemed a rare and inspiring didactic stance. His own opinions were expressed with such caution that you knew how carefully they had been measured.

For someone who claimed he didn't love to teach, he made a great deal of difference to a great many students. He certainly changed my life irrevocably and I have heard others say the same thing.

I'm still leaning forward with my head cocked to one side, straining to hear his voice.

JAMES A. McPHERSON

To Blacks and Jews: Hab Rachmones

FROM TIKKUN

ABOUT 1971, Bernard Malamud sent me a manuscript of a novel called *The Tenants.* Malamud had some reservations about the book. Specifically, he was anxious over how the antagonism between Harry Lesser, a Jewish writer, and Willie Spear, a Black writer, would be read. We communicated about the issue. On the surface, Malamud was worried over whether he had done justice to Willie Spear's Black idiom; but beneath the surface, during our exchange of letters, he was deeply concerned about the tensions that were then developing between Black intellectuals and Jewish intellectuals. I was living in Berkeley at the time, three thousand miles away from the fragmentation of the old civil rights coalition, the mounting battle over affirmative action, and most of the other incidents that would contribute to the present division between the Jewish and Black communities.

I was trying very hard to become a writer. As a favor to Malamud, I rewrote certain sections of the novel, distinguished Willie Spear's idiom from Harry Lesser's, and suggested several new scenes. I believed then that the individual human heart was of paramount importance, and I could not understand why Malamud had chosen to end his novel with Levenspiel, the Jewish slumlord who owned the condemned building in which the two antagonists lived, pleading with them *"Hab rachmones"* ("Have mercy"). Or why Levenspiel begs for mercy 115 times. Like Isaac Babel, I felt that a well-placed period was much more effective

than an extravagance of emotion. Malamud sent me an auto-
graphed copy of the book as soon as it was printed. Rereading
the book eighteen years later, I now see that, even after the 115th
plea for mercy by Levenspiel, there is no period and there is no
peace.

Well-publicized events over the past two decades have made it
obvious that Blacks and Jews have never been the fast friends
we were alleged to be. The best that can be said is that, at least
since the earliest decades of this century, certain spiritual elites
in the Jewish community and certain spiritual elites in the Black
community have found it mutually advantageous to join forces
to fight specific obstacles that block the advancement of both
groups: lynchings, restrictive housing covenants, segregation in
schools, and corporate expressions of European racism that target both groups. During the best of times, the masses of each
group were influenced by the moral leadership of the elites. From
my reading of the writers of the extreme right wing, in whose
works one can always find the truest possible expression of white
racist sentiment, I know that the Black and Jewish peoples have
historically been treated as "special cases." The most sophisticated of these writers tend to examine the two groups as "problems" in Western culture. Both share incomplete status. Both
are legally included in Western society, but for two quite different reasons each has not been fused into the "race."

Until fairly recently, Jews were considered a "sect-nation," a
group of people living within Western territorial states and committed to a specific religious identity. This extraterritorial status
allowed Jews to convert and become members of a confessional
community, as was often the case in Europe, or to drop any specific religious identification and become "white," as has often been
the case in the United States.

This second Jewish option is related, in very complex ways, to
the special status of Black Americans and thus to the core of the
present Black–Jewish problem. The romantic illusions of Black
nationalism aside, Black Americans have not been Africans since
the eighteenth century. Systematic efforts were made to strip
Black slaves of all vestiges of the African cultures from which
they came. The incorporation of European bloodlines, from the
first generations onward, gave the slaves immunities to the same

diseases, brought by Europeans to the Americas, that nearly dec-
imated America's indigenous peoples. The slave ancestors of today's thirty or so million Black Americans took their ideals from
the sacred documents of American life, their secular values from
whatever was current, and their deepest mythologies from the
Jews of the Old Testament. They were a self-created people,
having very little to look back on. The one thing they could not
acquire was the institutional protection, or status, that comes in
this country from being classified as "white." And since from its
very foundation the United States has employed color as a negative factor in matters of social mobility, we Black Americans
have always experienced tremendous difficulties in our attempts
to achieve the full rewards of American life. The structure of
white supremacy is very subtle and complex, but the most obvious thing that can be said about it is that it "enlists" psychologically those whites who view their status as dependent on it. It
has the effect of encouraging otherwise decent people to adopt
the psychological habits of policemen or prison guards.

Given this complex historical and cultural reality, most Black
Americans, no matter how wealthy, refined, or "integrated," have
never been able to achieve the mobility and security available to
whites. Jewish Americans, by contrast, have this option, whether
or not they choose to exercise it. Blacks recognize this fact, and
this recognition is the basis of some of the extreme tension that
now exists between the two groups. While Jews insist that they
be addressed and treated as part of a religious community, most
Black Americans tend to view them as white. When Jews insist
that Jewish sensitivities and concerns be recognized, Black
Americans have great difficulty separating these concerns from
the concerns of the corporate white community.

And yet, despite the radically different positions of the two
groups, there has been a history of alliances. Perhaps it is best to
say that mutual self-interest has defined the interaction between
Blacks and Jews for most of this century. In her little-known
study *In the Almost Promised Land,* Hasia R. Diner has traced the
meeting and mutual assessment of the two peoples as presented
in the Yiddish press to the two million Jewish immigrants from
Eastern Europe and Russia who came to the United States during the first four decades of this century. Community papers like

the *Tageblatt* and the *Forward* forged a socialistic language that brought together Jewish immigrants from different backgrounds, that helped them acculturate, and that advised them about the obstacles and opportunities they would find in America. These papers gave more attention to Black American life than to any other non-Jewish concern. They focused on Black marriage and family, on Black crime, on Black "trickery and deception," and on Black education, entertainment, and achievement. They linked Black suffering to Jewish suffering. Diner writes:

> The Yiddish papers sensed that a special relationship existed between blacks and Jews and because of this the press believed that the two groups were captivated by each other. . . . Jews believed that a history of suffering had predisposed Jews toward understanding the problems of blacks. ("Because we have suffered we treat kindly and sympathetically and humanly all the oppressed of every nation.")

The central theme was that Black people were America's Jews. Historical parallels were emphasized: the Black Exodus from the South was compared to the Jewish Exodus from Egypt and to the Jewish migration from Russia and Germany.

But there were much more practical reasons why the two groups — one called "white," the other defined by caste; one geared to scholarship and study, the other barely literate; one upwardly mobile, the other in constant struggle merely to survive — managed to find common ground during the first four decades of this century. There was the desperate Black need for financial, legal, and moral support in the fight against racism, lynchings, and exclusion from the institutions of American life. There was the Jewish perception that many of the problems of exclusion faced by Black people were also faced by Jews. Diner writes:

> Black Americans needed champions in a hostile society. Jewish Americans, on the other hand, wanted a meaningful role so as to prove themselves to an inhospitable [society]. . . . Thus, American Jewish leaders involved in a quest for a meaningful identity and comfortable role in American society found that one way to fulfill that search was to serve as the intermediaries between blacks and whites.

The Jewish magazines defined a mission for Jews to interpret the black world to white Americans and to speak for blacks and champion their cause.

Diner is describing the "interstitial" role, traditionally assumed by Jewish shopkeepers and landlords in Black communities, being extended into the moral sphere. Given the radical imbalance of potential power that existed between the two groups, however, such a coalition was fated to fail once American Jews had achieved their own goals.

For mutually self-interested reasons, I believe, the two groups began a parting of the ways just after the Six Day War of 1967. The rush of rationalizations on both sides — Jewish accusations of Black anti-Semitism, Black Nationalist accusations of Jewish paternalism and subversion of Black American goals — helped to obscure very painful realities that had much more to do with the broader political concerns of both groups, as they were beginning to be dramatized in the international arena, than with the domestic issues so widely publicized. Within the Black American community, even before the killing of Martin King, there arose a nationalistic identification with the emerging societies of newly liberated Africa. In the rush to identify with small pieces of evidence of Black freedom *anywhere* in the world, many Black Americans began to embrace ideologies and traditions that were alien to the traditions that had been developed, through painful struggle, by their earliest ancestors on American soil.

A large part of this romantic identification with Africa resulted from simple frustration: the realization that the moral appeal advocated by Martin King had authority only within those southern white communities where the remnants of Christian tradition were still respected. The limitations of the old civil rights appeal became apparent when King was stoned while attempting to march in Cicero, Illinois, in 1966. We Black Americans discovered that many ethnic Americans, not just southern whites, did not care for us. The retrenchment that resulted, promoted by the media as Black Nationalism, provided convenient excuses for many groups to begin severing ties with Black Americans. Expressions of nationalism not only alienated many well-meaning whites; they had the effect of discounting the Black American tradition of principled struggle that had produced the great leaders in the Black American community. To any perceptive listener, most of the nationalistic rhetoric had the shrillness of despair.

For the Jewish community, victory in the Six Day War of 1967 caused the beginning of a much more complex reassessment of the Jewish situation, one based on some of the same spiritual motivations as were the defeats suffered by Black Americans toward the end of the 1960s. The Israeli victory in 1967 was a *reassertion* of the nationhood of the Jewish people. But, like the founding of Israel in 1948, this reassertion raised unresolved contradictions. My reading teaches me that, until the twentieth century, Zion to most Jews was not a tangible, earthly hope, but a mystical symbol of the divine deliverance of the Jewish nation. Zion was a heavenly city that did not yet exist. It was to be planted on earth by the Messiah on the Day of Judgment, when historical time would come to an end. But the Jewish experience in Europe seems to have transformed the dream of a heavenly city into an institution in the practical world. This tension has turned the idea of the Jews as a nation existing as the community of the faithful into the idea of Israel as a Western territorial sovereign. Concerned for its survival, Israel has turned expansionist; but the price it has paid has been the erosion of its ethical identity. It is said that the world expects more from the Jews than from any other people. This deeply frustrating misconception, I believe, results from the dual premise (religious and political) of the State of Israel. I also believe that American Jews are extraordinarily frustrated when they are unable to make non-Jews understand how sensitive Jews are to uninformed criticism after six thousand years of relentless persecution.

The majority of Black Americans are unaware of the complexity of the meaning of Israel to American Jews. But, ironically, Afro-Zionists have as intense an emotional identification with Africa and with the Third World as American Jews have with Israel. Doubly ironic, this same intensity of identification with a "Motherland" seems rooted in the mythologies common to both groups. In this special sense — in the spiritual sense implied by "Zion" and "Diaspora" and "Promised Land" — Black Americans *are* America's Jews. But given the isolation of Black Americans from any meaningful association with Africa, extensions of the mythology would be futile. We have no distant homeland preparing an ingathering. For better or worse, Black Americans are *Americans*. Our special problems must be confronted and solved here, where they began. They cannot be solved in the international arena, in competition with Jews.

Related to the problem of competing mythologies is a recent international trend that, if not understood in terms of its domestic implications, will deepen the already complex crisis between Blacks and Jews. The period of European hegemony, mounted in the fifteenth century and consolidated in the nineteenth, imposed on millions of non-European people values and institutions not indigenous to their cultural traditions. One of these institutions was the nation-state. Since the end of World War II, the various wars of independence in India, Asia, Africa, and elsewhere have exposed the fact that a European invention does not always meet the mythological, linguistic, and cultural needs of different ethnic groups competing within artificial "territorial states." We sometimes forget that it took many centuries for Europeans to evolve political forms suited to their own habits. Since the 1950s, colonized people have begun to assert their own cultural needs. The new word coined to define this process is "devolutionism." While devolutionism is currently a Third World phenomenon, two of the most prominent groups within the territorial United States, because of their unique origins, can be easily drawn into this struggle: Black Americans, because of our African origins and our sympathy for the liberation struggle currently taking place in South Africa; and Jews, because of their intense identification with Israel. Given the extent of Israeli involvement in South Africa, and given the sympathy many Black Americans feel for Black South Africans and Palestinians, it is only predictable that some Black Americans would link the two struggles. My deepest fear is that the dynamics of American racism will force Black Americans into a deeper identification with the Palestinians, thus incorporating into an already tense domestic situation an additional international dimension we just do not need. The resulting polarization may well cause chaos for a great many people, Blacks and Jews included.

I have no solutions to offer beyond my feeling that we should begin talking with each other again.

I remember walking the streets of Chicago back in 1972 and 1973, gathering information for an article on Jewish slumlords who had "turned" white neighborhoods and then sold these homes at inflated prices to poor Black people, recent migrants from the South, on installment purchase contracts. I remember talking with Rabbi Robert Marx, who sided with the buyers against the Jewish sellers; with Gordon Sherman, a businessman who was deeply disturbed by the problem; with Marshall Patner, a lawyer in Hyde Park; and with other Jewish lawyers who had volunteered to work with the buyers in an attempt to correct the injustice. I spent most of a Guggenheim Fellowship financing my trips to Chicago. I gave the money I earned from the article to the organization created by the buyers. And although the legal case that was brought against the sellers was eventually lost in federal district court, I think that all the people involved in the effort to achieve some kind of justice found the experience very rewarding. I remember interviewing poor Black people, the victims, who did not see the sellers as Jews but as whites. I remember interviewing Mrs. Lucille Johnson, an elderly Black woman who seemed to be the spiritual center of the entire effort. Her influence could get smart Jewish and Irish lawyers to do the right thing, as opposed to the legal thing. I asked her about the source of her strength. I still remember her reply:

> The bad part of the thing is that we just don't have what we need in our lives to go out and do something, white or black. We just don't have *love*. . . . But this ain't no situation to get hung up on color; getting hung up on some of God's love will bail us out. I think of "Love one another" and the Commandments. If we love the Lord our God with all our hearts and minds, and love our neighbors as ourselves, we done covered them Commandments. And "Let not your heart be troubled; he that believes in God believes also in me."

I think there was, a generation or two ago, a group of stronger and wiser Black and Jewish people. I think they were more firmly grounded in the lived mythology of the Hebrew Bible. I think that, because of this grounding, they were, in certain spiritual dimensions, almost one people. They were spiritual elites. Later generations have opted for more mundane values and the rewards these values offer. Arthur Hertzberg told me, "Anti-Semitism is the way Blacks join the majority. Racism is the way Jews join the majority. Individuals in both groups have the capacity to package themselves in order to make it in terms the white majority can understand."

Certain consequences of the Black–Jewish alliance cannot be overlooked. The spiritual elites within both groups recognized, out of common memories of oppression and suffering, that the only true refuge a person in pain has is within another person's heart. These spiritual elites had the moral courage to allow their hearts to become swinging doors. For at least six decades these elites contributed to the soul of American democracy. Their influence animated the country, gave it a sense of moral purpose it had not known since the Civil War. The coalition they called into being helped to redefine the direction of the American experience and kept it moving toward transcendent goals. With the fragmentation of that coalition, and with the current divisions among its principals, we have fallen into stasis, if not into decadence. Bernard Malamud's Levenspiel the landlord would like to be rid of his two troublesome tenants. I have no solutions to offer. But, eighteen years later, I want to say with Malamud: Mercy, Mercy, Mercy, Mercy, Mercy, Mercy, Mercy, Mercy, Mercy, Mercy

I want to keep saying it to all my friends, and to all my students, until we are strong enough to put a period to this thing.

LEONARD MICHAELS

I'm Having Trouble
with My Relationship

FROM THE THREEPENNY REVIEW

THE WORD "relationship" appears for the first time in the 1743
edition of *The Dunciad*. Pope uses it in a way both funny and
cruel to identify his enemy Cibber with the insane. Cibber is said
to be related to famous heads, sculpted by his father, represent-
ing despondent and raving madness. The heads were affixed to
the front of Bedlam. Pope calls them Cibber's "brothers." Cibber
and the heads have the same father; they stand in a blood, brains,
"brazen," family "Relationship." The word effects a contemp-
tuous distance between Pope and Cibber, and makes Cibber one
with the sculpted heads. Funny in its concreteness; cruel in the
play of implications; luminous in genius. Before Pope, "relationship" may have been part of daily talk, but until he uses it nothing exists in this way, bearing the lineaments of his mind, the
cultural affluence of his self and time.

After 1743, "relationship" appears with increasing frequency,
with no joke intended, and it not only survives objections to its
redundant structure (two abstract suffixes), but, in the 1940s, it
begins to intrude into areas of thought and feeling where it never
belonged, gathering a huge constituency of uncritical users and
displacing words that once seemed more appropriate, precise,
and pleasing. Among them are "romance," "affair," "lover,"
"beau," "fellow," "girl," "boyfriend," "girlfriend," "steady date,"
etc. People now find these words more or less quaint or embar-
rassingly innocent. They use "relationship" to mean any of them

when talking about the romantic-sexual connection between a man and a woman or man, or woman and woman. In this liberal respect, Pope's use of the word is uncannily reborn.

People say, "I'm having trouble with my relationship," as though the trouble were not with Penelope or Max but with an object, like a BMW, a sort of container or psychological condition into which they enter and relate. By displacing the old words for romantic love, "relationship" indicates a new caution where human experience is extremely intense and ephemeral, or a distrust of concrete words in which our happiness might suffer any idea of limit, or perhaps a distrust of words in general. It could be argued that "relationship" is better than the old words, since it makes abstraction palpable, generously distributing it among four syllables; a feeling of love in the actions of sex; or philosophy in desire; and, as love is various, so are the syllables of "relationship," not one of them repeating another. Though intended to restrict reference to a single person, the word has the faint effect of suggesting many persons. In its palpableness, syllables bob like Bedlam heads. Strange images of mind.

People also say, "I can relate to that," where no person is intended or essentially involved, just an idea of some kind of experience. The expression is innocuous, and yet it is reminiscent of psychopathic thinking. In the same modern spirit, people say "mothering" to mean no particular person is essential to the action; that is, "mothering" does not flow from a mother as poetry flows only from a poet, or life from the sun god. "Fathering" has a sexual charge different from "mothering" and cannot be used like this. We talk, then, of "parenting." The political necessity for "mothering" and "parenting," which justifies the words, doesn't make them less grotesque. But this sort of judgment is precious. The antinomies of our culture cling to each other like breeders in a slow, violent divorce, and aesthetic considerations are irrelevant. We have no use, in our thinking, for the determining power of essences, or depths of soul, or ideas of value that inhere, like juice in grapes, in the quiddity of people. Mom is not by any means an inevitable source of love. She might well be a twisted bitch, and many vile creeps are Dad. The words no longer pack honorific content. Commitments built into blood are honored only by the Mafia. Philip Larkin writes: "They fuck you up, your mum and dad."

What conservatives, feminists, Marxists, and other contemporary thinkers have in common is the idea that value has fled the human particular. Larkin might agree. He might even say that, long ago, value went off someplace to vomit and it has not returned. If this is true, we have been abandoned to the allure of nonspecific possibility, or the thrill of infinite novelty. A lexical whorehouse shines in the darkness of the modern mind. (The "new," says Roland Barthes, is itself a value. No big surprise to the automobile industry.) To descend again to my theme: your hot lover has cooled into your "relationship," which in another aspect you have with your grocer or your cat.

This large disposition in our thinking and speaking arises from impersonal democratic passions, the last refuge of the supreme good. As Simone Weil says, thinking of God, "Only the impersonal is sacred." But it is a little crazy that "relationship," an uppity version of "relation," should be enormously privileged, lumbering across the landscape of English with prefix and two suffixes streaming from a tiny head of substance like ghostly remains of its Latin roots and Germanic ending (*referre*, maybe *latus*, and *ship*).

To have survived the guns of our grammarians and displaced more pleasant words in the natural history of English, it must answer to an exceptionally strong need. The other words may seem impossibly quaint, but it isn't only the sophistication of "relationship" that is needed. It is the whole word, including the four-syllable sound, which is a body stumbling downstairs, the last two — "shunship" — the flap of a shoe's loose sole, or loose lips and gossip. In fact, "relationship" flourished in the talky, psychological climate of the modern century as we carried it from the offices of our shrinks and, like a forgotten umbrella, left "romance" behind.

Notice well how the syllabic tumble of "relationship" makes a sound like sheer talk, or talking about something, emphasis on "about," not "something." Exactly here, in the eternally mysterious relation of sound and sense, "relationship" confers the dignity of thought upon referential promiscuity, its objects graced with interestingness, a sound basis in indeterminacy for interminable talk.

Philosophers might complain that it is a word without much "cash value." Heidegger, on the other hand, might take it as an expression of "the groundlessness and nullity of inauthentic everydayness." He means the nonstop impetuous trivialization, in "idle talk," of *Dasein,* by which he means anything real, by which he means that thing of which anyone who "is genuinely 'on the scent of' [it] will not speak." Certainly, then, in regard to "relationship," Heidegger might say:

> Being-with-one-another in the "they" is by no means an indifferent side-by-sideness in which everything has been settled, but rather an intent, ambiguous watching of another, a secret and reciprocal listening-in. Under the mask of "for-one-another," an "against-one-another" is in play.

By which he means, "I'm having trouble with my relationship."

"The secret king of thought," forerunner of deconstructionism, who spoke of the Nazis as "manufacturing corpses," Heidegger had the deepest grasp of what is authentic and inauthentic in human relations. (His literary descendants — as too often noted — manufacture "texts" out of "works.") But to feel what has been lost in thought, consider this text from a letter by Kafka to Milena, the woman he loved:

> Today I saw a map of Vienna. For an instant it seemed incomprehensible to me that they had built such a big city when you need only one room.

The incomprehensible city is "relationship," or what you have with everyone in the abstract and lonely vastness of our social reality. The room, all one needs, is romance, love, passionate intimacy, the unsophisticated irrational thing you have with someone; or what has long been considered a form of madness, if not the universal demonic of contemporary vision.

The city is also "relationship" in the movie *Last Tango in Paris,* where Marlon Brando texts to his lover, "Everything outside this room is bullshit." He makes the same point as Kafka, but the subtext of the movie is that, in our lust for relationship, we have shoveled all the bullshit into the room. This lust, which is basically for power, or control, or the illusion of possessing something that isn't there — *Dasein,* needless to say, but what the hell — makes us prefer Theory to novels, poems, and people, or flat surfaces in architecture to the various elaborations of material that once engaged our hearts.

Native speakers of Swedish say *förhållande* is close in meaning to "relationship," which suggests the Swedes are in the same boat as the English-speakers, especially since other native speakers say it is difficult to find a close equivalent to "relationship" in other European languages or in Asian languages. "Relationship," then, shouldn't be taken as a mere tendency of English where any noun might lust for sublimity in the abstract extension of itself. It isn't just another polysyllabic fascist on the left or right, but rather something that bespeaks a deeper tendency, in the soul, like what one sees in Andy Warhol's disquieting portraits of Marilyn Monroe and Mao, their faces repeating and vanishing into the static quality of their "look."

"Relationship" has a similarly reductive force, ultimately even an air of death worship. The "aura of death," says Georges Bataille, "is what denotes passion." It also denotes its absence, one might suppose, but this old notion isn't likely to seize our imagination, which is why "relationship" has slipped unnoticed into astounding prominence and ubiquitous banality. The word is no less common than death, and it is no less pathetically private; and we use it much as though, after consigning ourselves to the grave, we had lingered to love the undertaker, having had no such exquisitely personal attention before, nothing so convincing that one is.

MICHAEL POLLAN

Why Mow? The Case Against Lawns

FROM THE NEW YORK TIMES MAGAZINE

ANYONE NEW to the experience of owning a lawn, as I am, soon figures out that there is more at stake here than a patch of grass. A lawn immediately establishes a certain relationship with one's neighbors and, by extension, the larger American landscape. Mowing the lawn, I realized the first time I gazed into my neighbor's yard and imagined him gazing back into mine, is a civic responsibility.

For no lawn is an island, at least in America. Starting at my front stoop, this scruffy green carpet tumbles down a hill and leaps across a one-lane road into my neighbor's yard. From there it skips over some wooded patches and stone walls before finding its way across a dozen other unfenced properties that lead down into the Housatonic Valley, there to begin its march south to the metropolitan area. Once below Danbury, the lawn — now purged of weeds and meticulously coiffed — races up and down the suburban lanes, heedless of property lines. It then heads west, crossing the New York border; moving now at a more stately pace, it strolls beneath the maples of Scarsdale, unfurls across a dozen golf courses, and wraps itself around the pale blue pools of Bronxville before pressing on toward the Hudson. New Jersey next is covered, an emerald postage stamp laid down front and back of ten thousand split levels, before the broadening green river divides in two.

One tributary pushes south, and does not pause until it has

colonized the thin, sandy soils of Florida. The other dilates and spreads west, easily overtaking the Midwest's vast grid before running up against the inhospitable western states. But neither flinty soil nor obdurate climate will impede the lawn's march to the Pacific: it vaults the Rockies and, abetted by a monumental irrigation network, proceeds to green great stretches of western desert.

Nowhere in the world are lawns as prized as in America. In little more than a century, we've rolled a green mantle of grass across the continent, with scarcely a thought to the local conditions or expense. America has more than fifty thousand square *miles* of lawn under cultivation, on which we spend an estimated $30 billion a year — this according to the Lawn Institute, a Pleasant Hill, Tennessee, outfit devoted to publicizing the benefits of turf to Americans (surely a case of preaching to the converted).

Like the interstate highway system, like fast-food chains, like television, the lawn has served to unify the American landscape; it is what makes the suburbs of Cleveland and Tucson, the streets of Eugene and Tampa, look more alike than not. According to Ann Leighton, the late historian of gardens, America has made essentially one important contribution to world garden design: the custom of "uniting the front lawns of however many houses there may be on both sides of a street to present an untroubled aspect of expansive green to the passer-by." France has its formal, geometric gardens, England its picturesque parks, and America this unbounded democratic river of manicured lawn along which we array our houses.

It is not easy to stand in the way of such a powerful current. Since we have traditionally eschewed fences and hedges in America (looking on these as Old World vestiges), the suburban vista can be marred by the negligence — or dissent — of a single property owner. This is why lawn care is regarded as such an important civic responsibility in the suburbs, and why the majority will not tolerate the laggard. I learned this at an early age, growing up in a cookie-cutter subdivision in Farmingdale, Long Island.

My father, you see, was a lawn dissident. Whether owing to laziness or contempt for his neighbors I was never sure, but he could not see much point in cranking up the Toro more than once a month or so. The grass on our quarter-acre plot towered over the crew-cut lawns on either side of us and soon disturbed the peace of the entire neighborhood.

That subtle yet unmistakable frontier, where the closely shaved lawn rubs up against a shaggy one, is a scar on the face of suburbia, an intolerable hint of trouble in paradise. The scar shows up in *The Great Gatsby,* when Nick Carraway rents the house next to Gatsby's and fails to maintain his lawn according to West Egg standards. The rift between the two lawns so troubles Gatsby that he dispatches his gardener to mow Nick's grass and thereby erase it.

Our neighbors in Farmingdale displayed somewhat less class. "Lawn mower on the fritz?" they'd ask. "Want to borrow mine?" But the more heavily they leaned on my father, the more recalcitrant he became, until one summer — probably 1959, or 1960 — he let the lawn go altogether. The grass plants grew tall enough to flower and set seed; the lawn rippled in the breeze like a flag. There was beauty here, I'm sure, but it was not visible in this context. Stuck in the middle of a row of tract houses on Long Island, our lawn said *turpitude* rather than *meadow*, even though strictly speaking that is what it had become.

That summer I felt the hot breath of the majority's tyranny for the first time. No one said anything now, but you could hear it all the same: *Mow your lawn or get out.* Certain neighbors let it be known to my parents that I was not to play with their children. Cars would slow down as they drove by. Probably some of the drivers were merely curious: they saw the unmowed lawn and wondered if someone had left in a hurry, or perhaps died. But others drove by in a manner that was unmistakably expressive, slowing down as they drew near and then hitting the gas angrily as they passed — pithy driving, the sort of move that is second nature to a Klansman.

We got the message by other media, too. Our next-door neighbor, a mild engineer who was my father's last remaining friend in the development, was charged with the unpleasant task of conveying the sense of the community to my father. It was early on a summer evening that he came to deliver his message. I don't remember it all (I was only four or five at the time), but

I can imagine him taking a highball glass from my mother, squeaking out what he had been told to say about the threat to property values, and then waiting for my father — who next to him was a bear — to respond.

My father's reply could not have been more eloquent. Without a word he strode out to the garage and cranked up the rusty old Toro for the first time since fall; it's a miracle the thing started. He pushed it out to the curb and then started back across the lawn to the house, but not in a straight line: he swerved right, then left, then right again. He had cut an *S* in the high grass. Then he made an *M*, and finally a *P*. These are his initials, and as soon as he finished writing them he wheeled the lawn mower back to the garage, never to start it up again.

I wasn't prepared to take such a hard line on my new lawn, at least not right off. So I bought a lawn mower, a Toro, and started mowing. Four hours every Saturday. At first I tried for a kind of Zen approach, clearing my mind of everything but the task at hand, immersing myself in the lawn-mowing here-and-now. I liked the idea that my weekly sessions with the grass would acquaint me with the minutest details of my yard. I soon knew by heart the exact location of every stump and stone, the tunnel route of each resident mole, the address of every anthill. I noticed that where rain collected white clover flourished, that it was on the drier rises that crabgrass thrived. After a few weekends I had a map of the lawn in my head as precise and comprehensive as the mental map one has of the back of one's hand.

The finished product pleased me too, the fine scent and the sense of order restored that a new-cut lawn exhales. My house abuts woods on two sides, and mowing the lawn is, in both a real and metaphorical sense, how I keep the forest at bay and preserve my place in this landscape. Much as we've come to distrust it, the urge to dominate nature is a deeply human one, and lawn mowing answers to it. I thought of the lawn mower as civilization's knife and my lawn as the hospitable plane it carved out of the wilderness. My lawn was a part of nature made fit for human habitation.

So perhaps the allure of lawns is in the genes. The sociobiologists think so: they've gone so far as to propose a "Savanna

Syndrome" to explain our fondness for grass. Encoded in our DNA is a preference for an open grassy landscape resembling the short-grass savannas of Africa on which we evolved and spent our first few million years. This is said to explain why we have remade the wooded landscapes of Europe and North America in the image of East Africa.

Such theories go some way toward explaining the widespread appeal of grass, but they don't really account for the American Lawn. They don't, for instance, account for the keen interest Jay Gatsby takes in Nick Carraway's lawn, or the scandal my father's lawn sparked in Farmingdale. Or the fact that, in America, we have taken down our fences and hedges in order to combine our lawns. And they don't even begin to account for the unmistakable odor of virtue that hovers in this country over a scrupulously maintained lawn.

If any individual can be said to have invented the American lawn, it is Frederick Law Olmsted. In 1868, he received a commission to design Riverside, outside Chicago, one of the first planned suburban communities in America. Olmsted's design stipulated that each house be set back thirty feet from the road and it proscribed walls. He was reacting against the "high deadwalls" of England, which he felt made a row of homes there seem "as of a series of private madhouses." In Riverside, each owner would maintain one or two trees and a lawn that would flow seamlessly into his neighbors', creating the impression that all lived together in a single park.

Olmsted was part of a generation of American landscape designer-reformers who set out at midcentury to beautify the American landscape. That it needed beautification may seem surprising to us today, assuming as we do that the history of the landscape is a story of decline, but few at the time thought otherwise. William Cobbett, visiting from England, was struck at the "out-of-door slovenliness" of American homesteads. Each farmer, he wrote, was content with his "shell of boards, while all around him is as barren as the sea beach . . . though there is no English shrub, or flower, which will not grow and flourish here."

The land looked as if it had been shaped and cleared in a great hurry — as indeed it had: the landscape largely denuded of trees, makeshift fences outlining badly plowed fields, tree stumps everywhere one looked. As Cobbett and many other nineteenth-century visitors noted, hardly anyone practiced ornamental gardening; the typical yard was "landscaped" in the style southerners would come to call "white trash" — a few chickens, some busted farm equipment, mud and weeds, an unkempt patch of vegetables.

This might do for farmers, but for the growing number of middle-class city people moving to the "borderland" in the years following the Civil War, something more respectable was called for. In 1870, Frank J. Scott, seeking to make Olmsted's ideas accessible to the middle class, published the first volume ever devoted to "suburban home embellishment": *The Art of Beautifying Suburban Home Grounds,* a book that probably did more than any other to determine the look of the suburban landscape in America. Like so many reformers of his time, Scott was nothing if not sure of himself: "A smooth, closely shaven surface of grass is by far the most essential element of beauty on the grounds of a suburban house."

Americans like Olmsted and Scott did not invent the lawn; lawns had been popular in England since Tudor times. But in England, lawns were usually found only on estates; the Americans democratized them, cutting the vast manorial greenswards into quarter-acre slices everyone could afford. Also, the English never considered the lawn an end in itself: it served as a setting for lawn games and as a backdrop for flower beds and trees. Scott subordinated all other elements of the landscape to the lawn; flowers were permissible, but only on the periphery of the grass: "Let your lawn be your home's velvet robe, and your flowers its not too promiscuous decoration.

But Scott's most radical departure from Old World practice was to dwell on the individual's responsibility to his neighbors. "It is unchristian," he declared, "to hedge from the sight of others the beauties of nature which it has been our good fortune to create or secure." One's lawn, Scott held, should contribute to the collective landscape. "The beauty obtained by throwing front grounds open together, is of that excellent quality which enriches all who take part in the exchange, and makes no man poorer." Like Olmsted before him, Scott sought to elevate an unassuming patch of turfgrass into an institution of democracy.

With our open-faced front lawns we declare our like-mindedness to our neighbors — and our distance from the English, who surround their yards with "inhospitable brick wall, topped with broken bottles," to thwart the envious gaze of the lower orders. The American lawn is an egalitarian conceit, implying that there is no reason to hide behind fence or hedge since we all occupy the same middle class. We are all property owners here, the lawn announces, and that suggests its other purpose: to provide a suitably grand stage for the proud display of one's own house. Noting that our yards were organized "to capture the admiration of the street," one garden writer in 1921 attributed the popularity of open lawns to our "infantile instinct to cry 'hello!' to the passer-by, to lift up our possessions to his gaze."

Of course the democratic front yard has its darker, more coercive side, as my family learned in Farmingdale. In specifying the "plain style" of an unembellished lawn for American front yards, the midcentury designer-reformers were, like Puritan ministers, laying down rigid conventions governing our relationship to the land, our observance of which would henceforth be taken as an index of our character. And just as the Puritans would not tolerate any individual who sought to establish his or her own back-channel relationship with the divinity, the members of the suburban utopia do not tolerate the homeowner who establishes a relationship with the land that is not mediated by the group's conventions.

The parallel is not as farfetched as it might sound, when you recall that nature in America has often been regarded as divine. Think of nature as Spirit, the collective suburban lawn as the Church, and lawn mowing as a kind of sacrament. You begin to see why ornamental gardening would take so long to catch on in America, and why my father might seem an antinomian in the eyes of his neighbors. Like Hester Prynne, he claimed not to need their consecration for his actions; perhaps his initials in the front lawn were a kind of Emerald Letter.

Possibly because it is this common land, rather than race or tribe, that makes us all Americans, we have developed a deep distrust of individualistic approaches to the landscape. The land is too important to our identity as Americans to simply allow everyone to have his own way with it. And once we decide that the land should serve as a vehicle of consensus, rather than an arena of self-expression, the American lawn — collective, national, ritualized, and plain — begins to look inevitable.

After my first season of lawn mowing, the Zen approach began to wear thin. I had taken up flower and vegetable gardening, and soon came to resent the four hours that my lawn demanded of me each week. I tired of the endless circuit, pushing the howling mower back and forth across the vast page of my yard, recopying the same green sentences over and over: "I am a conscientious homeowner. I share your middle-class values." Lawn care was gardening aimed at capturing "the admiration of the street," a ritual of consensus I did not have my heart in. I began to entertain idle fantasies of rebellion: Why couldn't I plant a hedge along the road, remove my property from the national stream of greensward and do something else with it?

The third spring I planted fruit trees in the front lawn, apple, peach, cherry, and plum, hoping these would relieve the monotony and begin to make the lawn productive. Behind the house, I put in a perennial border. I built three raised beds out of old chestnut barnboards and planted two dozen different vegetable varieties. Hard work though it was, removing the grass from the site of my new beds proved a keen pleasure. First I outlined the beds with string. Then I made an incision in the lawn with the sharp edge of a spade. Starting at one end, I pried the sod from the soil and slowly rolled it up like a carpet. The grass made a tearing sound as I broke its grip on the earth. I felt a little like a pioneer subduing the forest with his ax; I daydreamed of scalping the entire yard. But I didn't do it — I continued to observe front-yard conventions, mowing assiduously and locating all my new garden beds in the back yard.

The more serious about gardening I became, the more dubious lawns seemed. The problem for me was not, as it was for my father, the relation to my neighbors that a lawn implied; it was the lawn's relationship to nature. For however democratic a lawn may be with respect to one's neighbors, with respect to nature it is authoritarian. Under the mower's brutal indiscriminate rotor, the landscape is subdued, homogenized, dominated utterly. I became convinced that lawn care had about as much to do with gardening as floor waxing or road paving. Gardening was a subtle process of give and take with the landscape, a search for some middle ground between culture and nature. A lawn was nature under culture's boot.

Mowing the lawn, I felt that I was battling the earth rather than working it; each week it sent forth a green army and each week I beat it back with my infernal machine. Unlike every other plant in my garden, the grasses were anonymous, massified, deprived of any change or development whatsoever, not to mention any semblance of self-determination. I ruled a totalitarian landscape.

Hot, monotonous hours behind the mower gave rise to existential speculations. I spent part of one afternoon trying to decide who, in the absurdist drama of lawn mowing, was Sisyphus. Me? A case could certainly be made. Or was it the grass, pushing up through the soil every week, one layer of cells at a time, only to be cut down and then, perversely, encouraged (with fertilizer, lime, etc.) to start the whole doomed process over again? Another day it occurred to me that time as we know it doesn't exist in the lawn, since grass never dies or is allowed to flower and set seed. Lawns are nature purged of sex and death. No wonder Americans like them so much.

And just where *was* my lawn, anyway? The answer's not as obvious as it seems. Gardening, I had come to appreciate, is a painstaking exploration of place; everything that happens in my garden — the thriving and dying of particular plants, the maraudings of various insects and other pests — teaches me to know this patch of land intimately, its geology and microclimate, the particular ecology of its local weeds and animals and insects. My garden prospers to the extent I grasp these particularities and adapt to them.

Lawns work on the opposite principle. They depend for their success on the *overcoming* of local conditions. Like Jefferson superimposing one great grid over the infinitely various topography of the Northwest Territory, we superimpose our lawns on the land. And since the geography and climate of much of this country is poorly suited to turfgrasses (none of which are native), this can't be accomplished without the tools of twentieth-century industrial civilization — its chemical fertilizers, pesticides, herbicides, and machinery. For we won't settle for the lawn that will grow here; we want the one that grows *there*, that dense springy supergreen and weed-free carpet, that Platonic ideal of a lawn we glimpse in the ChemLawn commercials, the magazine spreads, the kitschy sitcom yards, the sublime links and pristine diamonds. Our lawns exist less here than there; they drink from the national stream of images, lift our gaze from the real places we live and fix it on unreal places elsewhere. Lawns are a form of television.

Need I point out that such an approach to "nature" is not likely to be environmentally sound? Lately we have begun to recognize that we are poisoning ourselves with our lawns, which receive, on average, more pesticide and herbicide per acre than just about any crop grown in this country. Suits fly against the national lawn-care companies, and interest is kindled in "organic" methods of lawn care. But the problem is larger than this. Lawns, I am convinced, are a symptom of, and a metaphor for, our skewed relationship to the land. They teach us that, with the help of petrochemicals and technology, we can bend nature to our will. Lawns stoke our hubris with regard to the land.

What is the alternative? To turn them into gardens. I'm not suggesting that there is no place for lawns *in* these gardens or that gardens by themselves will right our relationship to the land, but the habits of thought they foster can take us some way in that direction.

Gardening, as compared to lawn care, tutors us in nature's ways, fostering an ethic of give and take with respect to the land. Gardens instruct us in the particularities of place. They lessen our dependence on distant sources of energy, technology, food, and, for that matter, interest.

For if lawn mowing feels like copying the same sentence over and over, gardening is like writing out new ones, an infinitely variable process of invention and discovery. Gardens also teach the necessary if rather un-American lesson that nature and culture can be compromised, that there might be some middle ground between the lawn and the forest — between those who would complete the conquest of the planet in the name of progress and those who believe it's time we abdicated our rule and left the earth in the care of its more innocent species. The garden suggests there might be a place where we can meet nature halfway.

Probably you will want to know if I have begun to practice what I'm preaching. Well, I have not ripped out my lawn entirely. But each spring larger and larger tracts of it give way to garden. Last year I took a half acre and planted a meadow of black-eyed Susans and oxeye daisies. In return for a single annual scything, I am rewarded with a field of flowers from May until frost.

The lawn is shrinking, and I've hired a neighborhood kid to mow what's left of it. Any Saturday that Bon Jovi, Twisted Sister, or Van Halen isn't playing the Hartford Civic Center, this large blond teenaged being is apt to show up with a forty-eight-inch John Deere mower that shears the lawn in less than an hour. It's $30 a week, but he's freed me from my dark musings about the lawn and so given me more time in the garden.

Out in front, along the road where my lawn overlooks my neighbors', and in turn the rest of the country's, I have made my most radical move. I built a split rail fence and have begun to plant a hedge along it — a rough one made up of forsythia, lilac, bittersweet, and bridal wreath. As soon as this hedge grows tall and thick, my secession from the national lawn will be complete.

Anything then is possible. I *could* let it all revert to meadow, or even forest, except that I don't go in for that sort of self-effacement. I could put in a pumpkin patch, a lily pond, or maybe an apple orchard. And I could even leave an area of grass. But even if I did, this would be a very different lawn from the one I have now. For one thing, it would have a frame, which means it could accommodate plants more subtle and various than the screaming marigolds, fierce red salvias, and musclebound rhododendrons that people usually throw into the ring against a big unfenced lawn. Walled off from the neighbors, no longer a tributary of the national stream, my lawn would now form a distinct and private space — become part of a garden rather than a substitute for one.

Yes, there might well be a place for a small lawn in my new garden. But I think I'll wait until the hedge fills in before I make a decision. It's a private matter, and I'm trying to keep politics out of it.

RANDY SHILTS

Talking AIDS to Death

FROM ESQUIRE

I'M TALKING TO my friend Kit Herman when I notice a barely percep-
tible spot on the left side of his face. Slowly, it grows up his cheekbone, down
to his chin, and forward to his mouth. He talks on cheerfully, as if noth-
ing is wrong, and I'm amazed that I'm able to smile and chat on, too, as
if nothing were there. His eyes become sunken; his hair turns gray; his
ear is turning purple now, swelling into a carcinomatous cauliflower,
and still we talk on. He's dying in front of me. He'll be dead soon if noth-
ing is done.

Dead soon if nothing is done.

"Excuse me, Mr. Shilts, I asked if you are absolutely sure, if
you can categorically state that you definitely can*not* get AIDS
from a mosquito."

I forget the early-morning nightmare and shift into my canned
response. All my responses are canned now. I'm an AIDS talk-
show jukebox. Press the button, any button on the AIDS question list, and I have my canned answer ready. Is this Chicago or
Detroit?

"Of course you can get AIDS from a mosquito," I begin.

Here I pause for dramatic effect. In that brief moment, I can
almost hear the caller murmur, "I *knew* it."

"If you have unprotected anal intercourse with an infected
mosquito, you'll get AIDS," I continue. "Anything short of that
and you won't."

The talk-show host likes the answer. All the talk-show hosts
like my answers because they're short, punchy, and to the point.

Not like those boring doctors with long recitations of scientific studies so overwritten with maybes and qualifiers that they frighten more than they reassure an AIDS-hysteric public. I give good interview, talk-show producers agree. It's amazing, they say, how I always stay so cool and never lose my temper.

"Mr. Shilts, has there ever been a case of anyone getting AIDS from a gay waiter?"

"In San Francisco, I don't think they allow heterosexuals to be waiters. This fact proves absolutely that if you could get AIDS from a gay waiter, all northern California would be dead by now."

I gave that same answer once on a Bay Area talk show, and my caller, by the sound of her a little old lady, quickly rejoined, "What if that gay waiter took my salad back into the kitchen and ejaculated into my salad dressing? Couldn't I get AIDS then?"

I didn't have a pat answer for that one, and I still wonder at what this elderly caller thought went on in the kitchens of San Francisco restaurants. Fortunately, this morning's phone-in — in Chicago, it turned out — is not as imaginative.

"You know, your question reminds me of a joke we had in California a couple of years back," I told the caller. "How many heterosexual waiters in San Francisco does it take to screw in a light bulb? The answer is both of them."

The host laughs, the caller is silent. Next comes the obligatory question about whether AIDS can be spread through coughing.

I had written a book to change the world, and here I was on talk shows throughout America, answering questions about mosquitoes and gay waiters.

This wasn't exactly what I had envisioned when I began writing *And the Band Played On*. I had hoped to effect some fundamental changes. I really believed I could alter the performance of the institutions that had allowed AIDS to sweep through America unchecked.

AIDS had spread, my book attested, because politicians, particularly those in charge of federal-level response, had viewed the disease as a political issue, not an issue of public health — they deprived researchers of anything near the resources that were needed to fight it. AIDS had spread because government health officials consistently lied to the American people about the need for more funds, being more concerned with satisfying their political bosses and protecting their own jobs than with telling the truth and protecting the public health. And AIDS had spread because indolent news organizations shunned their responsibility to provide tough, adversarial reportage, instead basing stories largely on the Official Truth of government press releases. The response to AIDS was never even remotely commensurate with the scope of the problem.

I figured the federal government, finally exposed, would stumble over itself to accelerate the pace of AIDS research and put AIDS prevention programs on an emergency footing. Once publicly embarrassed by the revelations of its years of shameful neglect, the media would launch serious investigative reporting on the epidemic. Health officials would step forward and finally lay bare the truth about how official disregard had cost this country hundreds of thousands of lives. And it would never happen again.

I was stunned by the "success" of my book. I quickly acquired all the trappings of bestsellerdom: *60 Minutes* coverage of my "startling" revelations, a Book-of-the-Month Club contract, a miniseries deal with NBC, translation into six languages, book tours on three continents, featured roles in movie-star-studded AIDS fund raisers, regular appearances on network news shows, and hefty fees on the college lecture circuit. A central figure in my book became one of *People* magazine's "25 Most Intriguing People of 1987," even though he had been dead for nearly four years, and the *Los Angeles Herald Examiner* pronounced me one of the "in" authors of 1988. The mayor of San Francisco even proclaimed my birthday last year "Randy Shilts Day."

And one warm summer day as I was sunning at a gay resort in the redwoods north of San Francisco, a well-toned, perfectly tanned young man slid into a chaise next to me and offered the ultimate testimony to my fifteen minutes of fame. His dark eyelashes rising and falling shyly, he whispered, "When I saw you on *Good Morning America* a couple weeks ago, I wondered what it would be like to go to bed with you."

"You're the world's first AIDS celebrity," enthused a friend at the World Health Organization, after hearing one of WHO's most eminent AIDS authorities say he would grant me an interview on one condition — that I autograph his copy of my book. "It must be great," he said.

It's not so great.

The bitter irony is, my role as an AIDS celebrity just gives me a more elevated promontory from which to watch the world make the same mistakes in the handling of the AIDS epidemic that I had hoped my work would help to change. When I return from network tapings and celebrity glad-handing, I come back to my home in San Francisco's gay community and see friends dying. The lesions spread from their cheeks to cover their faces, their hair falls out, they die slowly, horribly, and sometimes suddenly, before anybody has a chance to know they're sick. They die in my arms and in my dreams, and nothing at all has changed.

Never before have I succeeded so well; never before have I failed so miserably.

I gave my first speech on the college lecture circuit at the University of California at Los Angeles in January 1988. I told the audience that there were 50,000 diagnosed AIDS cases in the United States as of that week and that within a few months there would be more people suffering from this deadly disease in the United States than there were Americans killed during the Vietnam War. There were audible gasps. During the question-and-answer session, several students explained that they had heard that the number of AIDS cases in America was leveling off.

In the next speech, at the University of Tennessee, I decided to correct such misapprehension by adding the federal government's projections — the 270,000 expected to be dead or dying from AIDS in 1991, when the disease would kill more people than any single form of cancer, more than car accidents. When I spoke at St. Cloud State University in Minnesota three months later, I noted that the number of American AIDS cases had that week surpassed the Vietnam benchmark. The reaction was more a troubled murmur than a gasp.

By the time I spoke at New York City's New School for Social Research in June and there were 65,000 AIDS cases nationally, the numbers were changing so fast that the constant editing made my notes difficult to read. By then as many as 1,000 Americans a week were learning that they, too, had AIDS, or on the average, about one every fourteen minutes. There were new government projections to report, too: by 1993, some 450,000 Americans would be diagnosed with AIDS. In that year, one American will be diagnosed with the disease every thirty-six seconds. Again, I heard the gasps.

For my talk at a hospital administrators' conference in Washington in August, I started using little yellow stick-ons to update the numbers on my outline. That made it easier to read; there were now 72,000 AIDS cases. Probably this month, or next, I'll tell another college audience that the nation's AIDS case load has topped 100,000, and there will be gasps again.

The gasps always amaze me. Why are they surprised? In epidemics, people get sick and die. That's what epidemics do to people and that's why epidemics are bad.

When Kit Herman was diagnosed with AIDS on May 13, 1986, his doctor leaned over his hospital bed, took his hand, and assured him, "Don't worry, you're in time for AZT." The drug worked so well that all Kit's friends let themselves think he might make it. And we were bolstered by the National Institutes of Health's assurance that AZT was only the first generation of AIDS drugs, and that the hundreds of millions of federal dollars going into AIDS treatment research meant there would soon be a second and third generation of treatments to sustain life beyond AZT's effectiveness. Surely nothing was more important, considering the federal government's own estimates that between 1 and 1.5 million Americans were infected with the Human Immunodeficiency Virus (HIV), and virtually all would die within the next decade if nothing was done. The new drugs, the NIH assured everyone, were "in the pipeline," and government scientists were working as fast as they possibly could.

Despite my nagging, not one of dozens of public-affairs-show producers chose to look seriously into the development of those long-sought second and third generations of AIDS drugs. In fact, clinical trials of AIDS drugs were hopelessly stalled in the morass of bureaucracy at the NIH, but this story tip never seemed to cut it with producers. Clinical trials were not sexy. Clinical trials were boring.

I made my third *Nightline* appearance in January 1988 because new estimates had been released revealing that one in sixty-one babies born in New York City carried antibodies to the AIDS virus. And the link between those babies and the disease was intravenous drug use by one or both parents. Suddenly, junkies had become the group most likely to catch and spread AIDS through the heterosexual community. Free needles to junkies — now there was a sizzling television topic. I told the show's producers I'd talk about that, but that I was much more interested in the issue of AIDS treatments — which seemed most relevant to the night's program, since Ted Koppel's other guest was Dr. Anthony Fauci, associate NIH director for AIDS, and the Reagan administration's most visible AIDS official.

After fifteen minutes of talk on the ins and outs and pros and cons of free needles for intravenous drug users, I raised the subject of the pressing need for AIDS treatments. Koppel asked Fauci what was happening. The doctor launched into a discussion of treatments "in the pipeline" and how government scientists were working as fast as they possibly could.

I'd heard the same words from NIH officials for three years: drugs were in the pipeline. Maybe it was true, but when were they going to come out of their goddamn pipeline? Before I could formulate a polite retort to Fauci's stall, however, the segment was over, Ted was thanking us, and the red light on the camera had blipped off. Everyone seemed satisfied that the government was doing everything it possibly could to develop AIDS treatments.

Three months later, I was reading a week-old *New York Times* in Kit's room in the AIDS ward at San Francisco General Hospital. It was April, nearly two years after my friend's AIDS diagnosis. AZT had given him two years of nearly perfect health, but now its effect was wearing off, and Kit had suffered his first major AIDS-related infection since his original bout with pneumonia — cryptococcal meningitis. The meningitis could be treated, we all knew, but the discovery of this insidious brain infection meant more diseases were likely to follow. And the long-promised second and third generations of AIDS drugs were still nowhere on the horizon.

While perusing the worn copy of the *Times,* I saw a story about Dr. Fauci's testimony at a congressional hearing. After making Fauci swear an oath to tell the truth, a subcommittee headed by Congressman Ted Weiss of New York City asked why it was taking so long to get new AIDS treatments into testing at a time when Congress was putting hundreds of millions of dollars into NIH budgets for just such purposes. At first Fauci talked about unavoidable delays. He claimed government scientists were working as fast as they could. Pressed harder, he finally admitted that the problem stemmed "almost exclusively" from the lack of staffing in his agency. Congress had allocated funds, it was true, but the Reagan administration had gotten around spending the money by stingily refusing to let Fauci hire anybody. Fauci had requested 127 positions to speed the development of AIDS treatments; the administration had granted him eleven. And for a year, he had not told anyone. For a year, this spokesman for the public health answered reporters that AIDS drugs were in the pipeline and that government scientists had all the money they needed. It seemed that only when faced with the penalty of perjury would one of the administration's top AIDS officials tell the truth. That was the real story, I thought, but for some reason nobody else had picked up on it.

At the international AIDS conference in Stockholm two months later, the other reporters in "the AIDS pack" congratulated me on my success and asked what I was working on now. I admitted that I was too busy promoting the British and German release of my book to do much writing myself, and next month I had the Australian tour. But if I *were* reporting, I added with a vaguely conspiratorial tone, *I'd* look at the *scandal* in the NIH. Nobody had picked up that *New York Times* story from a few months ago about staffing shortages on AIDS clinical trials. The lives of 1.5 million HIV-infected Americans hung in the balance, and the only way you could get a straight answer out of an administration AIDS official was to put him under oath and make him face the charge of perjury. Where I went to journalism school, *that* was a news story.

One reporter responded to my tip with the question "But who's going to play *you* in the miniseries?"

A few minutes later, when Dr. Fauci came into the press room, the world's leading AIDS journalists got back to the serious business of transcribing his remarks. Nobody asked him if he was actually telling the truth, or whether they should put him under oath to ensure a candid response to questions about when we'd get AIDS treatments. Most of the subsequent news accounts of

Dr. Fauci's comments faithfully reported that many AIDS treatments were in the pipeline. Government scientists, he said once more, were doing all they possibly could.

The producer assured my publisher that Morton Downey, Jr., would be "serious" about AIDS. "He's not going to play games on this issue," the producer said, adding solemnly, "His brother has AIDS. He understands the need for compassion." The abundance of Mr. Downey's compassion was implicit in the night's call-in poll question: "Should all people with AIDS be quarantined?"

Downey's first question to me was, "You *are* a homosexual, aren't you?"

He wasn't ready for my canned answer: "Why do you ask? Do you want a date or something?"

The show shifted into an earnest discussion of quarantine. In his television studio, Clearasil-addled high school students from suburban New Jersey held up MORTON DOWNEY FAN CLUB signs and cheered aggressively when the truculent, chain-smoking host appeared to favor a kind of homespun AIDS Auschwitz. The youths shouted down any audience member who stepped forward to defend the rights of AIDS sufferers, their howls growing particularly vitriolic if the speakers were gay. These kids were the ilk from which Hitler drew his Nazi youth. In the first commercial break, the other guest, an AIDS activist, and I told Downey we would walk off the show if he didn't tone down his gay-baiting rhetoric. Smiling amiably, Downey took a long drag on his cigarette and assured us, "Don't worry, I have a fallback position."

That comment provided one of the most lucid moments in my year as an AIDS celebrity. Downey's "fallback position," it was clear, was the opposite of what he was promoting on the air. Of course, he didn't *really* believe that people with AIDS, people like his brother, should all be locked up. This was merely a deliciously provocative posture to exploit the working-class resentments of people who needed someone to hate. AIDS sufferers and gays would do for this week. Next week, if viewership dropped and Downey needed a new whipping boy, maybe he'd move on to Arabs, maybe Jews. It didn't seem to matter much to him, since he didn't believe what he was saying anyway. For

Morton Downey, Jr., talking about AIDS was not an act of conscience; it was a ratings ploy. He knew it, he let his guests know
it, his producers certainly knew it, and his television station knew
it. The only people left out of the joke were his audience.

The organizers of the Desert AIDS Project had enlisted actor
Kirk Douglas and CBS morning anchor Kathleen Sullivan to be
honorary co-chairs of the Palm Springs fund raiser. The main
events would include a celebrity tennis match pitting Douglas
against Mayor Sonny Bono, and a $1,500-a-head dinner at which
I would receive a Lucite plaque for my contributions to the fight
against AIDS. The next morning I would fly to L.A. to speak at
still another event, this one with Shirley MacLaine, Valerie Harper, and Susan Dey of *L.A. Law.*

The desert night was exquisite. There were 130 dinner guests,
the personification of elegance and confidence, who gathered on
a magnificent patio of chocolate-brown Arizona flagstone at the
home of one of Palm Springs's most celebrated interior design-
ers. A lot of people had come simply to see what was regarded
as one of the most sumptuous dwellings in this sumptuous town.

When I was called to accept my reward, I began with the same
lineup of jokes I use on talk shows and on the college lecture
circuit. They work every time.

I told the crowd about how you get AIDS from a mosquito.

Kirk Douglas laughed; everybody laughed.

Next, I did the how-many-gay-waiters joke.

Kirk Douglas laughed; everybody laughed.

Then I mentioned the woman who asked whether she could
get AIDS from a waiter ejaculating in her salad dressing.

That one always has my college audiences rolling in the aisles,
so I paused for the expected hilarity.

But in the utter stillness of the desert night air, all that could
be heard was the sound of Kirk Douglas's steel jaw dropping to
the magnificent patio of chocolate-brown Arizona flagstone. The
rest was silence.

"You've got to remember that most of these people came because they're my clients," the host confided later. "You said that,
and all I could think was how I'd have to go back to stitching
slipcovers when this was done."

It turned out that there was more to my lead-balloon remark

than a misjudged audience. Local AIDS organizers told me that a year earlier, a rumor that one of Palm Springs's most popular restaurants was owned by a homosexual, and that most of its waiters were gay, had terrified the elite community. Patronage at the eatery quickly plummeted, and it had nearly gone out of business. Fears that I dismissed as laughable were the genuine concerns of my audience, I realized. My San Francisco joke was a Palm Springs fable.

As I watched the busboys clear the tables later that night, I made a mental note not to tell that joke before dinner again. Never had I seen so many uneaten salads, so much wasted iceberg lettuce.

A friend had just tested antibody positive, and I was doing my best to cheer him up as we ambled down the sidewalk toward a Castro Street restaurant a few blocks from where I live in San Francisco. It seems most of my conversations now have to do with who has tested positive or lucked out and turned up negative, or who is too afraid to be tested. We had parked our car near Coming Home, the local hospice for AIDS patients and others suffering from terminal illnesses, and as we stepped around a nondescript, powder-blue van that blocked our path, two men in white uniforms emerged from the hospice's side door. They carried a stretcher, and on the stretcher was a corpse, neatly wrapped in a royal-blue blanket and secured with navy-blue straps. My friend and I stopped walking. The men quickly guided the stretcher into the back of the van, climbed in the front doors, and drove away. We continued our walk but didn't say anything.

I wondered if the corpse was someone I had known. I'd find out Thursday when the weekly gay paper came out. Every week there are at least two pages filled with obituaries of the previous week's departed. Each week, when I turn to those pages, I hold my breath, wondering whose picture I'll see. It's the only way to keep track, what with so many people dying.

Sometimes I wonder if an aberrant mother or two going to mass at the Most Holy Redeemer Church across the street from Coming Home Hospice has ever warned a child, "That's where you'll end up it you don't obey God's law." Or whether some youngster, feeling that first awareness of a different sexuality, has looked at the doorway of this modern charnel house with an awesome, gnawing dread of annihilation.

"Is the limousine here? Where are the dancers?"

The room fell silent. Blake Rothaus had sounded coherent until that moment, but he was near death now and his brain was going. We were gathered around his bed in a small frame house on a dusty street in Oklahoma City. The twenty-four-year-old was frail and connected to life through a web of clear plastic tubing. He stared up at us and seemed to recognize from our looks that he had lapsed into dementia. A friend broke the uncomfortable silence.

"Of course, we all brought our dancing shoes," he said. "Nice fashionable pumps at that. I wouldn't go out without them."

Everyone laughed and Blake Rothaus was lucid again.

Blake had gone to high school in a San Francisco suburb. When he was a sophomore, he told us, he and his best friend sometimes skipped school, sneaking to the city to spend their afternoons in the gay neighborhood around Castro Street.

It's a common sight, suburban teenagers playing hooky on Castro Street. I could easily imagine him standing on a corner not far from my house. But back in 1982, when he was eighteen, I was already writing about a mysterious, unnamed disease that had claimed 330 victims in the United States.

Blake moved back to Oklahoma City with his family after he graduated from high school. When he fell ill with AIDS, he didn't mope. Instead, he started pestering Oklahoma health officials with demands to educate people about this disease and to provide services for the sick. The state health department didn't recoil. At the age of twenty-two, Blake Rothaus had become the one-man nucleus for Oklahoma's first AIDS patient services. He was the hero of the Sooner State's AIDS movement and something of a local legend.

Though the state had reported only 250 AIDS cases, Oklahoma City had a well-coordinated network of religious leaders, social workers, health-care providers, gay-rights advocates, state legislators, and businessmen, all committed to providing a sane and humane response to this frightening new disease.

"I think it's the old Dust Bowl mentality," suggested one AIDS organizer. "When the hard times come, people pull together."

My past year's travels to twenty-nine states and talks with literally thousands of people have convinced me of one thing about
this country and AIDS: most Americans want to do the right
thing about this epidemic. Some might worry about mosquitoes
and a few may be suspicious of their salad dressing. But beyond
these fears is a reservoir of compassion and concern that goes
vastly underreported by a media that needs conflict and heart-
lessness to fashion a good news hook.

In Kalamazoo, Michigan, when I visited my stepmother, I was
buttonholed by a dozen middle-aged women who wondered
anxiously whether we were any closer to a vaccine or a long-term
treatment. One mentioned a hemophiliac nephew. Another had
a gay brother in Chicago. A third went to a gay hairdresser who,
she quickly added, was one of the finest people you'd ever meet.
When I returned to my conservative hometown of Aurora, Illinois, nestled among endless fields of corn and soy, the local health
department told me they receive more calls than they know what
to do with from women's groups, parishes, and community organizations that want to do something to help. In New Orleans,
the archconservative, pro-nuke, anti-gay bishop had taken up
the founding of an AIDS hospice as a personal mission because,
he said, when people are sick, you've got to help them out.

Scientists, reporters, and politicians privately tell me that of
course *they* want to do more about AIDS, but they have to think
about the Morton Downeys of the world, who argue that too
much research or too much news space or too much official sympathy is being meted out to a bunch of miscreants. They do as
much as they can, they insist; more would rile the resentments
of the masses. So the institutions fumble along, convinced they
must pander to the lowest common denominator, while the
women and men of America's heartland pull me aside to fret
about a dying cousin or co-worker and to plead, "When will there
be a cure? When will this be over?"

"I think I'll make it through this time," Kit said to me, "but I
don't have it in me to go through it again."

We were in room 3 in San Francisco General Hospital's ward
5A, the AIDS ward. The poplar trees outside Kit's window were
losing their leaves, and the first winter's chill was settling over

the city. I was preparing to leave for my fourth and, I hoped, final media tour, this time for release of the book in paperback and on audiocassette; Kit was preparing to die.

The seizures had started a week earlier, indicating he was suffering either from toxoplasmosis, caused by a gluttonous protozoa that sets up housekeeping in the brain; or perhaps it was a relapse of cryptococcal meningitis; or, another specialist guessed, it could be one of those other nasty brain infections that nobody had seen much of until the past year. Now that AIDS patients were living longer, they fell victim to even more exotic infections than in the early days. But the seizures were only part of it. Kit had slowly been losing the sight in his left eye to a herpes infection. And the Kaposi's sarcoma lesions that had scarred his face were beginning to coat the inside of his lungs. When Kit mentioned he'd like to live until Christmas, the doctors said he might want to consider having an early celebration this year, because he wasn't going to be alive in December.

"I can't take another infection," Kit said.

"What does that mean?"

"Morphine," Kit answered, adding mischievously, "lots of it."

We talked briefly about the mechanics of suicide. We both knew people who'd made a mess of it, and people who had done it right. It was hardly the first time the subject had come up in conversation for either of us. Gay men facing AIDS now exchange formulas for suicide as casually as housewives swap recipes for chocolate-chip cookies.

Kit was released from the hospital a few days later. He had decided to take his life on a Tuesday morning. I had to give my first round of interviews in Los Angeles that day, so I stopped on the way to the airport to say goodbye on Monday. All day Tuesday, while I gave my perfectly formed sound bites in a round of network radio appearances, I wondered: Is this the moment he's slipping out of consciousness and into that perfect darkness? When I called that night, it turned out he'd delayed his suicide until Thursday to talk to a few more relatives. I had to give a speech in Portland that day, so on the way to the airport I stopped again. He showed me the amber-brown bottle with the bubble-gum-pink morphine syrup, and we said another goodbye.

The next morning, Kit drank his morphine and fell into a

deep sleep. That afternoon, he awoke and drowsily asked what time it was. When told it was five hours later, he murmured, "That's amazing. I should have been dead hours ago."

And then he went back to sleep.

That night, Kit woke up again.

"You know what they say about near-death experiences?" he asked. "Going toward the light?"

Shaking his head, he sighed. "No light. Nothing."

His suicide attempt a failure, Kit decided the timing of his death would now be up to God. I kept up on the bizarre sequence of events by phone and called as soon as I got back to San Francisco. I was going to tell Kit that his theme song should be "Never Can Say Goodbye," but then the person on the other end of the phone told me that Kit had lapsed into a coma.

The next morning, he died.

Kit's death was like everything about AIDS — anticlimactic. By the time he actually did die, I was almost beyond feeling.

The next day, I flew to Boston for the start of the paperback tour, my heart torn between rage and sorrow. All week, as I was chauffeured to my appearances on *Good Morning America, Larry King Live,* and various CNN shows, I kept thinking, It's all going to break. I'm going to be on a TV show with some officious government health spokesman lying to protect his job, and I'm going to start shouting, "You lying son of a bitch. Don't you know there are people, real people, people I love out there dying?" Or I'll be on a call-in show and another mother will phone about her thirty-seven-year-old son who just died and it will hit me all at once, and I'll start weeping.

But day after day as the tour went on, no matter how many official lies I heard and how many grieving mothers I talked to, the crack-up never occurred. All my answers came out rationally in tight little sound bites about institutional barriers to AIDS treatments and projections about 1993 case loads.

By the last day of the tour, when a limousine picked me up at my Beverly Hills hotel for my last round of satellite TV interviews, I knew I had to stop. In a few weeks I'd return to being national correspondent for the *Chronicle,* and it was time to get off the AIDS celebrity circuit, end the interviews and decline the invitations to the star-studded fund raisers, and get back to work as a newspaper reporter. That afternoon, there was just one last radio interview to a call-in show in the San Fernando Valley, and then it would be over.

The first caller asked why his tax money should go toward funding an AIDS cure when people got the disease through their own misdeeds.

I used my standard jukebox answer about how most cancer cases are linked to people's behavior but that nobody ever suggested we stop trying to find a cure for cancer.

A second caller phoned to ask why her tax money should go to finding an AIDS cure when these people clearly deserved what they got.

I calmly put a new spin on the same answer, saying in America you usually don't sentence people to die for having a different lifestyle from yours.

Then a third caller phoned in to say that he didn't care if all those queers and junkies died, as did a fourth and fifth and sixth caller. By then I was shouting, "You stupid bigot. You just want to kill off everybody you don't like. You goddamn Nazi."

The talk-show host sat in stunned silence. She'd heard I was so *reasonable*. My anger baited the audience further, and the seventh and eighth callers began talking about "you guys," as if only a faggot like myself could give a shit about whether AIDS patients all dropped dead tomorrow.

In their voices, I heard the reporters asking polite questions of NIH officials. Of course, they had to be polite to the government doctors; dying queers weren't anything to lose your temper over. I heard the dissembling NIH researchers go home to their wives at night, complain about the lack of personnel, and shrug; this was just how it was going to have to be for a while. They'd excuse their inaction by telling themselves that if they went public and lost their jobs, worse people would replace them. It was best to go along. But how would they feel if *their* friends, *their* daughters, were dying of this disease? Would they be silent — or would they shout? Maybe they'll forgive me for suspecting they believed that ultimately a bunch of fags weren't worth losing a job over. And when I got home, I was going to have to watch my friends get shoved into powder-blue vans, and it wasn't going to change.

The history of the AIDS epidemic, of yesterday and of today, was echoing in the voices of those callers. And I was screaming at them, and the show host just sat there stunned, and I realized I had rendered myself utterly and completely inarticulate.

I stopped, took a deep breath, and returned to compound-complex sentences about the American tradition of compassion and the overriding need to overcome institutional barriers to AIDS treatments.

When I got home to San Francisco that night, I looked over some notes I had taken from a conversation I'd had with Kit during his last stay in the hospital. I was carping about how frustrated I was at the prospect of returning to my reporting job. If an internationally acclaimed best seller hadn't done shit to change the world, what good would mere newspaper stories do?

"The limits of information," Kit said. "There's been a lot written on it."

"Oh," I said.

Kit closed his eyes briefly and faded into sleep while plastic tubes fed him a cornucopia of antibiotics. After five minutes, he stirred, looked up, and added, as if we had never stopped talking, "But you don't really have a choice. You've got to keep on doing it. What else are you going to do?"

PAUL WEST

Portrait of the Artist as a Lion on Stilts

FROM TRIQUARTERLY

1

ONE LOVELY SUNNY morning in August 1984 I awoke rested and serene, but lazy enough to take my first cup of coffee in bed — or at least to try to. My lips refused to drink, to move. Within minutes my entire mouth was numb and the right side of my face was paralyzed. I could not swallow or speak clearly; I looked at my face in the mirror and saw the whole of it sagging jowly yellow, my eyes bulging, my expression ghoulish.

I was in fact having a Transient Ischemic Attack (said fast as TIA), or a mild stroke. A clot, whipped up inside the heart during fibrillation, had blocked part of the blood supply to my brain. My pulse was 200, my blood pressure 200 over 150 — maybe all three even higher to begin with. In the ambulance I found my speech coming back, but my left arm and hand becoming paralyzed. The clot was on the move. My heart's atria have continued to fibrillate ever since and they always will, spurred on by an electrical malfunction in the sinus node, where one's pulse begins. I had probably been fibrillating undiagnosed for twenty years.

Four years later, rat poison thins my blood and keeps it from coagulating too fast. A quinine derivative keeps my ventricles from fibrillating when the atria do. A substance also given for migraine and stage fright (of all things) keeps my atria fairly calm most of the time and lowers my blood pressure, blocking the deadly hormones called catecholamines. An amazing fudged-up contraption, I seem in some ways among the very lucky. Sometimes my speech will slur, but nobody notices. I now swim as much as three hours a day and have actually managed to thin down my hypertrophied heart. The sapping fear of the first eighteen months has all but gone, replaced by a cliffhanger's high.

What got me into all this? Spending half a year in Arizona, I had felt so well that I stopped taking the half aspirin daily that had no doubt kept me uncoagulated for eight years; the stroke followed in the same year. There is also talk of rheumatic fever, undiagnosed when I was a child, as well as of too much coffee, liquor, cigars, and so forth. I take no stimulants at all now and wonder why I took them in the first place; my brain is clearer, my mood sweeter, my stomach flatter. I have learned from children who laughingly correct their "funny feeling" (atrial fibrillation) by standing on their heads or splashing cold water on their wrists and necks. I regard my heart as a host regards an alien visitor trapped in his chest, but also as an irritable friend who has to be humored. Or else.

2

I had always had a sense of being intimately linked with stuff that I was not, if indeed I knew where I began and stuff left off. Possessed of an almost eerie sense of how different I was from earthworm, tree, and star, all of them opaque, I had an even eerier sense of overlap with them, not so much from reading as from primitive hunch. From my first chemistry set, I knew that I was an experiment too. I walked and breathed immersed in a world not mine, not made of *me*. With seemingly detached mind, I used a brain whose stuff was generally available. Something streamed through us all, and through other things, that was never itself, which is to say it had identities by proxy. It was permanent and we were expendable.

In Intensive Care, I who had never known a night in hospital found myself not merely a part of all I had ever seen and known,

as before; I was newly connected to it by wires, oscilloscopes,
tubing, and big drafts of chemicals whose nature I would eventually ponder and marvel at, like the medium contemplating his
or her own ectoplasm. Dispossessed is what I felt: dispossessed
of even that cozy old intimacy with nature. It had been a luxury,
a mental game, and now it was being played out, proven, on my
pulses, taken outside me and blown up big on screens and charts.
I felt as if my marrow were being sucked out of me and had only
been on loan. Nothing belonged to me that could not be revoked
here in this functional room with only a curtain for a door: things,
they, you, came in and out at speed. The transits were fast and
unimpeded. The world outside the doorway, beyond the curtain, looked somehow vertically down. I lay in a horizontal shaft
that not far away bent at a right angle to dispose of me. I hung
on, not a cut worm or a lightning-struck tree or a star starting to
run out of energy, but a something somehow without a destiny.
The atoms that owned me had come into their own, loud in the
squeak and ping of the big EKG machine close to my bed. I had
ignored the fibers in the sinus node of my heart, and now they
were thrashing in chaos. I had never even known about catecholamines that could surge and boost my blood pressure to an
almost lethal level. Now they had done their massive, silent roar
through me, and I was weaker for their dominance. I was what
things within me happened to. I was a guest in the throne room
of juices and sludges, and it was here that heparin, a substance
my own stomach made, was fed into me nonstop through an IV
needle. It was here that British propranolol blocked my adrenaline from reaching my sympathetic nervous system. It was here
that, in need, the speeding ventricle calmed down after a long
squirt of lidocaine, a liquid made from wood. It was a place in
which you had only a backstage identity and became only the
patient: the one who suffers, your first and last names all of a
sudden become Atrial Fib. Why, fib sounded like a lie, but the
straight truth was all around you as the EKG clamored when you
made the slightest move and an abortive attempt to move the
bowels set all the bells ringing all at once, from the bearing-down,
which I now understand affects the vagus nerve and can even
be used to quell the fibrillating heart. In Intensive Care, the place
in which, with whatever energy I could muster, I tried to take

an interest in what had happened to me: the pupil of my own mishap, asking the nurse to write out, for me to learn by heart, what propranolol is made of, and heparin, and Coumadin, and quinidine, those prompters of my latter life.

On the brink of nothing I began to think of myself in the third person: now the use is going from his left arm again and there is a runaway train in his chest.

But was too blurred even to maintain the consistency of that primal decorum. Hooked up by chest and wrist, I waited for the bed to slide away down that chute beyond the curtain. Where was the pain, anyway? The pain was in a recognition that I was lucky to be there, a thing thinking about the thing I was, but might not be for long. It was like being shoved back into the prehistory of humankind, waiting for my cells to move me up a rung.

I was safe; but I was only faintly ticking over, stalled between idle and stop, in a tiny way craving something to read (I remember wanting *Malone Dies*, for its outlandish appropriateness). I hovered. Sometimes I seemed to be levitating, whisked upward (or winched) while gravity tugged the other way in silent fury. At other times I seemed all of me to be one wince, all one shrug, as if my body had heard something appallingly sour and wanted to enact derision. The counterpoint to this sense of invasion or dispossession was not medical — or rather it was, yet not done by doctors. There, by my bed each day, was Diane Ackerman telling me, in a magnificent hyperbole of her poet's imagination, that I was a resting lion. No doubt of it, she insisted, I *was* a lion, and she brought me stuffed lions to play with, big pictures of lions to behold, and I half fancied I was Hemingway's old Santiago dreaming of them: in my case, as animations of an almost defunct body, picturesque extrusions from a ghost that had almost given up. In full view of the nurses, my lioness curled up on the narrow bed with me and persuaded me that I could still get somewhere from there, if only I would try. Feedback had not worked against the paralysis of my left arm, but I think it worked against the mental slough my body had lured me into. Somewhere in the back of my mind an equation failed to take shape, but I had heard it, or something like it: three weeks flat on your back equals three years of aging. I couldn't recall it, but the phantom of it scared me back to my feet, off which I fell. Dizzy, blacking or graying out, I clutched at my lioness and the wall, ever on the point of knocking the IV out of my arm. A week later, still dizzy, I was walking the steps within the wing while the nurses monitored my heart by telemetry. I had survived to faint another day. I had learned, in irrevocable terms, that a mind stretched to a new idea never returns to its original dimensions. Was that why, only a few months later, there began the most sustained period of creativity (and reward) I had ever known? In my livelier moments in hospital I had dreamed of, and listed, the books I would write if I got the chance. Well, the chance came and, off all stimulants, with a heart for once beating sometimes properly, and propranolol to give me Technicolor dreams as well as fend off migraine attacks, my brain worked better than before, I thought. No longer maltreated, it reformed and served me well.

I still have to sleep a lot, in some vague hope of nerve regeneration; I am supposed to swim just about daily; the rat-poison anticoagulant I have to take for life keeps my eyes bloodshot or pink; and Quinaglute keeps my arrhythmias to a minimum. I cannot pretend I am unscathed. Nor, oddly enough, in some moods, do I wish to be (in other moods I want to start afresh, of course, with a brand-new chemistry set to be myself with). I have become a body watcher, a devout auscultator, to whom every squeeze of persistalsis becomes a miracle of what Coleridge called is-ness, and every irregular beat ("an irregular irregularity," my cardiologist says) seems a heroic elegy evocative of the mood that Stevie Smith pinned down so well: waving while drowning. On the not-so-good days, when my unpushed blood pools away from my body's surface and I feel intolerably hot, I try a homemade maneuver: I "bear down," and this restores proper tone to the vagus nerve, which controls the heart's beat. Other maneuvers include coughing while holding my breath. When they don't work, I try to accept a sweat-soak as my portion and fill my mind with images of icebergs and the accursed cold pools with which cheap hotels trick out the landscape of the winter south.

I will probably never learn the full extent of what I have been through, or went through long before I had any idea that anything was wrong. Four years after the stroke, my cardiologist informs me that recurrences usually come in the first few months: something I am glad he kept to himself. "Benign cardiomyopathy" he writes on my appointment slips, warning me that it isn't *that* benign: my life has been shortened, he says, and the heart will one day slip into a fibrillation that, far from being fatal, will become a constant in my checkered life; in other words, for what it is worth, and it is worth a paradise, my habitual alternation of lovely sinus rhythm and chaotic arrhythmias will go downhill into being only the latter, and I will not feel quite so good so often. Meanwhile, I reason, the Samarkand of drugs gets bigger and cleverer; I might cheat the odds even yet — if they can quell cholesterol with gemfibrozil, surely the perfect anti-arrhythmic is only just around the corner. This is a very American faith I have in progress and remedy: God-given maladies call up and out God-given remedies. The beloved chemistry set of my boyhood has come back to me; but, in order to play with this one, you have to put your carcass on the line. I do. Each day is a pageant, an experiment, a ravishing communion. Death, as one of my students wrote, intending something quite different, is a plague for which there is no known anecdote. Perhaps. All I know is that not to have told the anecdote or story of it all, to oneself or to others, makes me feel less powerful than having told. We live in a precarious foison lent us. That is why the lion sleeps and roars.

3

Seven months after that frightening episode, my heart began to slow to thirty beats a minute; for some periods it was inert for as long as seven seconds, and it would soon be inert for longer. I had been to see Dr. Obeid up in Syracuse, and had stayed there overnight so as to wear a heart-monitoring device called a Holter for the required twenty-four hours. I was home, cooking a meal of Chinese vegetables, when the phone rang. "I want you here in hospital tonight," Obeid said, unusually dictatorial for him. "I feel fine," I told him. "We're just going to have a Chinese meal. I'm cooking it right now." He told me to have my dinner and then get my body through the sleet and fog to the Crouse-Irving Hospital, where a bed awaited me. "You're in trouble." I refused. He spoke with Diane and convinced her, and we were there by ten o'clock. The only thing that cheered me up was Obeid's standing order to all hospital staff to let me sleep in, at least until 8 A.M. Unheard of, this fiat brought patients and doctors alike from all over the hospital, just to gawp at the enormous placard outside my door. Obeid believes in the usefulness of sleep, but also in pacemakers too: I needed one, he said, as soon as possible. It was the only thing to do.

I had various questions for the surgeon, Dr. Pradhan, and he breezed through the answers, telling how many pacemakers he had implanted, in what kinds of patients, and where he had trained in Pakistan and the United States, and with whom. What he said was as interesting as informative. He jibbed, though, when I asked him if he would recommend this procedure for a member of his own family. Right now, he said, there was no case to consider; he could not deal with the question in the abstract, but he certainly dealt with another I posed: "Are there times when it is utterly imperative to implant a pacemaker?" Of course there were. This was one, and he talked about heart block, a phrase that hadn't come up before, although I had become familiar with such gems of cardiological jargon as *pulsus paradoxicus*, the footprints of Wenckebach, salvos and cannon waves, Mobitz 1 and 2, and bigeminal beats. Indeed, I had a strong emotional interest in such jargon; its esoteric poetry was about what went on inside *me*. I took a word lover's interest in such things, and in the superstitious way that seems peculiar to Western intellectuals from Faust on, I wanted to find out how things worked or did not work. If you have to go through all this, I reasoned, you're entitled to the whys and wherefores; they give you that sense of minimal but not altogether abolished control. You feel less passive, less of a victim. An illusion? Probably so, as I was to discover.

Then I asked about the complications attending the procedure, all of course in the interests of what I called knowledge for its own sake; but I also wanted to frighten myself to death, I suppose, and then prove myself to myself in setting such terrors aside and going ahead. With expressionless candor, Dr. Pradhan, who had just been chatting about his daughter's desire to study creative writing at one of several universities, went down the list, from an air embolism when the lead is threaded into the vein to myocardial hemorrhage when it passes into the first chamber of the heart. Fibrillation was possible, he said, when the lead goes into the heart. The target tip might also migrate or be rejected. The lead might erode. I might get an infection, or muscle spasms, or the hiccups. He had never had a fatality or a severe mishap, but he had colleagues who had. Nothing precluded some complications, some of the most unanticipated interactions of unknown factors. For half an hour he just explained the mainstream snags.

"Do I really need the thing?" I asked, as if I were in for a bypass; but the realization had bitten home. A pacemaker was another alien presence, an invader once in never out. The probe would always be in that intimate red nest of the heart. Pradhan reiterated my cardiologist's bleak prophecy that, one day soon, I was going to collapse because my heart had paused too long. Or I was going to drop dead. That was the nonanswer that overrode all my questions and quibbles, at least as Obeid and Pradhan saw it.

All the same, a big piece of me wanted to squirm away home and risk it. I felt well. My blood pressure had remained stable without medication. My mind was working a treat. I persuaded myself that I could sense when the wooziness was going to hit; all I had to do was sit down fast and wait it out. I felt chilled by Pradhan's unemotional recital of what could happen to you in even the most expert hands, but he was citing the odds, the body of knowledge. There are always odds, even to the most trivial procedure, and I marveled even then, wrought up as I was, at the human mind's capacity to want to know the unknowable, in Macbeth's brisk phrase "to jump the life to come." In fact I grilled Dr. Pradhan good and proper, but in truth badly and improperly, as any self-styled analytical mind might. He told Obeid he had never been so "sweated" in his life, and no doubt now avoids novelists like the plague. Before he left, I agreed tentatively to go through with the procedure, but he himself insisted that at any point up to about two in the afternoon tomorrow, I could back out, delay, or cancel. His ego was not in the least involved in my choice, any more than it had been in my questions, and it would not come into play during the operation either. An ap-

propriate card went up above my bed and I was told, just in case
I went ahead, presumably after an evening's thought, not to eat
anything after midnight.

Around dinnertime, Dr. Obeid stopped by and in his gently
imperative way (He Who Must Be Obeyed, I call him) told me
to pull back, to stop trying to summon up, warts and refinements
and all, a body of knowledge I had not been trained to understand. The answers to some questions were useful to me, he
thought; the patient is entitled to be vigilant and self-concerned;
but the answers to many other questions were so recondite, so
much involved with chance, that I had best leave them alone.
Theologies, I thought, will give you various answers as to the
nature of God; they don't hesitate to supply positive answers in
the absence of evidence. But theologies do not go to the operating room, not in that sense anyway.

How my mind buckled and flexed, asserted itself and then
cringed away. I wanted it and it alone to find out for me the
right thing to do, to be my surgeon and cardiologist in one, just
like that. The last thing it wanted to do was trust blindly; indeed,
I had been told that the state of the art of being a patient was to
take an interrogative interest in what went on. *Always ask.* Now
here was this top-notch humanist of a cardiologist telling me to
take him and the surgeon on trust. "We do not want you to *be*
an individual," he said, "not for such a purpose as this. We want
you to be average, typical. It is no use making the surgeon nervous or overcautious, feeling he has been put on his mettle and
must prove himself beyond measure." I could see the sense
in what he said, although part of me demurred. It was a bit
like second-to-second compounding of interest: impossible because the instant occupied by any calculation made the calculation obsolete, and because with time, as with a crumb or a bead
of water, there is no indivisible minimum. At any rate, what I
wanted was as hypothetical as that, just as theoretical. All I
could ever get was a list of known mishaps, but my impulse to
trifle with the minutiae of chance amounted, I eventually saw,
to morbid vanity. No doubt the two doctors would trust my
literary taste, but their lives would not depend on it, whereas,
in theory at least, to trust them was to gamble just a bit with my
life.

4

What shone in Pradhan's hands when he entered, shooting the white frost of his cuffs, was what I could have. At first I thought he had arrived with a bola, the rope used in Argentina to entangle a steer's legs as the weighted ends coil around them. Then it seemed an anchor, a yoyo, a silver disk on a string. Very much a toy. Then I saw that he had brought two of them. Maybe I didn't want to believe that he had brought the real thing, and I disliked the idea that something he could implant in my very own heart he could swing around in front of me with an airy playful motion that revealed his mystery, let him flaunt his wares.

I saw two pacemakers, each in convex titanium like small cigarette cases, from each of which curled a lead encased in pliable metal mesh with, at the tip, a tiny version of the chimney sweep's brush: a probe with a few flanges sloping backward at 45 degrees. *These,* he explained, would embed themselves in the wall of the ventricle and, if we were lucky, make themselves permanent by building up scar tissue around them.

How many beats my heart skipped, or threw in extra, at the sight I have no idea. I felt sickened. He would slide the probe through a vein and the flanges would bend back along the lead, giving easily as the probe passed from the vein into the left atrium, where most of my trouble was to begin with. Then through the tricuspid valve into the ventricle, the holy of holies. I fingered the flanges, wondering if they couldn't be made even more pliable, easier to smooth back as the probe slid ahead. Wouldn't they catch on something while going in? Once in the ventricle they were supposed to spring outward again, meant to snag the soft red pulp inside. Surely the lead would slip and then, like some zany metal butterfly waft around, touching off twitches and convulsions wherever it landed, scraping and abrading, making me gasp. Wouldn't there, *won't there*, I asked him, be a leakage when the tricuspid valve has the lead going through it? Good question, he said; but no, the pliable triple petals would mold themselves around it — no leak. I asked other questions. Asking questions, you feel less powerless, yet you end up not much the wiser or even better informed. No, this had a lithium iodide battery, not plutonium, no longer much used, and it might

last as long as ten years, depending on how much the heart demanded of it. This was a *demand* pacemaker, after all.

When, I wondered, would my mind stop going off on tangents, eager to escape a brutish truth? To me, the procedure
seemed barbaric, although of course not to him, who put in one
or two each day. What bothered me was not so much the slit
beneath the collarbone that would enable him to slide the shiny
shape into place amid the muscles and behind the subcutaneous
layer, leaving me with only a bulge whose crest was the sealed
smile of the scar. At that I jibbed not much. The thing that set
my teeth on edge was the slithering lead, when it went past the
defenseless portals at my core, silver interloper where the sun
had never shone and where there was never rest. My heart would
be cuddling a tiny propeller forever. If it came loose, could they
get it out, with what I thought of as the *barbs* going the wrong
way? Surely they would catch. I fondled the flanges, forcing them
forward toward the probe. Wouldn't they then tear things apart
if they had to come out again?

Then I realized that, instead of fending off all these images
and tangents, I must allow them full play as my head's means of
getting used to the idea; my imagination was translating for me,
the barbaric into the tender, and I broke through to the palatable comparison that had been at the back of my mind all along.
Instead of that chimney-brush lead, I was going to have the pink
and velvet-gentle pistil of a hibiscus slid into my vein, with five
red-spotted stamens in the vanguard, behind them the shank of
the pistil and the tiny wire whisk of pliant golden commas that
were the pollen. When the mind is desperate, it feeds itself some
bizarre things. It worked, though, almost like self-hypnosis, and
I felt very much outside myself, allowing them to do all this to
someone else into whose most private thoughts and sensations I
could peer. If I *had* to be implanted, then it would be with something like this, alien but somehow semifriendly. If being imaginative is what scares you most, then use imagination to come to
terms. I did. Once in, having graced its passage with an ocher
talc, the hibiscus-pacer would merge at once with the just-as-soft
mucosa at its destination, fusing heart of the flower with the heart
of me.

At first I hesitated at almost every turn. Would the thing break
loose and tear me apart? I must not bump into things, and cer-

tainly (the doctors said) I must avoid body-contact sports, excepting for the only one I cherished. I must not dive into the water anymore. Was I, like some possessors of this gadget, going to develop the so-called time-bomb complex, in which I thought it would explode or begin to tick? I had been told that, when it was functioning, I would perhaps feel a twitch or a tickle, a little throbbing, and I did. Indeed, even when it wasn't being *demanded* of, its presence might make my muscles spasm a bit. If I could only get my mind off it for long enough — a week, say, and then even longer — I might learn to live with it. I had coaxed myself to keep calm through the operation that implanted it, even though during it we had had an electrical failure and, at one hairy moment, an onset of ventricular tachycardia that made me feel as if I'd had a speeding dynamo in my chest that was going to break loose and scatter my viscera like so many sponges. At another point, because my heart kept kicking the pacemaker lead out, they had almost decided to cut their way through the front of my chest and install the electrodes directly on my heart. In the end, however, the tip of the lead bit and snagged, the ventricle failed to punch it loose, and the front of my abdomen stayed uncut.

I walk uneasily away from microwave ovens, though, knowing as I now do that only leaky ones can harm me, and I smile at the pseudo-VIP treatment meted out at airports, where I go around the magnetic sensors and get hand-scanned, braced ever for the litany that goes (often enough): "It wouldn't hurt you to go through, you know." They act with solicitude, I concluded, not so much because the magnetic sensors might start my pacemaker off or halt it as because I would keep their buzzers ringing forever. I would never get through, I thought, even if alive, until I had pretended to be my own hand baggage and allowed myself to be x-rayed so that they could see clearly what had been planted in my chest, below the collarbone. They want to spare me all that bother.

After my first year of being bionic, I rather began to relish the lore of it all, always having a good chat about titanium when I left from Heathrow or Ithaca, New York, learning to laugh when the uninitiated (who should have been schooled in the matter of pacemakers) yelled to a colleague down the line, "He's got a pacemaker, Frank."

"A *what?*"

"Pacemaker."

"Yeah. So what? What's that?"

"Pace-maker."

"*You* do him."

Any shred of embarrassment I ever felt in the beginning has long since gone. There was the woman security guard who said, "Don't mind if I feel you up some?" She did. "You're used to doing that," I said as she stiffened into her tunic, looked sideways, and told me to put my hand over my pacemaker and keep it there. The guards who know least about this bionic business are at the TWA terminal, JFK; at Lambert Airport, St. Louis; and at Sacramento, California. At all three there is no space for you to "go around" through, not until they make it, and as they do so they peer at you as if you have leprosy; you don't look old enough for this prop of the elderly, whereas many children have them and wear them with aplomb.

I had no sooner gotten accustomed to the weekly or fortnightly blood test, to check my clotting time and thus my dose of Coumadin, than I had to get used to another rigmarole that tests the pacemaker by telephone. With an electrode on each index finger, I transmit my pulse to the master computer in my cardiologist's office one or two hundred miles away, and then pass a big blue doughnut of a magnet over my pacemaker, setting it off, and it goes *cheep-cheep.* Or it should if the battery has not failed. If it has, my heart-block problems will recur and I will become dizzy in no time at all. After about ten years, the surgeon removes the old battery and implants a new one (it used to be only three years), which is bound to be smaller. If you last long enough, I presume, you ultimately receive a battery the size of a quarter and go into your grave with one of the cutest engines in the world frantically trying, in the very temple of your chest, to restart the arrested heart, as if it were two paddles and not just an accelerator. One almost senses a chance of immortality here, becoming a Frankensteinian metronome.

5

Having come this far, I want to become as mechanically foolproof as I can; but in order to become that you need to have

implanted in you a different kind of pacemaker that delivers a
powerful shock sufficient to halt a fibrillating ventricle (the easy
way to sudden death). People who have these in them go unconscious briefly, and fall, when the life-saving shock goes off, but
they get up in good shape. I sometimes wonder how many con-
traptions I will need to have, how many I can have before they
start getting in one another's way. My problem is electrical, and
that is perhaps why I have come to dote on Mary Shelley's famous book, on all the spin-offs from it, but most of all on the
passion to bring the dead back to life that dominated the fevered
imaginations colluding at the Villa Diodati in 1816. New Doctor
Frankensteins laid their hands on me when I was on the brink
of being naught and engineered me back, not with galvanome-
ters and lightning conductors but with little clever motors (and
those other little motors we call pills). I wish Mary Shelley, and
Percy, a pacemaker or two to play with, and I marvel not at the
eyes in Mary's nipples (although in Intensive Care you believe
anything) but at the toy that tweaks me.

Most of all, of course, I have become acquainted with death:
with how casual it can be, sidling in to have you just when you
feel not half bad and think you are going to get away with it after
all. Perhaps because I was not in pain I felt better than I really
was. I came close, I am told. I do recall seeing those who went
into Intensive Care with me going out under sheets on gurneys,
not in wheelchairs. I will never forget seeing how smoothly and
omnipotently death operated in there, having its way with us
almost at random, without any by-your-leave or warning or
overture. It claimed and claimed without, I thought, even *wanting* any of us. It was just in a habit of taking us off. Death was a
force with a tic. An eerie smoothness was among us at no one's
request, something mathematical and implacable: no fuss, just
naked and universal power, the power that comes to mind (oddly,
maybe) whenever I have to explain to someone the most puzzling part of my condition: my pacemaker remedies only the
heart block, it does nothing to curb the arrhythmias; in other
words, I am not going to keel over as Prokofiev did, because my
heart isn't beating fast enough, but I am going to feel sweaty and
claustrophobic from time to time because the ventricle is beating
chaotically. I wish there were some toy to put all things right; if

there ever is, my hunch is that it will be a chemical similar to propranolol, which is good for half a dozen things.

There is a lethal context to all this wising-up, which you have to get accustomed to, much as you get accustomed to the color of buttercups or the rank aroma of narcissi. One's quiet mania says: After all that, I intend to get away with as much as I can for as long as I can; tread quietly and applaud my body nonstop for its ability to survive. Politicians talk of the art of the possible. Doctors talk of the quality of life. I think about what my body achieved against the odds and what supports the rest of what I do: the art of the passable, and the high quality of that compared with the alternative. I keep managing to come to the end of another book, another essay (as now), and I marvel at the plenary gratitude the human spirit can feel after the Furies have had it and it has managed to slink away, back into the operating theater of words.

JOY WILLIAMS

Save the Whales,
Screw the Shrimp

FROM ESQUIRE

I DON'T WANT to talk about *me*, of course, but it seems as though
far too much attention has been lavished on *you* lately — that
your greed and vanities and quest for self-fulfillment have been
catered to far too much. You just want and want and want. You
haven't had a mandala dream since the eighties began. To have
a mandala dream you'd have to instinctively know that it was an
attempt at self-healing on the part of Nature, and you don't believe in Nature anymore. It's too isolated from you. You've ab-
stracted it. It's so messy and damaged and sad. Your eyes glaze
as you travel life's highway past all the crushed animals and the
Big Gulp cups. You don't even take pleasure in looking at nature
photographs these days. Oh, they can be just as pretty, as always,
but don't they make you feel increasingly . . . anxious? Filled
with more trepidation than peace? So what's the point? You see
the picture of the baby condor or the panda munching on a
bamboo shoot, and your heart just sinks, doesn't it? A picture of
a poor old sea turtle with barnacles on her back, all ancient and
exhausted, depositing her five gallons of doomed eggs in the
sand hardly fills you with joy, because you realize, quite rightly,
that just outside the frame falls the shadow of the condo. What's
cropped from the shot of ocean waves crashing on a pristine
shore is the plastics plant, and just beyond the dunes lies a parking lot. Hidden from immediate view in the butterfly-bright
meadow, in the dusky thicket, in the oak and holly wood, are the

surveyors' stakes, for someone wants to build a mall exactly
there — some gas stations and supermarkets, some pizza and
video shops, a health club, maybe a bulimia treatment center.
Those lovely pictures of leopards and herons and wild rivers,
well, you just know they're going to be accompanied by a text
that will serve only to bring you down. You don't want to think
about it! It's all so uncool. And you don't want to feel guilty
either. Guilt is uncool. Regret maybe you'll consider. *Maybe.* Regret is a possibility, but don't push me, you say. Nature photographs have become something of a problem, along with almost
everything else. Even though they leave the bad stuff out — maybe
because you *know* they're leaving all the bad stuff out — such
pictures are making you increasingly aware that you're a little
too late for Nature. Do you feel that? Twenty years too late,
maybe only ten? Not *way* too late, just a little too late? Well, it
appears that you are. And since you are, you've decided you're
just not going to attend this particular party.

Pascal said that it is easier to endure death without thinking about
it than to endure the thought of death without dying. This is
how you manage to dance the strange dance with that grim partner, nuclear annihilation. When the U.S. Army notified Winston
Churchill that the first atom bomb had been detonated in New
Mexico, it chose the code phrase BABIES SATISFACTORILY BORN.
So you entered the age of irony, and the strange double life
you've been leading with the world ever since. Joyce Carol Oates
suggests that the reason writers — *real* writers, one assumes —
don't write about Nature is that it lacks a sense of humor and
registers no irony. It just doesn't seem to be of the times — these
slick, sleek, knowing, objective, indulgent times. And the word
Environment. Such a bloodless word. A flat-footed word with a
shrunken heart. A word increasingly disengaged from its association with the natural world. Urban planners, industrialists,
economists, and developers use it. It's a lost word, really. A cold
word, mechanistic, suited strangely to the coldness generally felt
toward Nature. It's their word now. You don't mind giving it up.
As for *Environmentalist,* that's one that can really bring on the
yawns, for you've tamed and tidied it, neutered it quite nicely.
An environmentalist must be calm, rational, reasonable, and

willing to compromise, otherwise you won't listen to him. Still, his beliefs are *opinions* only, for this is the age of radical subjectivism. Not long ago, Barry Commoner spoke to the Environmental Protection Agency. He scolded them. They loved it. The way they protect the environment these days is apparently to find an "acceptable level of harm from a pollutant and then issue rules allowing industry to pollute to that level." Commoner suggested that this was inappropriate. An EPA employee suggested that any other approach would place limits on economic growth and implied that Commoner was advocating this. Limits on economic growth! Commoner vigorously denied this. Oh, it was a healthy exchange of ideas, healthier certainly than our air and water. We needed that little spanking, the EPA felt. It was refreshing. The agency has recently lumbered into action in its campaign to ban dinoseb. You seem to have liked your dinoseb. It's been a popular weed killer, even though it has been directly linked with birth defects. You must hate weeds a lot. Although the EPA appears successful in banning the poison, it will still have to pay the disposal costs and compensate the manufacturers for the market value of the chemicals they still have in stock.

That's ironic, you say, but farmers will suffer losses, too, oh dreadful financial losses, if herbicide and pesticide use is restricted.

Farmers grow way too much stuff anyway. They grow surplus crops with subsidized water created by turning rivers great and small into a plumbing system of dams and canals. Rivers have become *systems*. Wetlands are increasingly being referred to as *filtering systems* — things deigned *useful* because of their ability to absorb urban run-off, oil from roads, et cetera.

We know that. We've known that for years about farmers. We know a lot these days. We're very well informed. If farmers aren't allowed to make a profit by growing surplus crops, they'll have to sell their land to developers, who'll turn all that *arable land* into office parks. Arable land isn't Nature anyway, and besides, we like those office parks and shopping plazas, with their monster supermarkets open twenty-four hours a day with aisle after aisle after aisle of *products*. It's fun. Products are fun.

Farmers like their poisons, but ranchers like them even more. There are well-funded predominantly federal and cooperative programs like the Agriculture Department's Animal Damage Control Unit that poison, shoot, and trap several thousand animals each year. This unit loves to kill things. It was created to kill things — bobcats, foxes, black bears, mountain lions, rabbits, badgers, countless birds — all to make this great land safe for the string bean and the corn, the sheep and the cow, even though you're not consuming as much cow these days. A burger now and then, but burgers are hardly cows at all, you feel. They're not all *our* cows in any case, for some burger matter is imported. There's a bit of Central American burger matter in your bun. Which is contributing to the conversion of tropical rain forest into cow pasture. Even so, you're getting away from meat these days. You're eschewing cow. It's seafood you love, shrimp most of all. And when you love something, it had better watch out, because you have a tendency to love it to death. Shrimp, shrimp, shrimp. It's more common on menus than chicken. In the wilds of Ohio, far, far from watery shores, four out of the six entrées on a menu will be shrimp, for some modest sum. Everywhere, it's all the shrimp you can eat or all you *care* to eat, for sometimes you just don't feel like eating all you *can*. You are intensively *harvesting* shrimp. Soon there won't be any left and then you can stop. It takes that, often, to make you stop. Shrimpers shrimp, of course. That's their *business*. They put out these big nets and in these nets, for each pound of shrimp, they catch more than ten times that amount of fish, turtles, and dolphins. These, quite the worse for wear, they dump back in. There is an object called TED (Turtle Excluder Device), which would save thousands of turtles and some dolphins from dying in the nets, but the shrimpers are loath to use TEDs, as they say it would cut the size of their shrimp catch.

We've heard about TED, you say.

They want you, all of you, to have all the shrimp you can eat and more. At Kiawah Island, off the coast of South Carolina, visitors go out on Jeep "safaris" through the part of the island that hasn't been developed yet. ("Wherever you see trees," the guide says, "really, that's a lot.") The safari comprises six Jeeps, and these days they go out at least four times a day, with more trips promised soon. The tourists drive their own Jeeps and the guide talks to them by radio. Kiawah has nice beaches, and the guide talks about turtles. When he mentions the shrimpers' role in the decline of the turtle, the shrimpers, who share the same frequency, scream at him. Shrimpers and most commercial fishermen (many of them working with drift and gill nets anywhere from six to thirty miles long) think of themselves as an *endangered species*. A recent newspaper headline said, "Shrimpers Spared Anti-Turtle Devices." Even so, with the continuing wanton depletion of shrimp beds, they will undoubtedly have to find some other means of employment soon. They might, for instance, become part of that vast throng laboring in the *tourist industry*.

Tourism has become an industry as destructive as any other. You are no longer benign in your traveling somewhere to look at the scenery. You never thought there was much gain in just looking anyway, you've always preferred to *use* the scenery in some manner. In your desire to get away from what you've got, you've caused there to be no place to get away *to*. You're just all bumpered up out there. Sewage and dumps have become prime indicators of America's lifestyle. In resort towns in New England and the Adirondacks, measuring the flow into the sewage plant serves as a business barometer. Tourism is a growth industry. You believe in growth. *Controlled* growth, of course. Controlled exponential growth is what you'd really like to see. You certainly don't want to put a moratorium or a cap on anything. That's illegal, isn't it? Retro you're not. You don't want to go back or anything. Forward. Maybe ask directions later. Growth is *desirable* as well as being *inevitable*. Growth is the one thing you seem to be powerless before, so you try to be realistic about it. Growth is — it's weird — it's like cancer or something.

Recently you, as tourist, have discovered your national parks and are quickly *overburdening* them. Spare land and it belongs to you! It's exotic land too, not looking like all the stuff around it that looks like everything else. You want to take advantage of this land, of course, and use it in every way you can. Thus the managers — or *stewards,* as they like to be called — have developed *wise* and *multiple-use* plans, keeping in mind exploiters' interests (for they have their needs, too) as well as the desires of the backpackers. Thus mining, timbering, and ranching activities take place in the national forests, where the Forest Service maintains a system of logging roads eight times larger than the interstate highway system. The national parks are more of a public playground and are becoming increasingly Europeanized in their look and management. Lots of concessions and motels. You deserve a clean bed and a hot meal when you go into the wilderness. At least your stewards think that you do. You keep your stewards busy. Not only must they cater to your multiple and conflicting desires, they have to manage your wildlife *resources*. They have managed wildfowl to such an extent that the reasoning has become, If it weren't for hunters, ducks would disappear. Duck stamps and licensing fees support the whole rickety duck-management system. Yes! If it weren't for the people who killed them, wild ducks wouldn't exist! Managers are managing all wild creatures, not just those that fly. They track and tape and tag and band. They relocate, restock, and reintroduce. They cull and control. It's hard to keep it all straight. Protect or poison? Extirpate or just mostly eliminate? Sometimes even the stewards get mixed up.

This is the time of machines and models, hands-on management and master plans. Don't you ever wonder as you pass that billboard advertising another MASTER-PLANNED COMMUNITY just what master they are actually talking about? Not the Big Master, certainly. Something brought to you by one of the tiny masters, of which there are many. But you like these tiny masters and have even come to expect and require them. In Florida they've just started a ten-thousand-acre city in the Everglades. It's a *megaproject*, one of the largest ever in the state. Yes, they must have thought you wanted it. No, what you thought of as the Everglades, the Park, is only a little bitty part of the Everglades. Developers have been gnawing at this irreplaceable, strange land for years. It's like they just *hate* this ancient sea of grass. Maybe you could ask them about this sometime. Roy Rogers is the senior vice president of strategic planning, and the old cowboy says that every tree and bush and inch of sidewalk in the project has been planned. Nevertheless, because the whole thing will take twenty-five years to complete, the plan is going to be constantly changed. You can understand this. The important thing is that there be a blueprint. You trust a blueprint. The tiny masters know what you like. You like *a secure landscape* and *access to services.* You like grass — that is, lawns. The ultimate lawn is the golf course, which you've been told has "some ecological value." You believe this! Not that it really matters, you just like to play golf. These golf courses require a lot of watering. So much that the more inspired of the masters have taken to watering them with effluent, *treated* effluent, but yours, from all the condos and villas built around the stocked artificial lakes you fancy.

I really don't want to think about sewage, you say, but it sounds like progress.

It is true that the masters are struggling with the problems of your incessant flushing. Cuisine is also one of their concerns. Advances in sorbets — sorbet intermezzos — in their clubs and fine restaurants. They know what you want. You want A HAVEN FROM THE ORDINARY WORLD. If you're A NATURE LOVER in the West you want to live in a $200,000 home in A WILD ANIMAL HABITAT. If you're eastern and consider yourself more hip, you want to live in new towns — brand-new reconstructed-from-scratch towns — in a house of NINETEENTH-CENTURY DESIGN. But in these new towns the masters are building, getting around can be confusing. There is an abundance of curves and an infrequency of through streets. It's the new wilderness without any trees. You can get lost, even with all the "mental bread crumbs" the masters scatter about as visual landmarks — the windmill, the water views, the various groupings of landscape "material." You *are* lost, you know. But you trust a Realtor will show you the way. There are many more Realtors than tiny masters, and many of them have to make do with less than a loaf — that is, trying to sell stuff that's already been built in an environment already "enhanced" rather than something being planned — but they're everywhere, willing to show you the path. If Dante returned to Hell today, he'd probably be escorted down by a Realtor, talking all the while about how it was just another level of Paradise.

When have you last watched a sunset? Do you remember where you were? With whom? At Loews Ventana Canyon Resort, the Grand Foyer will provide you with that opportunity through lighting which is computerized to diminish with the approaching sunset!

The tiny masters are willing to arrange Nature for you. They will compose it into a picture that you can look at at your leisure,

when you're not doing work or something like that. Nature becomes scenery, a prop. At some golf courses in the Southwest,
the saguaro cacti are reported to be repaired with green paste
when balls blast into their skin. The saguaro can attempt to heal
themselves by growing over the balls, but this takes time, and the
effect can be somewhat . . . baroque. It's better to get out the
pastepot. Nature has become simply a visual form of entertainment, and it had better look snappy.

Listen, you say, we've been at Ventana Canyon. It's in the desert, right? It's very, very nice, a world-class resort. A totally self-
contained environment with everything that a person could possibly want, on more than a thousand acres in the middle of zip.
It sprawls but nestles, like. And they've maintained the integrity
of as much of the desert ecosystem as possible. Give them credit
for that. *Great* restaurant, too. We had baby bay scallops there.
Coming into the lobby there are these two big hand-carved coy-
otes, mutely howling. And that's the way we like them, *mute*. God,
why do those things howl like that?

Wildlife is a personal matter, you think. The attitude is up to
you. You can prefer to see it dead or not dead. You might want
to let it mosey about its business or blow it away. Wild things
exist only if you have the graciousness to allow them to. Just
outside Tucson, Arizona, there is a brand-new structure mod-
eled after a French foreign legion outpost. It's the *International
Wildlife Museum,* and it's full of dead animals. Three hundred
species are there, at least a third of them — the rarest ones —
killed and collected by one C. J. McElroy, who enjoyed doing it
and now shares what's left with you. The museum claims to be
educational because you can watch a taxidermist at work or touch
a lion's tooth. You can get real close to these dead animals, closer
than you can in a zoo. Some of you prefer zoos, however, which
are becoming bigger, better, and bioclimatic. New-age zoo de-
signers want the animals to *flow right out into your space.* In Dallas
there will soon be a Wilds of Africa exhibit; in San Diego there's
a simulated rain forest, where you can thread your way "down
the side of a lush canyon, the air filled with a fine mist from 300
high-pressure nozzles"; in New Orleans you've constructed a
swamp, the real swamp not far away on the verge of disappear-
ing. Animals in these places are abstractions — wandering relics

of their true selves, but that doesn't matter. Animal behavior in a zoo is nothing like natural behavior, but that doesn't really matter, either. Zoos are pretty, contained, and accessible. These new habitats can contain one hundred different species — not more than one or two of each thing, of course — on seven acres, three, one. You don't want to see *too much* of anything, certainly. An *example* will suffice. Sort of like a biological Crabtree & Evelyn basket selected with *you* in mind. You like things reduced, simplified. It's easier to take it all in, park it in your mind. You like things inside better than outside anyway. You are increasingly looking at and living in proxy environments created by substitution and simulation. *Resource economists* are a wee branch in the tree of tiny masters, and one, Martin Krieger, wrote, "Artificial prairies and wildernesses have been created, and there is no reason to believe that these artificial environments need be unsatisfactory for those who experience them. . . . We will have to realize that the way in which we experience nature is conditioned by our society — which more and more is seen to be receptive to responsible intervention."

Nature has become a world of appearances, a mere source of materials. You've been editing it for quite some time; now you're in the process of deleting it. Earth is beginning to look like not much more than a launching pad. Back near Tucson, on the opposite side of the mountain from the dead-animal habitat, you're building Biosphere II (as compared with or opposed to Biosphere I, more commonly known as Earth) — a 2½-acre terrarium, an artificial ecosystem that will include a rain forest, a desert, a thirty-five-foot ocean, and several thousand species of life (lots of microbes), including eight human beings, who will cultivate a bit of farmland. You think it would be nice to colonize other worlds after you've made it necessary to leave this one.

Hey, that's pretty good, you say, all that stuff packed into just 2½ acres. That's only about three times bigger than my entire *house*.

It's small all right, but still not small enough to be, apparently, useful. For the purposes of NASA, say, it would have to be smaller, oh much smaller, and energy-efficient too. Fiddle, fiddle, fiddle. You support fiddling, as well as meddling. This is how you learn. Though it's quite apparent the environment has been grossly polluted and the natural world abused and defiled, you seem to prefer to continue pondering effects rather than preventing causes. You want proof, you insist on proof. A Dr. Lave from Carnegie-Mellon — and he's an expert, an economist, and an environmental *expert* — says that scientists will have to prove to you that you will suffer if you don't become less of a "throw-away society." *If you really want me to give up my car or my air conditioner, you'd better prove to me first that the earth would otherwise be uninhabitable,* Dr. Lave says. *Me* is *you,* I presume, whereas *you* refers to them. You as in me — that is, *me, me, me* — certainly strike a hard bargain. Uninhabitable the world has to get before you rein in your requirements. You're a consumer after all, *the* consumer upon whom so much attention is lavished, the ultimate user of a commodity that has become, these days, everything. To try to appease your appetite for proof, for example, scientists have been leasing for experimentation forty-six pristine lakes in Canada.

They don't want to *keep* them, they just want to *borrow* them.

They've been intentionally contaminating many of the lakes with a variety of pollutants dribbled into the propeller wash of research boats. It's *one of the boldest experiments in lake ecology ever conducted.* They've turned these remote lakes into huge *real-world test tubes.* They've been doing this since 1976! And what they've found so far in these *preliminary* studies is that pollutants are really destructive. The lakes get gross. Life in them ceases. It took about eight years to make this happen in one of them, everything carefully measured and controlled all the while. Now the scientists are slowly reversing the process. But it will take hundreds of years for the lakes to recover. They think.

Remember when you used to like rain, the sound of it, the feel of it, the way it made the plants and trees all glisten. We needed that rain, you would say. It looked pretty too, you thought, particularly in the movies. Now it rains and you go, Oh-oh. A nice walloping rain these days means *overtaxing our sewage treatment plants.* It means *untreated waste discharged directly into our waterways.* It means . . .

Okay. Okay.

Acid rain! And we all know what this is. Or most of us do.

People of power in government and industry still don't seem to
know what it is. Whatever it is, they say, they don't want to curb
it, but they're willing to study it some more. Economists call air
and water pollution "externalities" anyway. Oh, acid rain. You
do get so sick of hearing about it. The words have already become a white-noise kind of thing. But you think in terms of *mit-
igating* it maybe. As for *the greenhouse effect,* you think in terms of
countering that. One way that's been discussed recently is the
planting of new forests, not for the sake of the forests alone, oh
my heavens, no. Not for the sake of majesty and mystery or of
Thumper and Bambi, are you kidding me, but because, as every
schoolchild knows, trees absorb carbon dioxide. They just soak
it up and store it. They just love it. So this is the plan: you plant
millions of acres of trees, and you can go on doing pretty much
whatever you're doing — driving around, using staggering
amounts of energy, keeping those power plants fired to the max.
Isn't Nature remarkable? So willing to serve? You wouldn't think
it had anything more to offer, but it seems it does. Of course
these "forests" wouldn't exactly be forests. They would be more
like trees. *Managed* trees. The Forest Service, which now manages our forests by cutting them down, might be called upon to
evolve in their thinking and allow these trees to grow. They would
probably be patented trees after a time. Fast-growing, uniform,
genetically-created-to-be-toxin-eating *machines.* They would be
new-age trees, because the problem with planting the old-fashioned variety to *combat* the greenhouse effect, which is caused by
pollution, is that they're already dying from it. All along the crest
of the Appalachians from Maine to Georgia, forests struggle to
survive in a toxic soup of poisons. They can't *help* us if we've
killed them, now can they?

All right, you say, wow, lighten up will you? Relax. Tell about
yourself.

Well, I say, I live in Florida . . .

Oh my God, you say. Florida! Florida is a joke! How do you
expect us to take you seriously if you still live there! Florida is
crazy, it's pink concrete. It's paved, it's over. And a little girl just
got eaten by an alligator down there. It came out of some swamp
next to a subdivision and just carried her off. That set your Endangered Species Act back fifty years, you can bet.

I . . .

Listen, we don't want to hear any more about Florida. We don't want to hear about Phoenix or Hilton Head or California's Central Valley. If our wetlands — our *vanishing* wetlands — are mentioned one more time, we'll scream. And the talk about condors and grizzlies and wolves is becoming too de trop. We had just managed to get whales out of our minds when those three showed up under the ice in Alaska. They even had *names*. Bone is the dead one, right? It's almost the twenty-first century! Those last condors are *pathetic*. Can't we just get this over with?

Aristotle said that all living beings are ensouled and striving to participate in eternity.

Oh, I just bet he said that, you say. That doesn't sound like Aristotle. He was a humanist. We're all humanists here. This is the age of humanism. And it has been for a long time.

You are driving with a stranger in the car, and it is the stranger behind the wheel. In the back seat are your pals for many years now — DO WHAT YOU LIKE and his swilling sidekick, WHY NOT. A deer, or some emblematic animal, something from that myriad natural world you've come from that you now treat with such indifference and scorn — steps from the dimming woods and tentatively upon the highway. The stranger does not decelerate or brake, not yet, maybe not at all. The feeling is that whatever it is *will get out of the way*. Oh, it's a fine car you've got, a fine machine, and oddly you don't mind the stranger driving it, because in a way, everything has gotten too complicated, way, way out of your control. You've given the wheel to the masters, the managers, the comptrollers. Something is wrong, *maybe*, you feel a little sick, *actually*, but the car is luxurious and fast and you're *moving*, which is the most important thing by far.

Why make a fuss when you're so comfortable? Don't make a fuss, make a baby. Go out and get something to eat, build something. Make *another* baby. Babies are cute. Babies show you have faith in the future. Although faith is perhaps too strong a word. They're everywhere these days, in all the crowds and traffic jams, there are the babies too. You don't seem to associate them with the problems of population increase. They're just babies! And you've come to believe in them again. They're a lot more tangi-

ble than the afterlife, which, of course, you haven't believed in
in ages. At least not for yourself. The afterlife now belongs to
plastics and poisons. Yes, plastics and poisons will have a far more
extensive afterlife than you, that's known. A disposable diaper,
for example, which is all plastic and wood pulp — you like them
for all those babies, so easy to use and toss — will take around
four centuries to degrade. Almost all plastics do, centuries and
centuries. In the sea, many marine animals die from ingesting
or being entangled in discarded plastic. In the dumps, plastic
squats on more than 25 percent of dump space. But your heart
is disposed toward plastic. Someone, no doubt the plastics industry, told you it was convenient. This same industry is now looking into recycling in an attempt to get the critics of their nefar-
ious, multifarious products off their backs. That should make
you feel better, because *recycling* has become an honorable word,
no longer merely the hobby of Volvo owners. The fact is that
people in plastics are born obscurants. Recycling (practically impossible) won't solve the plastic glut, only reduction of production will, and the plastics industry isn't looking into that, you can
be sure. Waste is not just the stuff you throw away, of course, it's
the stuff you use to excess. With the exception of *hazardous waste,*
which you do worry about from time to time, it's even thought
you have a declining sense of emergency about the problem.
Builders are building bigger houses because you want bigger.
You're trading up. Utility companies are beginning to worry about
your constantly rising consumption. Utility companies! You
haven't entered a new age at all but one of upscale nihilism, deluxe nihilism.

In the summer, particularly in *the industrial Northeast,* you did get
a little excited. The filth cut into your fun time. Dead stuff floating around. Sludge and bloody vials. Hygienic devices — ap-
pearing not quite so hygienic out of context — all coming in on
the tide. The air smelled funny, too. You tolerate a great deal,
but the summer of '88 was truly creepy. It was even thought for
a moment that the environment would become a political issue.
But it didn't. You didn't want it to be, preferring instead to continue in your politics of subsidizing and advancing avarice. The
issues were the same as always — jobs, defense, the economy,

maintaining and improving the standard of living in this greedy, selfish, expansionistic, industrialized society.

You're getting a little shrill here, you say.

You're pretty well off. You expect to be better off soon. You do. What does this mean? More software, more scampi, more square footage? You have created an ecological crisis. The earth is infinitely variable and alive, and you are killing it. It seems safer this way. But you are not safe. You want to find wholeness and happiness in a land increasingly damaged and betrayed, and you never will. More than material matters. You must change your ways.

What is this? *Sinners in the Hands of an Angry God?*

The ecological crisis cannot be resolved by politics. It cannot be solved by science or technology. It is a crisis caused by culture and character, and a deep change in personal consciousness is needed. Your fundamental attitudes toward the earth have become twisted. You have made only brutal contact with Nature, you cannot comprehend its grace. You must change. Have few desires and simple pleasures. Honor nonhuman life. Control yourself, become more authentic. Live lightly upon the earth and treat it with respect. Redefine the word *progress* and dismiss the managers and masters. Grow inwardly and with knowledge become truly wiser. Make connections. Think differently, behave differently. For this is essentially a moral issue we face and moral decisions must be made.

A *moral issue!* Okay, this discussion is now toast. A *moral* issue . . . And who's this *we* now? Who are *you* is what I'd like to know. You're not me, anyway. I admit, someone's to blame and something should be done. But I've got to go. It's getting late. That's dusk out there. That is dusk, isn't it? It certainly doesn't look like any dawn I've ever seen. Well, take care.

TOM WOLFE

Stalking the Billion-Footed Beast

FROM HARPER'S MAGAZINE

MAY I BE forgiven if I take as my text the sixth page of the fourth chapter of *The Bonfire of the Vanities*? The novel's main character, Sherman McCoy, is driving over the Triborough Bridge in New York City in his Mercedes roadster with his twenty-six-year-old girlfriend, not his forty-year-old wife, in the tan leather bucket seat beside him, and he glances triumphantly off to his left toward the island of Manhattan. "The towers were jammed together so tightly, he could feel the mass and stupendous weight. Just think of the millions, from all over the globe, who yearned to be on that island, in those towers, in those narrow streets! There it was, the Rome, the Paris, the London of the twentieth century, the city of ambition, the dense magnetic rock, the irresistible destination of all those who insist on being *where things are happening* —"

To me the idea of writing a novel about this astonishing metropolis, a big novel, cramming as much of New York City between covers as you could, was the most tempting, the most challenging, and the most obvious idea an American writer could possibly have. I had first vowed to try it in 1968, except that what I had in mind then was a nonfiction novel, to use a much-discussed term from the period. I had just written one, *The Electric Kool-Aid Acid Test,* about the psychedelic, or hippie, movement, and I had begun to indulge in some brave speculations about nonfiction as an art form. These were eventually recorded in a book called *The New Journalism*. Off the record, however, alone in my little apartment on East Fifty-eighth Street, I was worried that somebody out there was writing a big realistic fictional novel about the hippie experience that would blow *The Electric Kool-Aid Acid Test* out of the water. Somebody? There might be droves of them. After all, among the hippies were many well-educated and presumably, not to mention avowedly, creative people. But one, two, three, four years went by, and to my relief, and then my bafflement, those novels never appeared. (And to this day they remain unwritten.)

Meantime, I turned to the proposed nonfiction novel about New York. As I saw it, such a book should be a novel *of the city*, in the sense that Balzac and Zola had written novels *of Paris* and Dickens and Thackeray had written novels *of London*, with the city always in the foreground, exerting it relentless pressure on the souls of its inhabitants. My immediate model was Thackeray's *Vanity Fair*. Thackeray and Dickens had lived in the first great era of the metropolis. Now, a century later, in the 1960s, certain powerful forces had converged to create a second one. The economic boom that had begun in the middle of the Second World War surged through the decade of the sixties without even a mild recession. The flush times created a sense of immunity, and standards that had been in place for millennia were swept aside with a merry, rut-boar abandon. One result was the so-called sexual revolution, which I always thought was a rather prim term for the lurid carnival that actually took place.

Indirectly, the boom also triggered something else: overt racial conflict. Bad feelings had been rumbling on low boil in the cities ever since the great migrations from the rural South had begun in the 1920s. But in 1965 a series of race riots erupted, starting with the Harlem riot in 1964 and the Watts riot in Los Angeles in 1965, moving to Detroit in 1967, and peaking in Washington and Chicago in 1968. These were riots that only the sixties could have produced. In the sixties, the federal government had created the War on Poverty, at the heart of which were not alms for the poor but setups called CAPs, Community Action Programs. CAPs were something new in the history of political science. They were official invitations from the government to people in the slums to improve their lot by rising up and rebelling against the establishment, including the government itself. The government would provide the money, the headquarters, and the advisers. So people in the slums obliged. The riots were merely the most sensational form the strategy took, however. The more customary form was the confrontation. "Confrontation" was a sixties term. It was not by mere coincidence that the most violent of the sixties' confrontational groups, the Black Panther Party of America, drew up its ten-point program in the North Oakland poverty center. That was what the poverty center was there for.

Such was the backdrop one day in January of 1970 when I decided to attend a party that Leonard Bernstein and his wife, Felicia, were giving for the Black Panthers in their apartment at Park Avenue and Seventy-ninth Street. I figured that here might be some material for a chapter in my nonfiction *Vanity Fair* about New York. I didn't know the half of it. It was at this party that a ·Black Panther field marshal rose up beside the north piano — there was also a south piano — in Leonard Bernstein's living room and outlined the Panthers' ten-point program to a roomful of socialites and celebrities, who, giddy with *nostalgie de la boue*, entertained a vision of the future in which, after the revolution, there would no longer be any such thing as a two-story, thirteen-room apartment on Park Avenue, with twin grand pianos in the living room, for one family.

All I was after was material for a chapter in a nonfiction novel, as I say. But the party was such a perfect set piece that I couldn't hold back. I wrote an account of the evening for *New York* magazine entitled "Radical Chic" and, as a companion piece, an article about the confrontations the War on Poverty had spawned in San Francisco, "Mau-mauing the Flak Catchers." The two were published as a book in the fall of 1970. Once again I braced and waited for the big realistic novels that were sure to be written about this phenomenon that had played such a major part in American life in the late 1960s and early 1970s: racial strife in the cities. Once again the years began to roll by, and these novels never appeared.

This time, however, my relief was not very profound. I still had not written my would-be big book about New York. I had merely put off the attempt. In 1972 I put it off a little further. I went to Cape Canaveral to cover the launch of *Apollo 17*, the last mission to the moon, for *Rolling Stone*. I ended up writing a four-part series on the astronauts, then decided to spend the next five or six months expanding the material into a book. The five or six months stretched into a year, eighteen months, two years, and I began to look over my shoulder. Truman Capote, for one, had let it be known that he was working on a big novel about New York entitled *Answered Prayers*. No doubt there were others as well. The material was rich beyond belief and getting richer every day.

Another year slipped by . . . and, miraculously, no such book appeared.

Now I paused and looked about and tried to figure out what was, in fact, going on in the world of American fiction. I wasn't alone, as it turned out. Half the publishers along Madison Avenue — at that time, publishing houses could still afford Madison Avenue — had their noses pressed against their Thermopane glass walls, scanning the billion-footed city for the approach of the young novelists who, surely, would bring them the big novels of the racial clashes, the hippie movement, the New Left, the Wall Street boom, the sexual revolution, the war in Vietnam. But such creatures, it seemed, no longer existed.

The strange fact of the matter was that young people with serious literary ambitions were no longer interested in the metropolis or any other big, rich slices of contemporary life. Over the preceding fifteen years, while I had been immersed in journalism, one of the most curious chapters in American literary history had begun. (And it is not over yet.) The story is by turns bizarre and hilarious, and one day some lucky doctoral candidate with the perseverance of a Huizinga or a Hauser will do it justice. I can offer no more than the broadest outline.

After the Second World War, in the late 1940s, American intellectuals began to revive a dream that had glowed briefly in the 1920s. They set out to create a native intelligentsia on the French or English model, an intellectual aristocracy — socially unaffiliated, beyond class distinctions — active in politics and the arts. In the arts, their audience would be the inevitably small minority of truly cultivated people as opposed to the mob, who wished only to be entertained or to be assured they were "cultured." By now, if one need edit, the mob was better known as the middle class.

Among the fashionable European ideas that began to circulate was that of "the death of the novel," by which was meant the realistic novel. Writing in 1948, Lionel Trilling gave this notion a late-Marxist twist that George Steiner and others would elaborate on. The realistic novel, in their gloss, was the literary child of the nineteenth-century industrial bourgeoisie. It was a slice of life, a cross section, that provided a true and powerful picture of individuals and society — as long as the bourgeois order and the old class system were firmly in place. But now that the bourgeoisie was in a state of "crisis and partial rout" (Steiner's phrase) and the old class system was crumbling, the realistic novel was pointless. What could be more futile than a cross section of disintegrating fragments?

The truth was, as Arnold Hauser had gone to great pains to demonstrate in *The Social History of Art,* the intelligentsia have always had contempt for the realistic novel — a form that wallows so enthusiastically in the dirt of everyday life and the dirty secrets of class envy and that, still worse, is so easily understood and obviously relished by the mob, that is, the middle class. In Victorian England, the intelligentsia regarded Dickens as "the author of the uneducated, undiscriminating public." It required a chasm of time — eighty years, in fact — to separate his work from its vulgar milieu so that Dickens might be canonized in British literary circles. The intelligentsia have always preferred more refined forms of fiction, such as that long-time French intellectual favorite, the psychological novel.

By the early 1960s, the notion of the death of the realistic novel had caught on among young American writers with the force of revelation. This was an extraordinary turnabout. It had been only yesterday, in the 1930s, that the big realistic novel, with its broad social sweep, had put American literature up on the world stage for the first time. In 1930 Sinclair Lewis, a realistic novelist who used reporting techniques as thorough as Zola's, became the first American writer to win the Nobel Prize. In his acceptance speech, he called on his fellow writers to give America "a literature worthy of her vastness," and, indeed, four

of the next five Americans to win the Nobel Prize in literature —
Pearl Buck, William Faulkner, Ernest Hemingway, and John
Steinbeck — were realistic novelists. (The fifth was Eugene
O'Neill.) For that matter, the most highly regarded new novelists
of the immediate postwar period — James Jones, Norman Mailer,
Irwin Shaw, William Styron, Calder Willingham — were all real-
ists.

Yet by 1962, when Steinbeck won the Nobel Prize, young writers, and intellectuals generally, regarded him and his approach
to the novel as an embarrassment. Pearl Buck was even worse,
and Lewis wasn't much better. Faulkner and Hemingway still
commanded respect, but it was the respect you give to old boys
who did the best they could with what they knew in their day.
They were "squares" (John Gardner's term) who actually thought
you could take real life and spread it across the pages of a book.
They never comprehended the fact that a novel is a sublime literary game.

All serious young writers — "serious" meaning those who aimed
for literary prestige — understood such things, and they were
dismantling the realistic novel just as fast as they could think of
ways to do it. The dividing line was the year 1960. Writers who
went to college after 1960 . . . *understood*. For a serious young
writer to stick with realism after 1960 required contrariness and
courage.

Writers who had gone to college before 1960, such as Saul
Bellow, Robert Stone, and John Updike, found it hard to give
up realism, but many others were caught betwixt and between.
They didn't know which way to turn. For example, Philip Roth,
a 1954 graduate of Bucknell, won the National Book Award in
1960 at the age of twenty-seven for a collection entitled *Goodbye,
Columbus*. The title piece was a brilliant novella of manners —
brilliant . . . but, alas, highly realistic. By 1961 Roth was having second thoughts. He made a statement that had a terrific
impact on other young writers. We now live in an age, he said,
in which the imagination of the novelist lies helpless before what
he knows he will read in tomorrow morning's newspaper. "The
actuality is continually outdoing our talents, and the culture tosses
up figures daily that are the envy of any novelist."

Even today — perhaps especially today — anyone, writer or

not, can sympathize. What novelist would dare concoct a plot in which, say, a southern television evangelist has a tryst in a motel with a church secretary from Babylon, New York — did you have to make it *Babylon?* — and is ruined to the point where he has to sell all his worldly goods at auction, including his air-conditioned doghouse — *air-conditioned doghouse?* — whereupon he is termed a "decadent pompadour boy" by a second television evangelist, who, we soon learn, has been combing his own rather well-teased blond hair forward over his forehead and wearing headbands in order to disguise himself as he goes into Louisiana waterbed motels with combat-zone prostitutes — oh, *come on* — prompting a third television evangelist, who is under serious consideration for the Republican presidential nomination, to charge that the damning evidence has been leaked to the press by the vice president of the United States . . . while, meantime, the aforesaid church secretary has now bared her chest to the photographers and has thereby become an international celebrity and has gone to live happily ever after in a castle known as the Playboy Mansion . . . and her erstwhile tryst mate, evangelist number one, was last seen hiding in the fetal position under his lawyer's couch in Charlotte, North Carolina . . .

What novelist would dare dream up such crazy stuff and then ask you to suspend your disbelief?

The lesson that a generation of serious young writers learned from Roth's lament was that it was time to avert their eyes. To attempt a realistic novel with the scope of Balzac, Zola, or Lewis was absurd. By the mid-1960s the conviction was not merely that the realistic novel was no longer possible but that American life itself no longer deserved the term "real." American life was chaotic, fragmented, random, discontinuous; in a word, absurd. Writers in the university creative writing programs had long, phenomenological discussions in which they decided that the act of writing words on a page was the real thing and the so-called real world of America was the fiction, requiring the suspension of disbelief. "The so-called real world" became a favorite phrase.

New types of novels came in waves, each trying to establish an avant-garde position out beyond realism. There were Absurdist novels, Magical Realist novels, and novels of Radical Disjunction (the novelist and critic Robert Towers's phrase) in which plausible events and plausible characters were combined in fantastic or outlandish ways, often resulting in dreadful catastrophes that were played for laughs in the ironic mode. Irony was the attitude supreme, and nowhere more so than in the Puppet Master novels, a category that often overlapped with the others. The Puppet Masters were in love with the theory that the novel was, first and foremost, a literary game, words on a page being manipulated by an author. Ronald Sukenick, author of a highly praised 1968 novel called *Up*, would tell you what he looked like while he was writing the words you were at that moment reading. At one point you are informed that he is stark naked. Sometimes he tells you he's crossing out what you've just read and changing it. Then he gives you the new version. In a story called "The Death of the Novel," he keeps saying, à la Samuel Beckett, "I can't go on." Then he exhorts himself, "Go on," and on he goes. At the end of *Up* he tells you that none of the characters was real: "I just make it up as I go along."

The Puppet Masters took to calling their stories *fictions*, after the manner of Jorge Luis Borges, who spoke of his *ficciones*. Borges, an Argentinian, was one of the gods of the new breed. In keeping with the cosmopolitan yearnings of the native intelligentsia, all gods now came from abroad: Borges, Nabokov, Beckett, Pinter, Kundera, Calvino, García Márquez, and, above all, Kafka; there was a whole rash of stories with characters named H or V or T or P (but, for some reason, none named A, B, D, or E). It soon reached the point where a creative writing teacher at Johns Hopkins held up Tolstoy as a master of the novel — and was looked upon by his young charges as rather touchingly old-fashioned. As one of them, Frederick Barthelme, later put it, "He talked Leo Tolstoy when we were up to here with Laurence Sterne, Franz Kafka, Italo Calvino, and Gabriel García Márquez. In fact, Gabriel García Márquez was already *over* by then."

By the 1970s there was a headlong rush to get rid of not only realism but everything associated with it. One of the most highly praised of the new breed, John Hawkes, said, "I began to write fiction on the assumption that the true enemies of the novel were plot, character, setting, and theme." The most radical group, the Neo-Fabulists, decided to go back to the primal origins of fiction, back to a happier time, before realism and all its contaminations, back to myth, fable, and legend. John Gardner and John Irving both started out in this vein, but the peerless leader was John Barth, who wrote a collection of three novellas called *Chimera*, recounting the further adventures of Perseus and Andromeda and other characters from Greek mythology. *Chimera* won the 1972 National Book Award for fiction.

Other Neo-Fabulists wrote modern fables, à la Kafka, in which the action, if any, took place at no specific location. You couldn't even tell what hemisphere it was. It was some nameless, elemental terrain — the desert, the woods, the open sea, the snowy wastes. The characters had no backgrounds. They came from nowhere. They didn't use realistic speech. Nothing they said, did, or possessed indicated any class or ethnic origin. Above all, the Neo-Fabulists avoided all big, obvious sentiments and emotions, which the realistic novel, with its dreadful Little Nell scenes, specialized in. Perfect anesthesia; that was the ticket, even in the death scenes. Anesthetic solitude became one of the great motifs of serious fiction in the 1970s. The Minimalists, also known as the K Mart Realists, wrote about real situations, but very tiny ones, tiny domestic ones, for the most part, usually in lonely Rustic Septic Tank Rural settings, in a deadpan prose composed of disingenuously short, simple sentences — with the emotions anesthetized, given a shot of novocaine. My favorite Minimalist opening comes from a short story by Robert Coover: "In order to get started, he went to live alone on an island and shot himself."

Many of these writers were brilliant. They were virtuosos. They could do things within the narrow limits they had set for themselves that were more clever and amusing than anyone could have ever imagined. But what was this lonely island they had moved to? After all, they, like me, happened to be alive in what was, for better or for worse, the American century, the century in which we had become the mightiest military power in all history, capable of blowing up the world by turning two cylindrical keys in a missile silo but also capable, once it blew, of escaping to the stars in spaceships. We were alive in the first moment since the dawn of time in which man was able at last to break the bonds of Earth's gravity and explore the rest of the universe. And, on top of that, we had created an affluence that reached

clear down to the level of mechanics and tradesmen on a scale
that would have made the Sun King blink, so that on any given
evening even a Neo-Fabulist's or a Minimalist's electrician or air-
conditioner mechanic or burglar-alarm repairman might very
well be in St. Kitts or Barbados or Puerto Vallarta wearing a
Harry Belafonte cane-cutter shirt, open to the sternum, the better to reveal the gold chains twinkling in his chest hair, while he
and his third wife sit on the terrace and have a little designer
water before dinner . . .

What a feast was spread out before every writer in America!
How could any writer resist plunging into it? I couldn't.

In 1979, after I had finally completed my book about the astronauts, *The Right Stuff,* I returned at last to the idea of a novel
about New York. I now decided the book would not be a nonfiction novel but a fictional one. Part of it, I suppose, was curiosity
or, better said, the question that rebuked every writer who had
made a point of experimenting with nonfiction over the preceding ten or fifteen years: Are you merely ducking the big challenge — The Novel? Consciously, I wanted to prove a point. I
wanted to fulfill a prediction I had made in the introduction to
The New Journalism in 1973; namely, that the future of the fictional novel would be in a highly detailed realism based on reporting, a realism more thorough than any currently being attempted, a realism that would portray the individual in intimate
and inextricable relation to the society around him.

One of the axioms of literary theory in the seventies was that
realism was "just another formal device, not a permanent method
for dealing with experience" (in the words of the editor of *Par-
tisan Review,* William Phillips). I was convinced then — and I am
even more strongly convinced now — that precisely the opposite
is true. The introduction of realism into literature in the eighteenth century by Richardson, Fielding, and Smollett was like
the introduction of electricity into engineering. It was not just
another device. The effect on the emotions of an everyday realism such as Richardson's was something that had never been
conceived of before. It was realism that created the "absorbing"
or "gripping" quality that is peculiar to the novel, the quality that
makes the reader feel that he has been pulled not only into the

setting of the story but also into the minds and central nervous systems of the characters. No one was ever moved to tears by reading about the unhappy fates of heroes and heroines in Homer, Sophocles, Molière, Racine, Sydney, Spenser, or Shakespeare. Yet even the impeccable Lord Jeffrey, editor of *Edinburgh Review,* confessed to having cried — blubbered, boohooed, snuffled, and sighed — over the death of Little Nell in *The Old Curiosity Shop.* For writers to give up this power in the quest for a more up-to-date kind of fiction — it is as if an engineer were to set out to develop a more sophisticated machine technology by first of all discarding the principle of electricity, on the grounds that it has been used ad nauseam for a hundred years.

One of the specialties of the realistic novel, from Richardson on, was the demonstration of the influence of society on even the most personal aspects of the life of the individual. Lionel Trilling was right when he said, in 1948, that what produced great characters in the nineteenth-century European novel was the portrayal of "class traits modified by personality." But he went on to argue that the old class structure by now had disintegrated, particularly in the United States, rendering the technique useless. Again, I would say that precisely the opposite is the case. If we substitute for "class," in Trilling's formulation, the broader term "status," that technique has never been more essential in portraying the innermost life of the individual. This is above all true when the subject is the modern city. It strikes me as folly to believe that you can portray the individual in the city today without also portraying the city itself.

Asked once what three novels he would most recommend to a creative writing student, Faulkner said (or is said to have said), "*Anna Karenina, Anna Karenina,* and *Anna Karenina.*" And what is at the core of not only the private dramas but also the very psychology of *Anna Karenina?* It is Tolstoy's concept of the heart at war with the structure of society. The dramas of Anna, Vronsky, Karenin, Levin, and Kitty would be nothing but slow-moving romances without the panorama of Russian society against which Tolstoy places them. The characters' electrifying irrational acts are the acts of the heart brought to a desperate edge by the pressure of society.

If Trilling were here, he would no doubt say, But of course:

"class traits modified by personality." These are substantial characters ("substantial" was one of Trilling's favorite terms) precisely because Russian society in Tolstoy's day was so clearly defined by social classes, each with its own distinctive culture and traditions. Today, in New York, Trilling could argue, Anna would just move in with Vronsky, and people in their social set would duly note the change in their Scully & Scully address books; and the arrival of the baby, if they chose to have it, would occasion no more than a grinning snigger in the gossip columns. To which I would say, Quite so. The status structure of society has changed, but it has not disappeared for a moment. It provides an infinite number of new agonies for the Annas and Vronskys of the Upper East Side, and, as far as that goes, of Leningrad. Anyone who doubts that need only get to know them.

American society today is no more or less chaotic, random, discontinuous, or absurd than Russian society or French society or British society a hundred years ago, no matter how convenient it might be for a writer to think so. It is merely more varied and complicated and harder to define. In the prologue to *The Bonfire of the Vanities,* the mayor of New York delivers a soliloquy in a stream of consciousness as he is being routed from a stage in Harlem by a group of demonstrators. He thinks of all the rich white New Yorkers who will be watching this on television from within the insulation of their cooperative apartments. "Do you really think this is *your* city any longer? Open your eyes! The greatest city of the twentieth century! Do you think *money* will keep it yours? Come down from your swell co-ops, you general partners and merger lawyers! It's the Third World down there! Puerto Ricans, West Indians, Haitians, Dominicans, Cubans, Colombians, Hondurans, Koreans, Chinese, Thais, Vietnamese, Ecuadorians, Panamanians, Filipinos, Albanians, Senegalese, and Afro-Americans! Go visit the frontiers, you gutless wonders! Morningside Heights, St. Nicholas Park, Washington Heights, Fort Tryon — *por qué pagar más!* The Bronx — the Bronx is finished for you!" — and on he goes. New York and practically every other large city in the United States are undergoing a profound change. The fourth great wave of immigrants — this one from Asia, North Africa, Latin America, and the Caribbean — is now pouring in. Within ten years political power in most major

American cities will have passed to the nonwhite majorities. Does that render these cities incomprehensible, fragmented beyond the grasp of all logic, absurd, meaningless to gaze upon in a literary sense? Not in my opinion. It merely makes the task of the writer more difficult if he wants to know what truly presses upon the heart of the individual, white or nonwhite, living in the metropolis in the last decade of the twentieth century.

That task, as I see it, inevitably involves reporting, which I regard as the most valuable and least understood resource available to any writer with exalted ambitions, whether the medium is print, film, tape, or the stage. Young writers are constantly told, "Write about what you know." There is nothing wrong with that rule as a starting point, but it seems to get quickly magnified into an unspoken maxim: The only valid experience is personal experience.

Emerson said that every person has a great autobiography to write, if only he understands what is truly his own unique experience. But he didn't say every person had *two* great autobiographies to write. Dickens, Dostoevski, Balzac, Zola, and Sinclair Lewis *assumed* that the novelist had to go beyond his personal experience and head out into society as a reporter. Zola called it documentation, and his documenting expeditions to the slums, the coal mines, the races, the *folies,* department stores, wholesale food markets, newspaper offices, barnyards, railroad yards, and engine decks, notebook and pen in hand, became legendary. To write *Elmer Gantry,* the great portrait of not only a corrupt evangelist but also the entire Protestant clergy at a time when they still set the moral tone of America, Lewis left his home in New England and moved to Kansas City. He organized Bible study groups for clergymen, delivered sermons from the pulpits of preachers on summer vacation, attended tent meetings and Chautauqua lectures and church conferences and classes at the seminaries, all the while doggedly taking notes on five-by-eight cards.

It was through this process, documentation, that Lewis happened to scoop the Jim Bakker story by sixty years — and to render it totally plausible, historically and psychologically, in fiction. I refer to the last two chapters of *Elmer Gantry.* We see Elmer, the great evangelist, get caught in a tryst with . . . the church secretary (Hettie Dowler is her name) . . . who turns out to be in league with a very foxy lawyer . . . and the two of them present Elmer with a hefty hush-money demand, which he is only too eager to pay. With the help of friends, however, Elmer manages to turn the tables, and is absolved and vindicated in the eyes of humanity and the press. On the final page, we see Elmer on his knees beside the pulpit on Sunday morning before a packed house, with his gaze lifted heavenward and his hands pressed together in Albrecht Dürer mode, tears running down his face, loudly thanking the Lord for delivering him from the vipers. As the book ends, he looks toward the choir and catches a glimpse of a new addition, "a girl with charming ankles and lively eyes."

Was it reporting that made Lewis the most highly regarded American novelist of the 1920s? Certainly not by itself. But it was the material he found through reporting that enabled Lewis to exercise with such rich variety his insights, many of them exceptionally subtle, into the psyches of men and women and into the status structure of society. Having said that, I will now reveal something that practically every writer has experienced — and none, as far as I know, has ever talked about. The young person who decides to become a writer because he has a subject or an issue in mind, because he has "something to say," is a rare bird. Most make that decision because they realize they have a certain musical facility with words. Since poetry is the music of language, outstanding young poets are by no means rare. As he grows older, however, our young genius keeps running into this damnable problem of *material*, of what to write about, since by now he realizes that literature's main arena is prose, whether in fiction or the essay. Even so, he keeps things in proportion. He tells himself that 95 percent of literary genius is the unique talent that is secure inside some sort of crucible in his skull and 5 percent is the material, the clay his talent will mold.

I can remember going through this stage myself. In college, at Washington and Lee, I decided I would write crystalline prose. That was the word: crystalline. It would be a prose as ageless, timeless, exquisite, soaring, and transparently dazzling as Scarlatti at his most sublime. It would speak to the twenty-fifth century as lucidly as to my own. (I was, naturally, interested to hear, years later, that Iris Murdoch had dreamed of the same quality and chosen the same word, crystalline, at a similar point in her life.) In graduate school at Yale, I came upon the Elizabethan books of rhetoric, which isolated, by my count, 444 figures of speech, covering every conceivable form of word play. By analyzing the prose of writers I admired — De Quincey, I remember, was one of them — I tried to come up with the perfect sequences of figures and make notations for them, like musical notes. I would flesh out this perfect skeleton with some material when the time came.

Such experiments don't last very long, of course. The damnable beast, material, keeps getting bigger and more obnoxious. Finally, you realize you have a choice. Either hide from it, wish it away, or wrestle with it. I doubt that there is a writer over forty who does not realize in his heart of hearts that literary genius, in prose, consists of proportions more on the order of 65 percent material and 35 percent the talent in the sacred crucible.

I never doubted for a moment that to write a long piece of fiction about New York City I would have to do the same sort of reporting I had done for *The Right Stuff* or *Radical Chic & Mau-mauing the Flak Catchers,* even though by now I had lived in New York for almost twenty years. By 1981, when I started work in earnest, I could see that Thackeray's *Vanity Fair* would not be an adequate model. *Vanity Fair* deals chiefly with the upper orders of British society. A book about New York in the 1980s would have to deal with New York high and low. So I chose Wall Street as the high end of the scale and the South Bronx as the low. I knew a few more people on Wall Street than in the South Bronx, but both were terrae incognitae as far as my own experience was concerned. I headed forth into I knew not exactly what. Any big book about New York, I figured, should have at least one subway scene. I started riding the subways in the Bronx. One evening I looked across the car and saw someone I knew sitting there in a strange rig. He was a Wall Street broker I hadn't seen for nine or ten years. He was dressed in a business suit, but his pants legs were rolled up three or four hitches, revealing a pair of olive-green army surplus socks, two bony lengths of shin, and some decomposing striped orthotic running shoes. On the floor between his feet was an A&P shopping bag made of slippery white polyethylene. He had on a dirty raincoat and a greasy rain hat, and his eyes were darting from one end of the car to the other. I went over, said hello, and learned the following. He and his family lived in the far North Bronx, where there are to this day some lively, leafy Westchester-style neighborhoods, and he worked on Wall Street. The subways provided fine service, except that lately there had been a problem. Packs of young toughs had taken to roaming the cars. They would pick out a likely prey, close in on his seat, hem him in, and ask for money. They kept their hands in their pockets and never produced weapons, but their leering, menacing looks were usually enough. When this fellow's turn came, he had capitulated, given them all he had — and he'd been a nervous wreck on the subway ever since. He had taken to traveling to and from Wall Street in this pathetic disguise in order to avoid looking worth robbing. In the A&P shopping bag he carried his Wall Street shoes and socks.

I decided I would use such a situation in my book. It was here that I began to run into not Roth's Lament but Muggeridge's Law. While Malcolm Muggeridge was editor of *Punch*, it was announced that Khrushchev and Bulganin were coming to England. Muggeridge hit upon the idea of a mock itinerary, a lineup of the most ludicrous places the two paunchy, pear-shaped little Soviet leaders could possibly be paraded through during the solemn business of a state visit. Shortly before press time, half the feature had to be scrapped. It coincided exactly with the official itinerary, just released, prompting Muggeridge to observe: We live in an age in which it is no longer possible to be funny. There is nothing you can imagine, no matter how ludicrous, that will not promptly be enacted before your very eyes, probably by someone well known.

This immediately became my problem. I first wrote *The Bonfire of the Vanities* serially for *Rolling Stone,* producing a chapter every two weeks with a gun at my temple. In the third chapter, I introduced one of my main characters, a thirty-two-year-old Bronx assistant district attorney named Larry Kramer, sitting in a subway car dressed as my friend had been dressed, his eyes jumping about in a bughouse manner. This was supposed to create unbearable suspense in the readers. What on earth had reduced this otherwise healthy young man to such a pathetic state? This chapter appeared in July of 1984. In an installment scheduled for April of 1985, the readers would learn of his humiliation by a wolf pack, who had taken all his money plus his little district attorney's badge. But it so happened that in December of 1984 a young man named Bernhard Goetz found himself in an identical situation on a subway in New York, hemmed in by four youths who were, in fact, from the South Bronx. Far from caving in, he pulled out a .38-caliber revolver and shot all four of them and became one of the most notorious figures in America. Now, how could I, four months later, in April of 1985, proceed with my plan? People would say, This poor fellow Wolfe, he has no imagination. He reads the newspapers, gets these obvious ideas, and then gives us this wimp Kramer, who caves in. So I abandoned the plan, dropped it altogether. The *Rolling Stone* readers' burning thirst, if any, to know what accounted for Assistant D.A. Kramer's pitiful costume and alarming facial tics was never slaked.

In one area, however, I was well ahead of the news, and this lent the book a curious kind of alter-life. The plot turns on a severe injury to a black youth in an incident involving a white couple in an automobile. While the youth lies in a coma, various forces close in on the case — the press, politicians, prosecutors, real estate brokers, black activists — each eager, for private reasons, to turn the matter into a racial Armageddon. Supreme among them is Reverend Bacon, a Harlem minister, a genius at handling the press who soon has the entire city throbbing to the young man's outrageous fate. In the book, the incident casts its shadow across the upcoming elections and threatens to cost the white mayor City Hall.

The Bonfire of the Vanities reached bookstores in October of 1987, a week before the Wall Street crash. From the start, in the press, there was a certain amount of grumbling, some of it not very nice, about my depiction of Reverend Bacon. He was a grotesque caricature of a black activist, grotesque or worse. Then, barely three months later, the Tawana Brawley case broke. At the forefront of the Brawley case appeared an activist black minister, the Reverend Al Sharpton, who was indeed a genius at handling the press, even when he was in the tightest corners. At one point the *New York Post* got a tip that Sharpton was having his long Byronic hair coiffed at a beauty parlor in Brooklyn. A reporter and photographer waited until he was socketed in under the dryer, then burst in. Far from throwing up his hands and crying out about invasion of privacy, Sharpton nonchalantly beckoned to his stalkers. "Come on in, boys, and bring your cameras. I want you to see how . . . a real man . . . gets his hair done." Just like that! — another Sharpton media triumph, under the heading of "Masculinity to Burn." In fact, Sharpton was so flamboyant, the grumbling about Reverend Bacon swung around 180 degrees. Now I heard people complain, This poor fellow Wolfe, he has no imagination. Here, on the front page of every newspaper, are the real goods — and he gives us this little divinity student, Reverend Bacon.

But I also began to hear and read with increasing frequency that *The Bonfire of the Vanities* was "prophetic." The Brawley case turned out to be only one in a series of racial incidents in which young black people were, or were seen as, the victims of white brutality. And these incidents did, indeed, cast their shadow across the race for mayor in New York City. As in the prologue to the book, the mayor, in real life, was heckled, harassed, and shouted down by demonstrators in Harlem, although he was never forced to flee the podium. And perhaps these incidents were among the factors that cost the white mayor City Hall. But not for a moment did I ever think of *The Bonfire of the Vanities* as prophetic. The book only showed what was obvious to anyone who had done what I did, even as far back as the early eighties, when I began; anyone who had gone out and looked frankly at the new face of the city and paid attention not only to what the voices said but also to the roar.

This brings me to one last point. It is not merely that reporting is useful in gathering the *petits faits vrais* that create verisimilitude and make a novel gripping or absorbing, although that side of the enterprise is worth paying attention to. My contention is that, especially in an age like this, they are essential for the very greatest effects literature can achieve. In 1884 Zola went down into the mines at Anzin to do the documentation for what was to become the novel *Germinal*. Posing as a secretary for a member of the French Chamber of Deputies, he descended into the pits wearing his city clothes, his frock coat, high stiff collar, and high stiff hat (this appeals to me for reasons I won't delay you with), and carrying a notebook and pen. One day Zola and the miners who were serving as his guides were 150 feet below the ground when Zola noticed an enormous workhorse, a Percheron, pulling a sled piled with coal through a tunnel. Zola asked, "How do you get that animal in and out of the mine every day?" At first the miners thought he was joking. Then they realized he was serious, and one of them said, "Mr. Zola, don't you understand? That horse comes down here *once*, when he's a colt, barely more than a foal, and still able to fit into the buckets that bring *us* down here. That horse grows up down here. He grows blind down here after a year or two, from the lack of light. He hauls coal down here until he can't haul it anymore, and then he dies down here, and his bones are buried down here." When Zola transfers this revelation from the pages of his documentation notebook to the pages of *Germinal,* it makes the hair on your arms stand on end. You realize, without the need of amplification, that the horse is the miners themselves, who descend below the face of the earth as children and dig coal down in the pit until they can dig no more and then are buried, often literally, down there.

The moment of The Horse in *Germinal* is one of the supreme moments in French literature — and it would have been impossible without that peculiar drudgery that Zola called documentation. At this weak, pale, tabescent moment in the history of American literature, we need a battalion, a brigade, of Zolas to head out into this wild, bizarre, unpredictable, Hog-stomping Baroque country of ours and reclaim it as literary property. Philip Roth was absolutely right. The imagination of the novelist is powerless before what he knows he's going to read in tomorrow morning's newspaper. But a generation of American writers has drawn precisely the wrong conclusion from that perfectly valid observation. The answer is not to leave the rude beast, the material, also known as the life around us, to the journalists but to do what journalists do, or are supposed to do, which is to wrestle the beast and bring it to terms.

Of one thing I am sure. If fiction writers do not start facing the obvious, the literary history of the second half of the twentieth century will record that journalists not only took over the richness of American life as their domain but also seized the high ground of literature itself. Any literary person who is willing to look back over the American literary terrain of the past twenty-five years — look back candidly, in the solitude of the study — will admit that in at least four years out of five the best nonfiction books have been *better literature* than the most highly praised books of fiction. Any truly candid observer will go still further. In many years, the most highly praised books of fiction have been overshadowed *in literary terms* by writers whom literary people customarily dismiss as "writers of popular fiction" (a curious epithet) or as genre novelists. I am thinking of novelists such as John le Carré and Joseph Wambaugh. Leaving the question of talent aside, le Carré and Wambaugh have one enormous advantage over their more literary confreres. They are not only willing to wrestle the beast; they actually love the battle.

In 1973, in *The New Journalism*, I wrote that nonfiction had displaced the novel as American literature's "main event." That was not quite the same as saying that nonfiction had dethroned the novel, but it was close enough. At the time, it was a rash statement, but *como Fidel lo ha dijo*, history will absolve me. Unless some movement occurs in American fiction over the next ten years that is more remarkable than any detectable right now, the pioneering in nonfiction will be recorded as the most important experiment in American literature in the second half of the twentieth century.

I speak as a journalist, with some enthusiasm, as you can detect, a journalist who has tried to capture the beast in long narratives of both nonfiction and fiction. I started writing *The Bonfire of the Vanities* with the supreme confidence available only to a writer who doesn't know quite what he is getting into. I was soon plunged into despair. One very obvious matter I had not reckoned with: in nonfiction you are very conveniently provided with the setting and the characters and the plot. You now have the task — and it is a huge one — of bringing it all alive as convincingly as the best of realistic fiction. But you don't have to concoct the story. Indeed, you can't. I found the sudden freedom of fiction intimidating. It was at least a year before I felt comfortable enough to use that freedom's advantages, which are formidable. The past three decades have been decades of tremendous and at times convulsive social change, especially in large cities, and the tide of the fourth great wave of immigration has made the picture seem all the more chaotic, random, and discontinuous, to use the literary clichés of the recent past. The economy with which realistic fiction can bring the many currents of a city together in a single, fairly simple story was something that I eventually found exhilarating. It is a facility that is not available to the journalist, and it seems more useful with each passing month. Despite all the current talk of "coming together," I see the fast-multiplying factions of the modern cities trying to insulate themselves more diligently than ever before. However brilliant and ambitious, a nonfiction novel about, say, the Tawana Brawley case could not get all of New York in 1989 between two covers. It could illuminate many things, most especially the press and the workings of the justice system, but it would not reach into Wall Street or Park Avenue, precincts even the resourceful Al Sharpton does not frequent. In 1970 the Black Panthers *did* turn up in Leonard Bernstein's living room. Today, there is no chic, radical or otherwise, in mixing colors in the grand salons.

So the doors close and the walls go up! It is merely another open invitation to literature, especially in the form of the novel. And how can any writer, in fiction or nonfiction, resist going to the beano, to the rout! At the end of *Dead Souls*, Gogol asks, "Whither art thou soaring away to, then, Russia? Give me an answer!" Russia gives none but only goes faster, and "the air, rent to shreds, thunders and turns to wind," and Gogol hangs on, breathless, his eyes filled with wonder. America today, in a headlong rush of her own, may or may not truly need a literature worthy of her vastness. But American novelists, without any doubt, truly need, in this neurasthenic hour, the spirit to go along for that wild ride.

Biographical Notes
Notable Essays of 1989

Biographical Notes

MICHAEL ARLEN is the author of numerous books, including *Exiles* (nominated for a National Book Award in 1970); *Passage to Ararat,* which won a National Book Award in 1975; *Thirty Seconds;* and *Say Goodbye to Sam,* a novel published in 1982. He has been a frequent contributor to *The New Yorker* since 1960, where for many years he wrote a television column called "The Air."

JACQUES BARZUN is a cultural historian and critic who has written a series of works setting forth the evolution of ideas in Western civilization since the Renaissance and offering at the same time a critique of contemporary culture. His latest book is *The Culture We Deserve;* his next, which carries the discussion of attitudes and feelings forward into the era of modernism, is *An Essay on French Verse for Readers of English Poetry,* to be published by New Directions in the coming season.

ANATOLE BROYARD was a daily book critic for the *New York Times* for thirteen years and an editor and columnist for the Sunday *Times Book Review* for five years. He has published two collections of essays and is now working on a memoir of Greenwich Village and a book on being a cancer patient.

ALAN M. DERSHOWITZ is professor of law at Harvard Law School. He is the author of several books, the most recent of which is *Taking Liberties.* He writes a weekly syndicated column, as well as occasional magazine articles. In addition to his teaching and writing, Professor Dershowitz is an active criminal defense and civil liberties lawyer. He is currently working on a book about the empirical assumptions underlying freedom of expression and censorship.

ANNIE DILLARD is the author of *The Writing Life, An American Childhood, Teaching a Stone to Talk,* and other books. *Pilgrim at Tinker Creek* won the Pulitzer Prize in general nonfiction for 1975.

STANLEY ELKIN is Merle King Professor of Modern Letters at Washington University in St. Louis. A member of the American Academy and Institute of Arts and Letters, he has published a dozen works of fiction, including *George Mills,* for which he won the National Book Award. His ninth novel, *The MacGuffin,* will be published in spring 1991 by Simon and Schuster. A collection of essays, *My Tuxedo and Other Meditations,* is also forthcoming.

JOSEPH EPSTEIN is the editor of *The American Scholar.* His essays and stories have appeared in *Commentary, The New Criterion, The Hudson Review,* and *Encounter.* A new book of his familiar essays, *A Line Out for a Walk,* will appear from W. W. Norton in the winter of 1990.

STEPHEN JAY GOULD teachers biology, geology, and the history of science at Harvard University. He is the author of *Ontogeny and Phylogeny, The Mismeasure of Man, Wonderful Life,* and five collections of essays: *Ever Since Darwin, The Panda's Thumb, Hens' Teeth and Horses' Toes, The Flamingo's Smile,* and *An Urchin in the Storm.* A MacArthur Prize Fellow, he writes a monthly scientific essay for *Natural History* magazine.

ANN HODGMAN is a contributing editor at *Spy* and at *Eating Well,* for which she writes a regular food column called "Sweet and Sour." She is the author or co-author of several humor books, including *Tiny Tales of Terror* and *The Reagan Report,* and has also written more than twenty children's books. She is currently working on a twelve-book children's series called *Lunchroom,* a Nancy Drew mystery, and a book for middle-schoolers called *My Babysitter Is a Vampire.*

SUE HUBBELL is the author of *A Country Year* and *Book of Bees.* She writes occasional pieces for *The New Yorker,* in which "The Vicksburg Ghost" appeared, the *New York Times,* and *Smithsonian* magazine. She lives in the Ozarks of southern Missouri, where she runs a commercial bee farm, and in Washington, D.C., where her husband lives.

STUART KLAWANS reviews films for *The Nation* and writes the "American Notes" column for the *Times Literary Supplement.* His reviews of books and films also appear frequently in *The Village Voice.* Recent publications include the short story "Svengali's Line-Up" in *Grand Street* (where "The Corpse in the Mirror" appeared) and the essay "Rose-Tinted Spectacles" in *Seeing Through Movies* (Pantheon Books). With Amelia Arenas, he is the co-author of a series of booklets for the Museum of Modern Art, New York, offering guides to the permanent collection.

NATALIE KUSZ teaches creative writing at Bethel College in St. Paul, Minnesota. She has been the recipient of a 1989 Whiting Writer's Award and a 1990 General Electric Award for Younger Writers. Her autobiographical book, *Road Song*, of which "Vital Signs" is a part, will be published by Farrar, Straus and Giroux in the fall of 1990.

URSULA K. LE GUIN was born in California and lives in Oregon. She has published poetry, essays, short fiction, and novels (including *The Left Hand of Darkness, The Dispossessed,* and *A Wizard of Earthsea*), has written film and radio scripts, and has taught at a number of writing workshops and conferences. Her two most recent books are: a collection, *Buffalo Gals and Other Animal Presences* (Capra Press) and *Tehanu: The Last Book of Earthsea* (Atheneum).

JAY MCINERNEY's best-selling novels, *Bright Lights, Big City* and *Ransom,* have been published in fifteen languages. His recent fiction has appeared in *Esquire* and *The Atlantic Monthly,* among other magazines, and he also wrote the screenplay for the movie version of *Bright Lights, Big City.* A graduate of Williams College, he has held fellowships from Princeton and Syracuse universities. He lives in New York City.

JAMES ALAN MCPHERSON is the author of *Hue and Cry, Railroad,* and *Elbow Room.* His articles and short stories have appeared in numerous periodicals, including *The Atlantic Monthly, Esquire, The Nation, Ploughshares,* and *The Iowa Review.* A graduate of Morris Brown College and Harvard Law School, he has received a Guggenheim Fellowship, a Pulitzer Prize, and a MacArthur Prize Fellows Award. He is professor of English at the University of Iowa.

LEONARD MICHAELS is the author of two story collections, *Going Places* and *I Would Have Saved Them If I Could,* and a novel, *The Men's Club.* He has received an award from the American Academy and Institute of Arts and Letters, a Guggenheim Fellowship, and various awards for his short stories, several of which have appeared in the O. Henry Prize collections. His work has been translated into a dozen languages. His latest book, largely autobiographical, is *Shuffle;* his next book, an adventure novel, is *Viva la Tropicana.* He teaches in the English department at the University of California at Berkeley.

MICHAEL POLLAN is executive editor of *Harper's Magazine,* where he has worked since 1983. Several of his essays have appeared in *The New York Times Magazine.* In the spring of 1991 the Atlantic Monthly Press will publish his book on gardens and nature, from which "Why Mow?" was adapted. Pollan grew up on Long Island, and now lives in New York City and Cornwall Bridge, Connecticut.

RANDY SHILTS is national correspondent of the *San Francisco Chronicle.* His critically acclaimed first book, *The Mayor of Castro Street: The Life and Times of Harvey Milk,* described the rise of gay political power against the backdrop of a turbulent era of social change in San Francisco. His second book, *And the Band Played On: Politics, People, and the AIDS Epidemic,* was an international best seller documenting the failings of the government and the public health and scientific establishment in fighting the burgeoning AIDS epidemic. The American Society of Authors and Journalists named Shilts the Outstanding Author of 1988 for that work.

PAUL WEST was educated at Oxford and Columbia universities and is the author of some twenty books, most recently *Rat Man of Paris, The Place in Flowers Where Pollen Rests,* and *Lord Byron's Doctor,* all novels. His nonfiction works include *Words for a Deaf Daughter* and *Sheer Fiction.* A former Guggenheim Fellow, he has won two National Endowment for the Arts Fellowships in Fiction Writing, the Arts and Letters Prize from the American Academy and Institute of Arts and Letters, the Aga Khan Fiction Prize, the Hazlett Award for Excellence in the Arts, and other awards. In 1988 he was inducted as a Literary Lion of the New York Public Library. His next novel, due in 1991, is about Jack the Ripper, and his next book is *Portable People* (1990), eighty-one portraits of familiar and unfamiliar public figures. He is a fiction judge this year for the National Book Award.

JOY WILLIAMS is the author of three novels and two collections of stories, *Taking Care* and *Escapes,* as well as a history and guide to the Florida Keys. Her story "The Little Winter" is included in *The Best American Short Stories 1990.*

TOM WOLFE holds a Ph.D. in American studies from Yale University and is the author of many books, including *The Kandy-Kolored Tangerine-Flake Streamline Baby, The Electric Kool-Aid Acid Test, Radical Chic & Mau-Mauing the Flak Catchers, The Painted Word,* and *From Bauhaus to Our House. The Right Stuff* won the American Book Award for general nonfiction in 1980. He received the Columbia Journalism Award in 1980 and the John Dos Passos Award in 1984. His first novel, *The Bonfire of the Vanities,* was published in 1987.

Notable Essays of 1989

SELECTED BY ROBERT ATWAN

JOEL AGEE
A Fury of Symbols. *Harper's Magazine,*
January.

ROGER ANGELL
No, But I Saw the Game. *The New
Yorker,* July 31.

TED ANTON
Great Books, Great Battles. *Chicago
Times Magazine,* September-October.

TIMOTHY GARTON ASH
The German Revolution. *New York
Review of Books,* December 21.

M. R. AXELROD
PIZD'oSH: Nikolai Gogol, Abner
Doubleday, and the Russian
Origins of American Baseball. *Iowa
Review,* Fall.

WILL BAKER
The Making of a Little Man. *Georgia
Review,* Summer.

MED BENNETT
Choosing the Public Interest. *Northern
Lights,* April.

MARSHALL BERMAN
Taking to the Streets. *Boston Review,*
June.

ANNE BERNAYS
A Poet's Safe Haven in Amherst. *New
York Times Magazine* (supplement),
October 1.

BILL BERRY
Class Southerner. *Virginia Quarterly
Review,* Spring.

CARMEL BIRD
Getting My Mother's Sewing Machine
Across Bass Street. *Grand Street,*
Autumn.

SVEN BIRKERTS
On the Road to Nowhere. *Harper's
Magazine,* July.

ROBERT BOYERS
Political Thought, Political Discourse.
Salmagundi, Winter.

ANTHONY BRANDT
Days. *Southwest Review,* Autumn.

JOSEPH BRODKEY
Isaiah Berlin at Eighty. *New York Review of Books,* August 17.

CLEANTH BROOKS
John Crowe Ransom: As I Remember
Him. *American Scholar,* Spring.

FRANKLIN BURROUGHS, JR.
Of Moose and a Moosehunter. *Georgia Review,* Summer.

FREDERICK BUSH
Public or Purloined? *Harper's Magazine*, August.

PHILIP CAPUTO
Death Goes to School. *Esquire*, December.

JUDITH ORTIZ COFER
Casa: A Partial Remembrance of a Puerto Rican Childhood. *Prairie Schooner*, Fall.

BERNARD COOPER
Fever. *Gettysburg Review*, Spring.

JAMES M. COX
Trial for a Southern Life. *Sewanee Review*, Spring.

MIDGE DECTER
The Professor and the L-Word. *Commentary*, February.

JOAN DIDION
Letter from Los Angeles. *The New Yorker*, April 24.

MICHAEL DORRIS
Life Stories. *Antaeus*, Autumn.

ANDRE DUBUS
Under the Lights. *The Village Voice*, September 19.

STUART DYBEK
The Woman Who Fainted. *The Critic*, Winter.

GERALD EARLY
Weight Watching: A Course in Women's Studies. *Antaeus*, Autumn.

GRETEL EHRLICH
A Season of Portents. *Harper's Magazine*, August.

STANLEY ELKIN
Talk Up! The First Amendment As an Art Form. *Grand Street*, Winter.

My Shirt Tale, *Harper's Magazine*, April.

RALPH ELLISON
On Being the Target of Discrimination. *New York Times Magazine* (supplement), April 16.

JOHN ENGELS
Making the Connections. *New England Review and Bread Loaf Quarterly*, Autumn.

JOSEPH EPSTEIN
Waiter, There's a Paragraph in My Soup. *The American Scholar*, Summer.
Smoke Gets in Your Eyes. *The American Scholar*, Winter.

ROBERT ERWIN
The Man Who Discovered America. *Yale Review*, March.

LESTER FAIGLEY
Nepal Diary: Where the Global Village Ends. *North Dakota Quarterly*, Summer.

HENRY FAIRLIE
Fear of Living. *The New Republic*, January 23.

FRANCES FITZGERALD
Memoirs of the Reagan Era. *The New Yorker*, January 16.

KITTY FLOREY
The Thirsty Deer. *North American Review*, Summer.

PETER FREUNDLICH
Confessions of a Head Case. *Esquire*, September.

GEORGE GARRETT
Under Two Flags. *Sewanee Review*, Fall.

PHILIP GARRISON
The Tour Guide. *Northwest Review*, Vol. 27, No. 2.

HENRY LOUIS GATES, JR.
Whose Canon Is It, Anyway? *New York Times Book Review,* February 26.

BRENDAN GILL
The Faces of Joseph Campbell. *New York Review of Books,* November 28.

ALBERT GOLDBARTH
The Space. *Georgia Review,* Summer.
Wind-up Sushi: With Catalogues and Instructions for Assembly. *Denver Quarterly,* Summer.

VIVIAN GORNICK
Twice an Outsider: On Being Jewish and a Woman. *Tikkun,* March-April.

STEPHEN JAY GOULD
Dark Outcasts, Cast in Bronze. *New England Monthly,* October.

PHILIP GRAHAM
A Writer in a World of Spirits. *Poets & Writers Magazine,* May-June.

PAUL GRUCHOW
The Ancient Faith of Cranes. *Audubon,* May.

ALLAN GURGANUS
Two Essays for Aloud. *Iowa Review,* Vol. 19, No. 1.

RACHEL HADAS
The Cradle and the Bookcase. *Southwest Review,* Spring.

DONALD HALL
The Poet of Fort Juniper. *Yankee,* June.

ROBERT HEILBRONER
The Triumph of Capitalism. *The New Yorker,* January 23.

ROBERT B. HEILMAN
Three Generations of English Studies: An Impression. *Sewanee Review,* Fall.

RICHARD HILL
Could We Please Have Some Quiet, Please? *The American Voice,* Winter.

EDWARD HOAGLAND
Too Much, Too Blindly, Too Fast. *Harper's Magazine,* June.
A World Worth Saving. *Life,* October.

DIANE HORTON
Apprenticed. *Iowa Woman,* Summer.

GERALD HOWARD
Mistah Perkins—He Dead (Publishing Today). *The American Scholar,* Summer.

PAT C. HOY II
Mosaics of Southern Masculinity: Small-Scale Mythologies. *Sewanee Review,* Spring.

JOHN HUTCHISON
Midseasonal. *San Francisco Flier,* September 29.

EDITH JENKINS
The Following Wind. *Threepenny Review,* Fall.

JUNE JORDAN
Waiting for a Taxi. *The Progressive,* June.

ROBERT KAREN
The Revenge of the Wounded. *Yale Review,* March.

GARRISON KEILLOR
When You Kick a Liberal. *Harper's Magazine,* January.

JAMES KILGO
Indian Givers. *Gettysburg Review,* Spring.

JUDITH KITCHEN
Hide-and-Go-Seek. *Georgia Review,* Spring.

PERRI KLASS
Ending. *TriQuarterly,* Spring-Summer.

MELVIN KONNER
Art of Darkness. *The Sciences,* November-December.

LEONARD KRIEGEL
From the Burning Bush: The Autobiographical "I." *Sewanee Review,* Fall.

PHILIP KUBERSKI
Proust's Brain. *Yale Review,* March.

LEWIS H. LAPHAM
A Political Opiate. *Harper's Magazine,* December.

CHRISTOPHER LASCH
Progress: The Last Superstition. *Tikkun,* May-June.

DAVID LAVERY
How to Gut a Book. *Georgia Review,* Winter.

MICHAEL LERNER
Looking Forward to the Nineties. *Tikkun,* November-December.

JONATHAN LIEBERSON
TV: A Day in the Life. *New York Review of Books,* April 13.

SAMUEL LIPMAN
Redefining Culture and Democracy. *The New Criterion,* December.

PHILLIP LOPATE
Suicide of a Schoolteacher. *Boulevard,* Spring.

BARRY LOPEZ
Life and Death in Galápagos. *North American Review,* Summer.
Our Frail Planet in Cold, Clear View. *Harper's Magazine,* May.

NANCY MAIRS
I'm Afraid. I'm Afraid. I'm Afraid. *The American Voice,* Winter.

DAVID MAMET
Fighting Words. *Playboy,* December.

GERALD MARZORATI
Salman Rushdie: Fiction's Embattled Infidel. *New York Times Magazine,* January 29.

FRANCES MAYES
Namesake. *Gettysburg Review,* Spring.

JOHN MCGOWAN
Can Marxism Survive? *Southern Humanities Review,* Summer.

WILLIAM MCGOWAN
My Half Year of Living Dangerously. *GQ,* January.

DAPHNE MERKIN
Dreaming of Hitler. *Esquire,* August.

DON MITCHELL
Fairy Tales. *Boston,* May.

SCOTT L. MONTGOMERY
Ultramarathon: An Immoderate Destiny. *Georgia Review,* Summer.

JUDITH MOORE
Cries and Whispers. *East Bay Express,* December 1.

SUSAN P. MOREHOUSE
Imagining Flight When I Am Still. *Southern Review,* Autumn.

WILLE MORRIS
Faulkner's Mississippi. *National Geographic,* March.

ROBERT NEWTON
Zeus the Friendly. *Grand Street,* Autumn.

JOYCE CAROL OATES
My Father, My Fiction. *New York Times Magazine,* March 19.

KEVIN ODERMAN
My Last Caribou. *Northwest Review,* Vol. 27, No. 3.

A Voice from the South. *Sewanee Review*, Fall.

SUSAN ALLEN TOTH
Missing: A Man with a Briefcase. *Mpls/St. Paul*, June.

CALVIN TRILLIN
Abigail y Yo. *The New Yorker*, June 26.

GORE VIDAL
Our Television Politburo: Cue the Green God, Ted. *The Nation*, August 7–14.

GEOFFREY WARD
The House at Eighth and Jackson. *American Heritage*, April.

RICHARD WATSON
On the Zeedijk. *Georgia Review*, Spring.

ALLON WHITE
Too Close to the Bone: Autobiographical Fragments. *Raritan*, Spring.

RICHARD WILBUR
Riddles. *Yale Review*, December.

ELLEN WILLIS
Coming Down Again: After the Age of Excess. *Salmagundi*, Winter.

S. L. WISENBERG
Separate Vacations. *The Sun*, September.

TOBIAS WOLFF
Raymond Carver. *Esquire*, September.

ERIC ZENCEY
Cartography: A Memoir. *North American Review*, Summer.

NOTE: Many essays of literary interest were included in two 1989 book collections (and were not considered for this volume): *Family Portraits: Remembrances by Twenty Distinguished Writers*, edited by Carolyn Anthony; and *Testimony: Contemporary Writers Make the Holocaust Personal*, edited by David Rosenberg.